THERE USED TO BE ORDER

AFRICAN PERSPECTIVES

Kelly Askew and Anne Pitcher
Series Editors

African Performance Arts and Political Acts
Naomi André, Yolanda Covington-Ward, and Jendele Hungbo, Editors

There Used to Be Order:
Life on the Copperbelt after the Privatisation of the
Zambia Consolidated Copper Mines
Patience Mususa

Animated by Uncertainty: Rugby and the
Performance of History in South Africa
Joshua D. Rubin

Filtering Histories: The Photographic Bureaucracy
in Mozambique, 1960 to Recent Times,
by Drew A. Thompson

Aso Ebi: Dress, Fashion, Visual Culture, and
Urban Cosmopolitanism in West Africa,
by Okechukwu Nwafor

Unsettled History: Making South African Public Pasts,
by Leslie Witz, Gary Minkley, and Ciraj Rassool

Seven Plays of Koffi Kwahulé: In and Out of Africa,
translated by Chantal Bilodeau and Judith G. Miller
edited with Introductions by Judith G. Miller

The Rise of the African Novel:
Politics of Language, Identity, and Ownership,
by Mukoma Wa Ngugi

Black Cultural Life in South Africa:
Reception, Apartheid, and Ethics,
by Lily Saint

A complete list of titles in the series can be found at www.press.umich.edu

There Used to Be Order

*Life on the Copperbelt after the
Privatisation of the Zambia
Consolidated Copper Mines*

Patience Mususa

University of Michigan Press
Ann Arbor

For questions or permissions, please contact um.press.perms@umich.edu

Published in the United States of America by the
University of Michigan Press
Manufactured in the United States of America
Printed on acid-free paper
First published October 2021

A CIP catalog record for this book is available from the British Library.

Library of Congress Cataloging-in-Publication data has been applied for.

ISBN: 978-0-472-07499-0 (hardcover : alk. paper)
ISBN: 978-0-472-05499-2 (paper)
ISBN: 978-0-472-12936-2 (e-book)

Publication of this volume has been partially funded by the African Studies Center,
University of Michigan.

In memory of my father Joseph

CONTENTS

Preface   ix

INTRODUCTION   1

CHAPTER 1
Mining, Welfare, and Urbanisation: The Wavering Urban
Character of Zambia's Copperbelt   18

CHAPTER 2
"You Can't Plan": Dreams, Practice, and Order   43

CHAPTER 3
"Getting By": "Improvising a Life" on the
Post-privatisation Copperbelt   78

CHAPTER 4
Contesting Illegality: Women in the Informal Copper Business   105

CHAPTER 5
Performing Gender on the Copperbelt   129

CHAPTER 6
"Topping Up": Life amidst Hardship and Death   169

CONCLUSION
Making Life out of Disorder   190

Bibliography   203

Index   217

Digital materials related to this title can be found on the Fulcrum platform
via the following citable URL: https://doi.org/10.3998/mpub.9441475

When I moved back to the Copperbelt in 2005, six years after my undergraduate degree in architecture there, I was struck by all the self-organised
building activity happening in the neighbourhoods and places that had previously been tightly regulated by the state mining company, the Zambia Consolidated Copper Mines. I was running an undergraduate architecture studio
in housing at the time, and was interested in how self-builders were negotiating varying planning and building regulations and finding the resources to
build in highly straitened economic circumstances. I was fascinated by how
all these changes materialised in the landscape and what it meant for people's
experience of place.

This book stems from this interest. It examines what happened to the
texture of place and the experience of life on a Zambian Copperbelt town
when Zambia Consolidated Copper Mines (ZCCM) was privatised beginning 1997 following the implementation of structural adjustment policies that
introduced free market policies and drastically reduced social welfare. The
Copperbelt has long been a locus for innovative research on urbanisation in
Africa. My study in its examination of middle-income decline directs us to
thinking of the Copperbelt not only as an extractive locale for copper whose
activities are affected by the market, but also as a place where the residents'
engagement with the reality of losing jobs and struggling to earn a living after
the withdrawal of mine welfare is re-texturing simultaneously both the material and the social character of the place.

It builds on an established anthropological engagement with the region
that began with the Manchester school, which had done much to develop a
theoretical approach to social change. The book contributes to this literature
by reflecting on how landscape and the art of living are interwoven and co-
produce possibilities that, owing to both historical contingencies and social
formation, make certain forms of inhabiting the world more or less successful
for some.

Ethnographic fieldwork was conducted over a two-year period between

2007 and 2009, and intermittently thereafter. This was complemented with two neighbourhood surveys.

In the book, I make a case for an anthropology of "trying," an expression often made in response by Copperbelt residents to how they are getting on. It is one that indicates an improvised life and offers an analytical approach to exploring the backstory to the residents' observation that in the (ZCCM) past there used to be order.

This book is made possible by several persons and institutions. I am especially grateful to Fiona Ross, my doctoral supervisor, who provided not only guidance on the study but also financial support through a South Africa National Research Foundation supervisor attached grant. The Wenner Gren Foundation provided generous support through a Wadsworth Africa Fellowship. Through the process of research and writing, I am indebted to colleagues who along the way directed me to readings and provided feedback, namely Deborah Bryceson, Sian Butcher, Divine Fuh, Jeremy Gould, Karen Tranberg Hansen, Hugh Macmillan, Francis Nyamnjoh, Sophie Oldfield, Robin Palmer, Ann Schlyter, Owen Sichone, and Megan Vaughan. Miles Larmer and Alistair Fraser brought together a community of Copperbelt scholars in the aftermath of privatisation. I am also grateful for the support of various institutions, namely Copperbelt University, University of Cape Town, and the Nordic Africa Institute. I would also like to thank Kapepa Hendrick, Kasonde Mwenda, David Chola, and Emmanuel Kamuna, who assisted with the research surveys. I would also like to thank the reviewers of the manuscript and the editor Anne Pitcher, who encouraged me in getting the book project out.

I am thankful to the Tembo and Nyati families, Xoliswa Kayumba, Sue Cavanna, Susan Hunter, Paul Physick, Manyanyato Kamoto, Mwansa and Finzi Saidi, and Liz and Brian Baldwin, who have provided their friendship and support in the book's journey. I am especially grateful to my family. Vito, my husband who has critically engaged with the work. My brothers, Tabuli, Mulemwa and Mufalo, with whom we share stories of the Copperbelt. My father Joseph, with whom I checked on ZCCM's institutional culture and who regularly visited my field site and was as interested as I was in the changing landscape of the region. Maureen, my mother, who has not only provided care and logistical support throughout the process of writing, but also, ever politically engaged, encouraged me to be attuned to issues of power.

My heartfelt gratitude goes to the residents of the Copperbelt who shared their stories of living through drastic change.

Introduction

The sale of the Zambian state-owned mining conglomerate, the Zambia Consolidated Copper Mines (ZCCM), in the mid-1990s left a majority of mine town residents anxious about making a living and sustaining life. In the formerly middle-class suburban area that is the focus of this book, residents dug wells in their backyard for water and cut trees that lined the streets to fire bricks moulded from the clay of anthills that dot the landscape. They also planted crops in their backyard and in the open spaces of the parks and golf club lawns. The book explores people's experiences of the texture of place and the shaping of life in a Zambian Copperbelt town following this sale, part of the widespread implementation of structural adjustment policies that introduced free market policies[1] and drastically reduced social welfare in Zambia.

It is based on a study, which focussed on a low-density former mine suburb in the Copperbelt town of Luanshya, where I lived in the years 2007 to 2010, and demonstrates how this transformation has influenced the urban character of the mine town; how its inhabitants seek a livelihood in very trying times; and how they gain skills, negotiate the moral and spatial boundaries of the free market, and make sense of their lives and change. Copperbelt residents say that in their recent past "there used to be order," whereas the present is characterised by uncertainty and incoherence. This book describes how they navigate this present to "get by" and "get on with life." I use an exploratory ontology that values *trying* as a way to open up possibilities, even in the likelihood of encountering impossibilities.

It departs from previous ethnographies on the Copperbelt that, although they have done much to highlight the social and political situation, have paid less attention to describing how its inhabitants engage with it as a place. By drawing on theoretical and methodological perspectives in anthropology and urban studies that emphasise performance and movement, I break from the systemic representations of the Copperbelt that do not account for the effort, experimental action, and poetic and textural engagement with place and the authority of everyday life in constrained circumstances.

THE COPPERBELT AS PLACE

To open, an extract from my journal.

Walking in the early morning, on the streets of the Copperbelt town, Luanshya, I get fleeting moments of the same buoyancy I felt as a child walking down the roads of the Copperbelt. It rained in the night; the light is soft and the air is fresh. I watch the children emerge from their homes, heading to school in their school uniforms. They seem so pensive. I watch them, they watch me, and I dodge the potholes full of water. I cross to the other side of the road, away from the house with the manhole that spews sewerage onto the road. I approach the house with the lovely garden and the only reasonable stretch of flamboyant trees on the road. I walk past it. On these walks, I go past the shiny new little metal Coca-Cola shop selling bread and cell phone talk-time. The shop is in front of a house painted with Mickey Mouse and Donald Duck cartoons; I think it also serves as a nursery school. I walk past another little shop, a wood off-cut cabin with a vividly and naively painted side profile of a man with a "table" cut. It is a barber shop located near the road and outside a house shaded by mango trees.

There is a stretch of the walk I do not like and that I particularly dislike at midday when the hot sun beats on my head. A road largely devoid of trees, its apparent barrenness broken by the termite-eaten stumps of yesterday's trees. Then there is the detour I like. It is to a place framed by memory; it reminds me of my childhood summer afternoons at the public pool, of picnics and fountains. It is the town's public pool. Amidst everything else, I find it a truly beautiful place, an Olympic-size pool and pared-down Grecian-like change rooms set on the shorter sides of the pool, palm trees, fountains, and more, looking like yesterday, like the Copperbelt I knew then! I have been to the pool on many mornings, the guards there allowing me to walk around it. I have not swum in it, though I have wanted to and planned to on many occasions, because I am not sure it is cleaned. It looks clean, and one morning I found one person swimming in it. The thing is, I have seen the overgrown tennis courts, rat-infested recreation halls, the desolate but still beautiful golf course and wondered, can the swimming pool have escaped their fate? Is there something I am missing?

There is a stretch of the walk I like. On most mornings on this stretch of the road a rooster struts, followed by some hens. During school holidays, I also see the little group of children who sit out early by the road, outside their home, watching people go by. I remember as a child being curious about where people went, my world bounded by the routines that did not take me very far—other than the imaginaries of places beyond my experience. One morning, while walking the rooster's stretch of road, I happened to look to the house on my left, which had a street shop, this one a metal cargo container painted red. The house was a large old red brick bungalow in the same style as most others in the area, and, from its long front veranda, to my surprise, streamed out a flutter of chickens, ushered out by three children. I was amazed at the sheer number of chickens that streamed out of the house.

THE COPPERBELT AS I REMEMBER IT

I spent most of my childhood on the Copperbelt, growing up in a small mining company town called Kalulushi that had been built in the 1950s. A third-generation Copperbelt resident, I considered the Copperbelt my home. My paternal grandfather, born in 1918 in what was then known as Fort Johnstone in Nyasaland (now Malawi), had migrated in his early twenties to work in the Wankie coal mines in Southern Rhodesia (now Zimbabwe), and then on to the Copperbelt town of Mufulira in 1948, where he had been employed as a general worker on the mines. He met my paternal grandmother while she was visiting an older sister who had married a mineworker. My paternal grandmother's family had moved from then Fiera (now known as Luangwa), a border town between Zambia, Malawi, and Mozambique, to Southern Rhodesia, where my great-grandfather had worked before moving to Livingstone, where he was employed as a shop assistant for the Susman brothers (see Macmillan 2005) and then moving with them in 1940 to Broken Hill (Kabwe), where they had opened a store. My father was born to my grandparents on the Copperbelt in 1949 and had grown up in a mine township in Mufulira, experiencing the Africanisation policies described in the latter part of this chapter that saw an improvement in mineworkers' welfare. He described to me how his parents, my grandparents, had moved from a three-room earth-block house with communal ablution facilities to a four-room brick house with internal ablution and electricity in 1955.

My father, also a former ZCCM mine employee, had worked as a mechanical engineer at the mines. He had been employed to work with Roan Copper

Mines in the 1970s. The Roan Copper Mines together with Nchanga Consolidated Copper Mines later merged to form the fully nationalised ZCCM. I provide a background to the mines in the next chapter. My father's training and tertiary education were sponsored by the mining company.[2] This was in the period following independence in 1964 from British colonial rule, and part of a broader policy of Zambianisation (see Burawoy 1972) that sought to expand the pool of a skilled local labour force so as to become less reliant on expatriate skilled migrant labour.

I attended a primary school that was run by ZCCM in Kalulushi. Throughout my seven years of education there, I had only one locally trained teacher, and that only in my last year. All the other teachers were British and Irish migrants trained in their countries.

As strange as it might sound today—this was at the height of the new postcolonial nation-building led by Kenneth Kaunda, then president of Zambia—it did not strike me, my parents, my classmates, or my neighbours as anything out of the ordinary. These schools were built after the colonial period, under Kaunda's proactive education policy. He believed that he could mix the best of all worlds by providing excellent formal education modelled on the Western system while preserving and nurturing African principles of solidarity, conviviality, and reciprocal exchange. The school population was also mixed: one-third of the children were from the families of British migrant miners and mining cadres working and living in the Copperbelt; another third from migrant mining workers from Indian subcontinent and the Philippines; the other third local Zambians. The provision of excellent education also served the purpose of attracting skilled labourers and managers in the mines who would have otherwise sent their children to boarding schools overseas, at a much higher cost. Compared to most other state schools founded during the colonial period, there was no corporal punishment, and I was glad for that. Teachers did try to anglicise our names, but in retrospect, while it seems quite odd and even ludicrous, I don't think my friends whose names were anglicised made much of this at the time.[3]

This melting pot of subtle oddities and creative opportunities was well in line with Kaunda's syncretic approach to nation-building. As we were constantly reminded about "One Zambia, One Nation," the catchy chorus to Kaunda's public speeches, we felt, consciously or not it was inappropriate to delve into our differences. Despite the long-term economic decline that started in the early 1980s and peaked toward the end of the 1990s, people like my family in the mining welfare system, with its large net of benefits ranging from housing to health and education, were the most protected. When riots about food shortages started in the urban areas in the mid-1980s, the people who had been most affected by the decline were from the non-mining sectors of the urban population.

Kaunda's socialist liberal dream was best symbolised by the mining system, which was nationalised progressively from 1969 (see Chapter 1). My school was one of the examples. With its idiosyncratic mix of African humanism, liberal socialism, Western standards of education and skill, and ecumenical religious spirit, Kaunda had created one of the most successful experiments in middle-class formation outside the West. I only realised much later that we were de facto an elite, despite the humble backgrounds of my family and many of my classmates' families. At the same time, Kaunda's nationalism did not allow for global consumerism to penetrate in any major way the life of most Zambians until the change of regime to multiparty democracy in the early 1990s. Consumer goods were scarce, and Tip Top, produced by the state-owned company that offered a substitute[4] for Western soft drinks, and DPB ice cream, also locally produced, were the most we could crave for. Protected by our benevolent dictator and a relatively stable welfare system, and shielded from the frills and trivialities of a fully free-market economy, my classmates and I had a carefree childhood, passing large parts of our time in a school system that fostered creativity and skill through a comprehensive program that included arts and sports. School competitions in the arts stimulated children to produce poetry, short stories, plays, paintings and sculptures. At that stage, my aspiration was to become an artist-scientist. At school or at home, nobody told me I couldn't. The era embodied the possibility of dreams in the future.

This idyllic view of my childhood sat in contrast to those of my parents, in particular my mother, who had not been raised on the Copperbelt and had worked outside the mine system. In her accounts of life on the Copperbelt, she remembers queuing for basic commodities like sugar, soap, flour, and cooking oil, which were not available in the stores because of the inefficiencies of what was then a centrally controlled economy. These shortages made the running of domestic life a stressful activity. In addition, she felt that aspects of Copperbelt sociality, like the mine recreation clubs, provided men (the majority of the mine workforce) with an escape mechanism that prevented them from dealing with the day-to-day difficulties of life in this period, as James Ferguson has eloquently described in his ethnography *Expectations of Modernity* (1999). For my parents, and others of their generation who came of age during the optimistic post-independence years that lasted until the late 1970s, the economic decline of the 1980s that Ferguson describes was a big blow to their social and material expectations of modernity. In addition, Kaunda's one-party state that limited free speech and the inefficient management of parastatals (Woldring 1983) were also a source of general discontent.

My mother's expression of this discontent led her to become a trade unionist, forming part of the movement that was instrumental in bringing the end of Kaunda's rule. Her involvement in labour strike activity, though formal in this case, was characteristic of many women who, often with their children, took to the Copperbelt streets to voice their discontent and were crucially important in negotiating better conditions for mineworkers. However, like Jacob Dlamini (2009) writing about growing up during the years of South Africa's apartheid, our memories of the past were not coloured predominantly by strife but by the texture of other aspects of life. In the same way, the Kaunda years as they are predominantly narrated (Burnell 1994; Geisler 1992; Mills 1992) not only were a period of economic mismanagement and political repression, but also comprised other memories. Thus, for me, and many of the children who grew up within the mine system in the declining years of the 1980s, this past was not viewed in the same way as my mother saw it, variously as one of consumer deprivation and political repression, but one of simpler pleasures.

While the colonial past, prior to independence in 1964, is woven into Copperbelt life in the landscape and layout of the towns, I argue that it is more of a sub-texture, one that is not as often referred to in Copperbelt residents' nostalgic memories of the past. What Copperbelt residents often refer to were the optimistic post-independence years of the Kaunda era, characterised by welfare largesse and a large developmental agenda, until the decline beginning the 1980s that makes the subject of Ferguson's ethnography. For Copperbelt residents today, the past is remembered as having been characterised by order, while the present and its future are characterised by uncertainty.

My idea of a seamless future that unravelled to reveal one's aspirations was disrupted in 1995, when my father, who was then working for a ZCCM subsidiary company and based in Lusaka, was retrenched. This was just a few months after I finished high school at the ZCCM-run Mpelembe Secondary School in Kitwe, on the Copperbelt. I remember it as a time of great uncertainty that underlined the precariousness of the middle-class life we had lived. Our family lived in rented accommodation, subsidised by the ZCCM subsidiary. We owned no other property. The majority of the household assets were owned by the mines. My three younger siblings were still enrolled at mine schools that were heavily subsidised by ZCCM. My mother's income as a personal assistant in another parastatal that was yet to be privatised was not enough to sustain a middle-income way of life and status. Our situation was no different from what other former formal sector employees and their families were going through. People downscaled, found other ways of earning a living, and attempted to cope with life, while others struggled or passed on. However, I was struck, and still am, at people's capacity to attempt to create new combinations for survival amidst great physical and psychosocial hardship.

The Copperbelt, so familiar to me, had, in its economic crisis, also become an unfamiliar place to me. It is this that made me want to undertake study of the Copperbelt. This is the way I went about it.

If I had to describe the moment that I began my fieldwork, I would say it began with the renovation of my fieldwork home, a process that I describe in Chapter 2. As focal point, the house coalesces not only the social, but the political, economic, and material aspects of a place. An edited collection by Carsten and Hugh-Jones (1995) focussing on the analytical significance of the house highlights that the "house" allows us to explore the social organisation of society, as houses have genealogies, reflect status, and signify ideological inclinations.[5] The renovation of the house gave me the opportunity to become a direct continuous participant observer as it engaged me in a process of "doing." Bernard argued that this method of research is "worth the effort" if "you want to know what people do, and won't settle for what they say" (1994, 312). Tim Ingold (2000) made a similar point, saying that understanding skill cannot really be accomplished only by observing but requires doing. With my interest in housing and background in architecture, the renovation of the house was also the entry point to my fieldwork that felt most natural. As I engaged in the making of my fieldwork home habitable in as short as possible a time, I became more aware of the constraints that hindered this process. It provided me the avenue to reflect on the difficulties that my Copperbelt informants had trying to get things done amidst social difficulties and uncertainties in the post-privatisation era. It also made me aware of the opportunities that emerged out of this context and the varying situations and skills that made some people better or less able to cope with their changed circumstances.

To depart from my own reflections on the Copperbelt as a place, I engaged in conversation with people I met on my walks, on public transport and in other public spaces to solicit their views on the Copperbelt today, the past and future, and their own life stories. Through this process, as well as the activity of renovating the house, I identified my key informants, who are presented in the various cases throughout the book. I conducted both informal and semi-structured interviews to elicit stories of their lives in relation to their experiences of the Copperbelt. Sandercock (2005) writes of the importance of telling the story of place from the perspective of those who experience it. Sandercock argues that the experience and story told of a particular place will vary according to the background and even world view. Stories of place, much like Ato Quayson's (2014) descriptions of life of Oxford Street in Accra, will capture provisional moments—when multiple economies, languages, and styles jostle amongst another, indicating the multiple itineraries for its users and the improvisational ways in which they come together. These experiences are more ephemeral but find their traces in representations within popular culture. In Chapter 6, I describe how Copperbelt youth deal with the momentary and ongoing stresses that followed the radical changes that ensued following the sale of the mines. I also show how youths' actions and views of a future are influenced not only by the ongoing political economic situation, but also by the gendered and intergenerational dynamics of the times.

Some of these experiences are hard to explain in words. Henrietta Moore's (1986) call for attention to metaphors of people's everyday practice was useful in overcoming this problem. It was these metaphors, often presented in the lingua franca of the Copperbelt, Bemba, in which I am fluent, that provided a conceptual understanding of people's views of the social changes that the sale of the ZCCM mines wrought. In the stories, they told of place they also allowed me to explore how power relations were enacted and how people's interests and values were framed, understood, and justified. Tim Cresswell (2004) argues that stories about specific sites, such as in this context the Copperbelt, are significant in that they are what make places meaningful, and help distinguish one place from another.

I spent a significant portion of my research "hanging out" with my key informants, observing as they went about their everyday activities, and noting my own and their impressions of social situations we encountered. I looked at what went on and what they did, but also how people behaved, tones of voice, bodily gestures, drawing loosely from Ervin Goffman's (1959) *Presentation of Self in Everyday Life* and Gregory Bateson's (1972) analysis of human communication. These observations are reflected in Chapter 5, which focuses on the performance of gender on the Copperbelt. The time spent with my key informants and their families also allowed me to build detailed case stories. I encountered many of my informants daily, enabling me to observe in close proximity their goings-on.

To establish the extent and scale of observed phenomena, I conducted two surveys in the "low-density" former mine suburb[6] of Luanshya, which formed the main hub of my research. The Manchester school anthropologists who did much urban anthropological research found this a useful method for collecting basic biographical data on income, household composition, and social affiliations and people's perceptions. For example, a key material change that occurred with the re-privatisation of the mines was the sale of mine-owned housing to former ZCCM employees. In my initial survey of fifty-six households, conducted in July and August 2008, I asked questions regarding house ownership because my observations and interviews with key informants suggested that the privatisation of housing starting from the mid-1990s might have affected settlement patterns. In the survey, I asked residents whether they were the owners of the house or were renting, and if renting, where the owners of the house lived; if there were people considered part of the household but who were currently not living there; and if residents had a backyard garden, field, or farm where they grew food and if so, where it was located. In a follow-up survey, this one of one hundred households conducted in August 2009, I included questions on family composition and bereavements after hearing many accounts of death following the sale of the ZCCM mines.

In addition to the survey, I drew from secondary statistical data such as the national census conducted by the Central Statistical Office, and archival information housed in Lusaka at the National Archives and in Ndola at the mining archives.

Prior to the re-privatisation of the mines, the mining companies kept very good archives. However, in the post-privatisation period, in particular in the case of the Luanshya mines, the gaps in the archives reflected some of the problems that beset the sale of these mines. Miles Larmer (2004) notes that the post-privatisation mining data and materials remain un-archived due to a lack of resources. From the archives, I drew on news items from the *Mining Mirror* and the minutes of the town management board. These provided insights into my informants' views on the extent of the role that the mining company played in miners' lives.

Divine Fuh[7] argues that ethnographers, as pliable tools for the observation and description of society, should be aware of their foibles, as well as how their background influences their analysis. I became aware that my interest in doing fieldwork on the Copperbelt was influenced by the anxieties of change wrought by the drastic shift in the political economy of the region during my early adulthood. I came to fieldwork with skills that came predominantly from years of working in architectural practice and education, such as an attention to patterns and how things come together. Accordingly, this book reflects less on the religious, historical, and political aspects of the Copperbelt—these aspects are better represented by other scholars[8] of the region. Rather, it focusses on the poetics and texture of place and describes a situation of drastic social change.

There is a dearth of descriptive material about social differentiation and coping during the transition period to a market-based economy and beyond in Zambia. Recently, a number of anthropologists have warned against the current trend towards highly theoretical work with little empirical content and have called for a return to ethnographic description as both a useful endeavour and as the basis from which to explore and build theoretical concepts (Englund 2002; Hart 2008; Hart and Oritz 2008; Da Col and Graeber 2011).[9] This work is an attempt to move in this direction. Nevertheless, many of the issues discussed here resonate with previous ethnographies, like James Ferguson's (1999) *Expectations of Modernity* and the works of the Manchester school scholars (e.g., Epstein 1958; Powdermaker 1962; Wilson 1968). The study contributes to scholarship on everyday life in African towns and cities (see Simone 2004; Kihato 2013; Quayson 2014), particularly within the context of the collapse of states following the end of the Cold War and widespread implementation of economic liberalisation policies (De Boeck and Plissart 2006; Piot 2010). It draws on theoretical insights on place and place-making from anthropology, human geography, and urban studies (Tuan 1977; Casey 1997; Creswell 2004; Ingold 2009), to describe the Copperbelt as I have come to understand it.

SOCIAL VARIATION AND CHANGE: AFTER FERGUSON

The long run of mine operations since the end of the Great Depression in the 1930s (the biggest recession to hit the mining industry until the long slow decline of the industry in the 1970s) lent to the general perception of the relative stability of the mines and the company welfare system. A number of the key anthropological studies were conducted during this period.

These included Godfrey Wilson's (1968) account that covered the economic effects of industrialisation in the region and its interrelationship to the local, regional, and global political economy; Clyde Mitchell's (1954, 1969) work on the perceptions of new urban dwellers of urban life, social status and urban social networks; Arnold Leonard Epstein's (1958, 1981) examinations of urban identity and political affiliation in the urban areas; and Hortense Powdermaker's (1962) descriptive observations of urban life on the Copperbelt. Most of these studies, other than Powdermaker's, which drew on multiple modes of analysis, were in the structural-functionalist tradition that was in vogue then, but differed from the prevailing model in that all addressed questions of social change within urban contexts. The cohort of these studies, collectively referred to as the Manchester school, advanced methodologies that dealt with social change and with scalar analyses that linked their informants to a wider macro-political context, both regional and global. Situational analysis and the "extended case" method were notable methodologies developed for exploring the more complex dynamics of urban life. Here individual and group interactions and their networks were observed in order to elucidate social structure.

However, James Ferguson's (1999) major critique of these earlier studies was that they assumed that social change was linked to a developmental discourse that was seen as progressive, and thus adhered to a problematic belief in the myth of modernity. A key aspect of the myth that Ferguson questions had to do with the belief that as people migrated from the rural areas to the Copperbelt towns, they progressively became permanent urban dwellers with weakened rural ties. Ferguson challenged this belief by drawing on his ethnography of the region in the late 1980s, exploring the life trajectories of retiring mineworkers, whom he followed over a number of years. Through cases of retiring miners, Ferguson shows that miners had either maintained rural kin ties and went on to settle in their rural homelands, and that even when they had opted out of a rural homeland retirement and had settled on the outskirts of the Copperbelt, they had reasons as to why they would not retire to their rural homeland. Amongst these reasons, Ferguson notes, was a real material, and not just psychological, fear of witchcraft that stemmed in the cases he describes from a failure to consistently maintain rural kin relations. Through these cases Ferguson challenges the linear notion of rural-to-urban migration and permanence in the towns, showcasing the range of strategies that Copperbelt retirees undertook to get by. These clearly showed a straddling and negotiation of rural life. He underlines how a rural retirement was an option even for long-term residents of the towns.

Ferguson further sets about demystifying the myth by drawing attention to the social variations that could be seen on the Copperbelt. Variation for Ferguson was not only to be seen in retiring miners' livelihood and spatial strategies, but also in representations of themselves. He draws on a stylistic notion of personhood that draws from Judith Butler's notion of performativity and Pierre Bourdieu's concept of habitus as embodied competence in practice to show the variation in Copperbelt residents' stylistic representations of themselves. Whereas the Manchester school had used situational analysis to explain stylistic presentation of the urban and the rural as located within a framed structural social context, Ferguson locates his within an individualistic agency that does not give primacy to structure, but describes a more fluid social setting and wider range of performative practices. Ferguson describes Copperbelt residents' self-presentations as ranging from the cosmopolitan to the localist, and as signifying a repertoire of town-like and rural-like behavioural competencies that, he says, are dispositions learned through circumstance and choice of social interactions.

It is here that Owen Sichone (2001) takes issue with Ferguson's ethnography of the Copperbelt, arguing that Ferguson downplays the social historical context that affords Copperbelt residents their options and behaviours. Similarly, Francis Nyamnjoh (2001) calls attention to the dichotomous trap that Ferguson finds himself in when he categorises people's stylistic repertoires into cosmopolitan and localist. Nyamnjoh argues that rather than a choice of drawing from here or out there, people draw from a repertoire of things that have themselves been so mixed it is hard to conclude where they are coming from. Ferguson's work on the Copperbelt (1990, 1992, 1999) has thus spurred debate on the academic orthodoxy about rural-urban migration patterns (see Palmer 2000; Potts 1995; Macmillan 1993) and also drawn attention to Copperbelt residents' own conceptualisations of their world—their sense of loss, nostalgia for a modern past, and their characterisation of various styles of personal representation.

In the context of Copperbelt residents' settlement patterns Ferguson has made a strong case that the standard narrative of linear progression from rural to urban migration did not account for the myriad ways that Copperbelt residents straddled these spaces and drew on them to get by. What this meant in practice was that even though Copperbelt residents themselves may have mapped out some kind of trajectory in the form of a "plan," as Ferguson's inquiry into what mineworkers planned to do following their retirement suggests, what happened in reality was what Ferguson describes as a "bush"

(1999, 78) or a "full spread" in options and variation that resisted being neatly mapped (1999, 20–21). An example of this departure from the plan is particularly well presented in Ferguson's case of Mr Paul Mukande (1999, 152–158), who, in his post-retirement plan of returning to "the land" settled on the outskirts of rural Copperbelt and set about establishing a farm. Initially all seemed to go well. Mr Mukande also had grander plans that included a small emerald-mining venture and a larger more permanent house to replace the temporary structure he was living in. However, several things went wrong. His farm was on land with ambiguous tenure, the cement for building the permanent house was damaged when soaked by the rains, and he failed to find emeralds in his digs. In an ideal world of well-laid plans, Mr Mukande would have conducted some background work to ensure his land was on secure tenure, bought a tent to keep his bags of cement dry, and known that the odds of finding emeralds were stacked against him. But in the world of the Copperbelt, as Ferguson observed, plans tended to be based on unrealistic expectations, and enterprises often did not end well.

Here I will be exploring similar expectations with the view to developing an analytical approach that accounts for Copperbelt residents' aspirations and efforts. I refer to this as "*trying.*" I show how, for Copperbelt residents in times of hardship, the unpredictability in the outcomes of their efforts made them increasingly perceptive of the opportunities and possibilities that had the potential to emerge from chance encounters. My aim is to engage with questions of social change and variation, but unlike Ferguson, engage too with the people's perceptions and engagements within a changing *material*, and not only *social*, landscape. From this approach and building on Ferguson's example of Mr Mukande, I posit an ecological approach drawn from Ingold (2000), in which residents are immanent in the environment, and, in turn, the environment is immanent in them. This position sees people and environment not as separate but as mutually constituting. Just as persons' characters or personalities are seen or perceived in relation to other persons, so too is the character of the Copperbelt as a place perceived in relation to what it affords to the persons who live there. Also, just as persons are affected by one another's moods, so too do the energies of a place, mutually comprising people and things in movement, in rhythm, affect persons and the character of place.

Chapter 1 focuses on the changing character of life and social welfare services in the mining towns of what was once the most urbanised country in central Africa, describing the variation of services provided by mining companies over the years. These ranged from minimal, at the time of the industry's establishment in the 1920s, to a period of largesse between the 1950s and the late 1970s, and then a slow decline following the slide in world copper prices. It shows how the withdrawal of the mines from welfare provision from the mid-1990s to the present has radically altered not only people's well-being, but also the character of the urban areas, leading to the observation that towns have lost their order and have become like "villages."

Chapter 2 engages with the methodological and theoretical ways that the Copperbelt has been presented, in particular with the most recent ethnography of the Copperbelt, James Ferguson's (1999) *Expectations of Modernity*. It argues for a phenomenological engagement and analysis of the Copperbelt. From the point of view of method, I argue that understanding places, in particular how people engage with them, requires the researcher engage in a process of "doing." As mentioned above, for me this was the renovation of a house in the former low-density mine suburb within which I focused my research. It was through this process that I got to know most of my research informants, and learnt through practice what my informants often told me, "You can't plan." This notion challenged my ideas of agency that had strongly been influenced by my architectural training and the anthropological work of Alfred Gell: the idea that if one can impose order and establish patterns, then in turn one can trace out a network of patterns and relationships. It was difficult to "order" the field, but I argue that rather than giving up entirely any attempt to do so, fieldwork and analysis should be approached as a continual process of "trying"; experimentation, and in turn agency, should be seen as a blob of blurred signifiers that indicates an ever-moving intent that is entangled within the also ever-changing environment. These arguments emerge throughout the book and are addressed again in the conclusion.

In Chapter 3 I trace the trajectories of former ZCCM employees living in a low-density former mine neighbourhood. I also detail how they attempt to make a life in what has become a difficult economic context. Despite the long economic decline from the 1970s, the privatisation of the Zambia Consolidated Copper Mines beginning 1997 brought to an almost complete halt one of the biggest experiments in middle-class formation in sub-Saharan Africa. The disappearance of the old ZCCM system and its de facto control of socioeconomic differentiation sparked new processes of "class" formation. The new classes have come to rely on working for oneself and an ethos of self-reliance. With the absence of a formalised work structure, the erosion of welfare, and amidst a difficult economic reality there has been a resort to improvisational strategies in an attempt to make a living. Some have made it, others have not, and the middle class has dwindled.

Copperbelt women have long played an important role in supplementing incomes from wages from the mines and lobbying through their participation in strike action for better living conditions. Until the privatisation of the mines, much of what women did took a back seat to the core business of mining. Increasingly, on the periphery of formal mining in Zambia, it is not uncommon to find women and children working at mining dump sites, spaces that in the Zambian imaginary are occupied by young male copper thieves, popularly known as Jerabos (jail boys). Chapter 4 describes women's work at these sites that fall outside the regulatory boundaries of legality. Here workers are called illegal miners, but workers have crafted an alternative moral economy to justify what they do. The chapter examines how Copperbelt residents see and engage with the copper industry after its re-privatisation. It explores local understandings of private and public ownership, and how an ideology of accumulation is received after decades of state and local narratives against selfishness. Women working at these sites ask, if the market for copper is open, why is it not open to them? Their question and the substance of the chapter provide a perspective on residents' engagement with copper from the home and yard to the copper-mining sites.

The proliferation of housekeeping courses that had been offered to women near the mines underlined the expectations of their role in the town and the ideal of domesticity. The representation of the Copperbelt as home to "loose women," eager to extort the wages of miners through vice, which had been perpetuated in the early days of mining, persisted well into Ferguson's (1999) ethnography, decades after the 1930s, when the mining companies were not sure whether to let women into mining towns. In the present context, many former male mine employees say they do not know how they would have survived the harshest periods that followed the sale of the mines were it not for the industriousness of women, a value strongly linked to the traditional or customary ideal of womanhood. Chapter 5 thus explores how Copperbelt women straddle these gendered expectations of domesticity and describes where they find places for pleasure and harmony. It reflects on Copperbelt women's communicative modus operandi and shows how the nuances of this affect spill into their broader economic and social life.

Chapter Six draws on Zambian popular music to explore how Copperbelt residents conceptualise life in difficult times. For many residents, life has been hard and also mired with the experience of death. While they describe themselves as "suffering," there is also the hope that this suffering may end. This belief does not necessarily play out as a clear plan for a future. The possibilities of what the future may bring emerge from the environment and people's engagement with it and each other. This may be good or bad; it cannot be predetermined. Zambian popular music urges people simply to go on, to endure. The extension of this temporal experience of life is expressed in the urging of people to literally "top up" on their lives.

In the conclusion, I call for an anthropology of *trying*. Especially in contexts of uncertainty, this approach assumes that there are numerous paths and journeys that can be embarked on in learning about the world. These multiple paths create different rhythms and resonances that are perceived beyond objective observation. It is an approach that resonates with Copperbelt residents' own approach to life. Lives of hardship, no longer under the attempted regulatory control of the mines, have become an exploration of how to survive and maybe become successful. In understanding the spatial boundaries of transition, Copperbelt residents do not edge around prescribed boundaries such as private property; they are prone to trespass. People's improvisational activities unfold in variation within the environment. This is perceived as villagisation, a visible marker of the changed urban character, which also points to the numerous attempts at trying in a context unconstrained by strong regulatory structures.

NOTES

1. In 1991, after its first multiparty elections since it became a one-party state in 1972, Zambia adopted full-scale free-market policies.

2. Though my father had gone to state-run schools in Mufulira, the mines had provided support to them and had, at secondary school level, recruited pupils from there to join their jobs on training program or offered scholarships for tertiary education in mining-related disciplines. My father had opted for an in-house training program with the Roan Copper Mines as an engineering draughtsperson. This had also entailed enrolment in a City and Guilds Technicians program. In-house trainees in such programs were accommodated in furnished single flats in a low-density area of the mine township. After my father completed his in-house training he applied to pursue a mechanical engineering degree with the University of Zambia, sponsored by the mines in 1974, and on graduation in 1979 returned to work on the mines.

3. It was at the ZCCM-run secondary school, Mpelembe, where the teachers, the majority Zambians of African origin, made a point in the first year of ensuring we learnt and used the correct pronunciations of our names.

4. Ann Seidman (1974) describes how following independence from British rule, Zambia pursued a policy of import substitution that intensified from the 1970s, when falling copper prices necessitated foreign currency controls that limited importation of goods.

5. Garth Myers (2003), writing on the planning of towns in colonial Africa, describes how colonial-era planners and architects sought to reflect colonial domination through the built environment.

6. The low-density neighbourhood comprised approximately just over one thousand lots.

7. At an anthropology seminar held 20 May 2014 at the University of Cape Town, South Africa.

8. Recent studies of the Copperbelt have included historical works on labour (Larmer 2007), medicine (Kalusa 2011; Schumaker 2008), and sports (Chipande 2016), as well as political economic studies on privatisation (Lungu and Fraser 2006; Kazimbaya 2007) and on foreign investment (Haglund 2008; Lee 2010; Negi 2013). They have also included studies on religion (Haynes 2012) and gender (Evans 2014).

9. Harri Englund (2002) in his work on the experience of migrancy in Malawi calls not just for an analysis of what he refers to as the rhetoric of globalism but for its exploration in relation to how it is "embodied and situated" in place. Hart and Oritz (2008) argue that an exploration of the political economy of the free market should move beyond the analysis of its ideology to look at its empirical realities. Da Col and Graeber (2011) in the foreword to the first issue of *HAU: The Journal of Ethnographic Theory* call contemporary anthropologists' attention to the theoretical richness to be found within ethnographic concepts.

CHAPTER 1

Mining, Welfare, and Urbanisation

The Wavering Urban Character of Zambia's Copperbelt

Zambia's changing fortunes in copper mining are mirrored in its urban growth and welfare trajectory.[1] The fluctuating world market price for copper has had a direct bearing on the urban population's levels of material welfare and deprivation. In this chapter, I explore this in two main parts: the first a historical review of mining's impact on urbanisation, the second an overview of the current urban and welfare circumstances of the population following the privatisation of Zambia Consolidated Copper Mines (ZCCM). This account sets the stage for the discussions in subsequent chapters.

Urbanisation on the Copperbelt since the mines came into production in the 1930s was synonymous with rural-to-urban migration, spurred on by the idea of a better "modern" life in the towns. Several studies from the 1990s suggest that the decline of the industry affected urban processes. These argue that Copperbelt residents were moving from urban to rural areas, settling, and seeking subsistence livelihoods in the "bush" on the outskirts of Copperbelt towns (Ferguson 1999; Hansangule, Feeney, and Palmer 1998; Potts 1995). The 2010 census indicates that Copperbelt residents were moving to the capital city, Lusaka, which would tally with the perceptible shift of Lusaka's lingua franca from Nyanja to Bemba. Furthermore, data from the 2000 census show shifts in regional livelihood diversification patterns, with the economically active in mining falling from 3.4% of the country's total labour force in 1990 to 1.3% in 2000, while those active in agricultural activities grew from 50% in 1990 to 72% in 2000 (CSO 2003). On the other hand, since approximately 2004, some rural areas have emerged as small-scale mining outposts, such as those in the new mining area of the North Western Province. They are becoming more "town-like" as former subsistence farmers and semi-foragers turn to small-scale mining joined by "old" Copperbelt in-migrants and others from as far away as Lusaka who are moving in to benefit from a boom in copper.

While these trends have not changed the cosmopolitan nature of the Copperbelt, which, from its early years, attracted a migrant population composed of various African groups and transient Europeans, they have influenced Copperbelt residents' perception of the "urban." This has been in the context of the acute urban poverty that followed the mines' privatisation, retrenchments, and withdrawal of social welfare provisions. Copperbelt residents complain that their urban areas have lost their sense of "urban order."

These changes have laid bare the fallacy of the idea of the urban as modern, which the former neat facade of the Copperbelt towns could imply. Myers (2003, 56), when considering African colonial cities, notes that the planned ideal of the modern city never materialised, as these places "became reframed within the African idioms of urban life, dependant on uneven and unequal development of power by individual householders, or religious institutions, or ideas of space and on customary neighbourly understanding." I explore these ideas further in later chapters.

Following Zambia's independence in 1964, President Kaunda tried to address the relation between the rural and urban through his philosophy of humanism, attempting to reframe urban life by transposing "African" values based on the idealisation of village life into the towns, and encouraging an African conviviality of giving across extended urban and rural kin, devolving the welfare of the state in urban areas to the rural through the "family" (Kaunda and Morris 1966). This theme informed Zambian state policies for the first few decades of national independence when copper underwrote the country's economic prosperity.

COPPER: HISTORICAL CONDUIT OF URBANISATION AND SOCIAL WELFARE

Emergence of the Copperbelt

Artisanal copper mining had long been practiced in the region between the Zambezi and the Congo basin. Nineteenth- and early twentieth-century European prospectors' accounts attest to extensive ancient copper working, and writers speculated that copper had flourished as a currency during the slave trade and thereafter become dormant with the abolition of slavery

(Bradley 1952). This suggests a centuries-long history of copper production, affected by dips and rises in international trade.

Industrial copper mining in Zambia was facilitated by Cecil Rhodes through dubiously[2] acquired concessions, for example Lochner's, which was held by the British South Africa Company (BSAC) and which erroneously covered most of the western half of Northern Rhodesia / Zambia. The confirmation of copper deposits by Frederick Burnham, a scout of the BSAC, was the catalyst for mining development. The nature of the ore deposits necessitated deep-shaft mining, and the lack of a transport infrastructure to take the minerals to ports delayed investment in the area for a decade (Coleman 1971).

The construction of a "Cape to Cairo" rail line reached Ndola in 1909, creating a corridor along which towns with an urban character were destined to develop. The BSAC's concession was exploited by the two mining houses, Rhodesian Selection Trust (RST) and the Anglo American Corporation (AAC), which were dominant until the early 1970s. Large-scale commercial farming did not emerge in the area due to the acidity of the soils of the copper-mining region, as Clifford Darby (1931) had already noted in the 1930s. Thus, there was a stark contrast between the urban mining strip and the rural subsistence-farming zone adjacent to it.

Coalescing Urban Growth and Welfare Awareness in the Copperbelt, 1909–1939

Many of the early African migrant mineworkers stayed in unhealthy camps that, as in the case of Luanshya, were plagued by malaria and blackwater fever associated with swampy areas (Schumaker 2008) and by unsanitary conditions associated with poor urban infrastructure (Kalusa 1997). By the 1930s some of these camps had been improved by the efforts of public-health experts, engineers, and vanguard town-planners, who were influenced by the garden-city movement[3] and endeavoured to apply these ideas to build small, liveable mining towns. The towns that developed around mining activity included Kabwe (formerly Broken Hill) in the Central Province, where lead was mined; Luanshya; Kitwe; Mufulira (my father's birthplace); Chingola; Chililabombwe; Kalulushi; and Ndola, which served as the administrative and commercial centre. As African settlement increased on the Copperbelt, it attracted considerable academic interest (Mitchell 1954; Epstein 1958; Powdermaker 1962). The parallel setting-up of colonial administrative centres resulted in towns with a dual administrative system consisting of the mines and local councils (Mutale 2004).

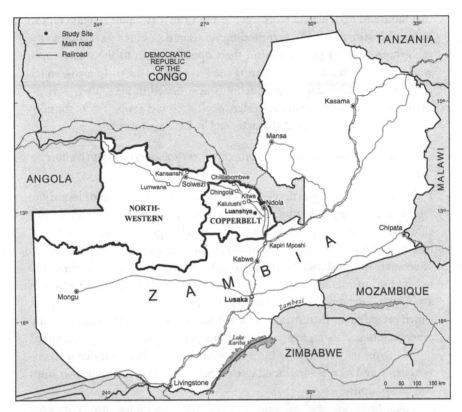

Figure 1. Map of Zambia, showing the Copperbelt and its towns, and the new mining regions in North Western Province. Source: Cartography by Mike Shand, University of Glasgow, based on United Nations Population Division map.

This early mining period was not characterised by any coherent plans for the welfare of African miners. In fact, the mining companies had a negative attitude towards the permanent settlement of African miners in the towns. They preferred to use male migrant labour, discouraging the presence of African women and children. Despite this attitude, the competition for labour with the more established mines in the region and the need to feed workers meant that the mining companies actively supported agricultural activity, carried out primarily by women cultivators who sold food to the mineworkers; and thus, in turn implicitly accepted the presence of women (Chauncey 1981). Subsistence plots were provided by some of the mines, first in Broken Hill (Kabwe), then more widely by Roan Antelope mine in Luanshya, where two thousand agricultural plots were in use in 1935 (Chauncey 1981; Wilson 1968). This stimulus to the surrounding agrarian economy was helpful to the indigenous African population on the Copperbelt and to the unemployed workers who remained in situ during the recession of the early 1930s, which occurred soon after copper production was initiated in 1929. Their agricultural activity provided a vital subsistence resource and a supplement for miners' families until the period characterised by ZCCM control.

Centrality of Large-Scale Mining Companies as Providers of Urban Welfare, 1940–1960s

Following major strike actions in the 1940s and a commission of inquiry to look into concerns raised by the workers, the mines adopted a welfare orientation. This was at a time when copper was bought at a stable fixed price by the British colonial government to support the Second World War effort. Thereafter, the post-war boom in world demand for copper enabled the resumption of market-based trade. The colonial government's adoption of a welfare orientation was outlined in the first ten-year development plan, which provided for infrastructural developments such as urban housing and other facilities. The implementation of this plan improved living conditions in the towns, particularly for Europeans and some African service workers, as housing and recreational facilities were built outside of the mine townships and compounds.

Conditions for the African workforce in the mines also somewhat improved as the mining companies, spearheaded by Sir Ronald Prain and RST, built housing for families and provided the opportunity to progress into skilled jobs as part of a policy of Africanisation. Prain (1956) argued that this was developed for the long-term stability of the Copperbelt mining industry and that it fostered development of a pool of skilled Africans in towns. Africanisation was based on the pragmatic policy of employing African workers in skilled jobs to replace European migrant workers, who were costlier to hire. However, as Walima Kalusa (1993) points out in a historical study on the health conditions of mineworkers at the RST mines, while improvements in living conditions accrued to an emergent middle class of African workers, the majority of African labourers suffered ill health connected to poor living conditions and pay; and from occupational illnesses such as silicosis and tuberculosis.

Mining revenue played an important role in funding infrastructural development in the country. During the colonial period, the mining houses paid mineral royalties on copper production to the BSAC and a tax on company profits to the state. After independence and the expropriation of the BSAC's mining rights, the mining companies paid royalty taxes of 13.5% and export taxes of 40% when the price of copper went beyond US$300 per long tonne, and corporate tax of 45% to the state (Lungu 2008). This revenue financed the implementation of the five-year transitional development plan that followed the country's independence in 1964. Despite many attempts both before and after independence to distribute this revenue evenly across the country for the development of the sparsely populated and infrastructure-poor rural areas, mining revenue was mainly spent on the urban areas of the Copperbelt Province and the capital city, Lusaka.[4] This use of government revenue for the development of urban areas was remarkable in view of the colonial government's concern that "over-urbanisation" would result in the rural areas being drained of people, and the urban areas being unable to cope with the influx of large numbers of people (Heisler 1971).

The towns on the Copperbelt, in what many describe as the golden era of the 1950s to the 1970s, had much to offer in terms of the residential lifestyle of those who stayed in the areas administered by the mine companies, particularly for workers of European heritage who lived in the better-serviced suburbs (see Phimister 2011). For African workers, too, there were significant improvements. There was decent subsidised housing that had been transformed since the 1940s from African mineworkers' bachelor quarters (measuring about twenty square metres with communal ablution facilities) to family homes (measuring over fifty square metres with indoor plumbing by 1952—see Mutale 2004). For recreation, mine employees had the option of sports clubs, libraries, theatres, cinemas, and ballroom-dancing facilities, which were also open to their families. Hortense Powdermaker (1962) provides a vivid description of life on the Copperbelt in these times. The mines also had good schools and health facilities and offered various skills-training programmes, including adult literacy. While the wage disparities between Africans and Europeans that characterised the colonial period prevailed even in the post-independence era, wages for better-paid African workers were high enough to enable them to save towards the purchase of more expensive consumer items like cars. This prosperity, particularly in the immediate post-independence decade, contributed to the self-confidence of the country (Fraser 2010).

However, it was also this period that consolidated architectonically the spatial order of modernism and thus the texturing of colonial hierarchies within the environment and, in the process, inscribed these as natural. Between the years 1940 and 1970, a whole series of acts and ordinances governing spatial practice were codified. These included the passing of the Urban Housing African Ordinance in 1948, the creation of the Local Government Act in 1949, and the Town and Country Planning Act in 1961 (see Makasa 2010). Under guise of public health, these laws prescribed the distances not only between industry and residence, but also between African and European settlements, creating "buffer" zones twelve kilometres wide. The new laws also indicated the types of buildings allowed, placing restrictions on the construction of buildings in African vernacular style and materials, and thus effectively imposing an aesthetic on the built environment influenced by those in vogue in Euro-America. This ordering of space and spatial activity through public health regulations, the promotion of certain recreational activities, and training based on notions of ideal domestic life are what Devisch, writing on similar processes of colonial state-building in the Congo, refers to as a form of social engineering (1998, 225). Thus, the welfare orientation of the mines not only was a material manifestation of the pragmatic benevolence of the mines, but also had, as Devisch (1998, 225) argues, a discursive character that attempted to etch into the environment the categorisations and ideologies of colonialism.[5]

Following the country's independence in 1964, efforts were made by the postcolonial state to address the problematic racial and classist categories of the colonial state through a humanist philosophy branded in the phrase "One Zambia, One Nation," as well as significantly to expand welfare. It failed to undo colonial legacies and colonialism's categories, in particular those pertaining to class and race, which continue to colour the character of place.

Mine Nationalisation and Gradual Decline of Urban Welfare, 1970 to Mid-1990s

Various reasons have been given for the decline of urban welfare in Zambia, and the Copperbelt in particular, as world copper prices plunged in the mid-1970s. First, the Matero economic reforms of August 1969 allowed the Zambian government to take over the mining companies by buying a majority stake in them and tied politics to economics in a way that reduced the flexibility of the business sector. Partial nationalisation of the RST and AAC mines in 1970, and the cancellation of the mining companies' management contracts in 1973, allowed the state to influence the running of the mines, with the state drawing on mining revenue for the continued expansion of welfare policies, even amidst uncertainties such as the closure in 1973 of the copper export route through Southern Rhodesia (now Zimbabwe).[6]

Second, the Zambian state failed to diversify its economy, dooming the country to over-reliance on a single commodity, copper. Third, the price of copper was subject to flexible market pricing, making the country, and the Copperbelt in particular, extremely vulnerable to the rise and fall of the market. Fourth, following independence, the country failed to create an alternative to the flexible market pricing of copper. A cartel of copper-producing countries, Cipec, was created, but it did not succeed in cushioning Zambia from the vagaries of the world market (Fraser 2010). Fifth, bad timing and poor luck prevented Zambia from benefiting from policies intended to increase state revenue from copper (Fraser 2010). Soon after the partial nationalisation of the mines in 1970, when the state could have benefited from a mineral tax of 51% and a corporation tax of 45%, a global recession began. This setback forced the Zambian government to reconsider its tax system and offer incentives to investors through a lower tax rate (Lungu 2008).

In spite of these handicaps, the state extended the Zambianisation program, a continuation of earlier Africanisation policies. The mines expanded in-house job training and built new trades schools for the mines and a technical secondary school, Mpelembe, that in 1983 served a third generation of Copperbelt residents, many of whom went on to study engineering subjects to service demand for skilled labour in the mines. In an attempt to reduce the wage bill for expatriate workers on which the mining industry was still dependent, ZCCM built primary schools offering superior quality education in each Copperbelt town so as not to have to pay for schools abroad for expatriate workers' children. If there had been a change of fortunes in the world price for copper, this continued investment in education and building skills could have paid off for the country. As it was, world copper prices did not improve.

In an attempt to reduce the country's foreign exchange spending as earnings from copper dwindled, the government scaled up import substitution, encouraging the fabrication of industrial components and consumer products locally. Towards the late 1970s, the country began to be besieged by regular shortages of basic commodities like bread, cooking oil, and soap as the country's national debt deepened. In the mid-1980s, under pressure from the International Monetary Fund and World Bank, the state sought to reduce the amount spent on subsidising maize meal for urban residents by introducing a coupon system for the urban poor, and many urban residents had to queue for hours for their supply of maize meal. People working for the mines, however, did not have to do so, as they had a separate distribution system, one of several privileges mine employees enjoyed.

Kaunda's failure to see these reform through was put down to the vulnerability of his government, which had become a one-party system in 1971 under his continued leadership since independence, and which was increasingly viewed as overly repressive. However, in 1989, with rising food prices and discontent over the lack of political freedom, popular riots started by the university union on the Copperbelt forced Kaunda to declare early elections in 1991. Frederick Titus Chiluba, leader of the Movement for Multi-Party Democracy, won by a landslide vote, dislodging Kaunda from his long sojourn as president.

Despite the heavy criticism of the mismanagement of the country's economy and mining sector by Kaunda's government between 1970 and 1991, in retrospect many Copperbelt residents remember it as a time when they could at least eat a daily meal. While a few Copperbelt residents over the age of 50, such as one of my key informants, Mr Mubita,[7] a former ZCCM employee resident in Luanshya, attribute the decline of the economy to the departure of the "whites," with reference to the nationalisation of the mines and "too much politicking," some of the younger generation, born in the 1970s, who experienced childhood in the lean years of Kaunda's socialist-cum-capitalist experiment, blame the abandonment of the African socialist model for the decline in the economy. Bissell's (2005) cautionary note on nostalgia is valid here in that it is useful to take into account "multiple strands of remembrance" (2005, 216). The years of decline that followed were, for the younger generation, recalled in an article in the Lusaka Times (26 March 2010), "Zambia: Those Were the Days!," as times of simpler pleasures, free from the anxieties of a consumer culture that took root in the privatisation era. Zambians of this generation, never having experienced the "golden era," are sometimes critical of re-privatisation, which is seen as an interruption of the Kaunda government's attempts towards self-determination.

The full extent of social welfare provision by the ZCCM mines was well captured in a 2000 Rights and Accountability in Development (RAID) report that estimated the social cost of privatisation of the mines. The report estimates that in the early 1990s the large ZCCM mine divisions such as Luanshya had been spending approximately US$20 million a year on social welfare (RAID 2000, 162). Expressing the extent of ZCCM companywide social provisioning, it reports on what was spent on in the years between 1990 and 1997:

The array of capital purchases or facilities rehabilitated is astonishing: the re-laying of sewers, the replacement of municipal pumping stations, water retic-ulation, the sinking of boreholes, the provision of a new chlorination plant and a one million gallon reservoir; the installation of an electricity substation to power a local cinema, floodlights at a local sports ground, the upgrading of electrical supply systems; home ownership schemes, the demolition of de-funct housing, the building of new houses, road rehabilitation, the repair of streetlights, expenditure on the local market, money to revamp a telephone exchange; the provision of libraries, training and youth schemes, the rehabili-tation of women's centres, the building of shelters for mourners at local ceme-teries; hospital refurbishments, the purchase of X-ray equipment, ventilators, blood banks, mortuary chambers, pathology labs, the construction of entire health centres; the purchase of laundry equipment, furniture, typewriters, fridges and cookers, kennels for the dogs of the mine police, a lawn mower, a fish pond, and three Tata buses. (RAID 2000, 162)

The end of this array of services and facilities following privatisation was experienced by Copperbelt residents as a loss of a way of life.

Privatisation Policy: 1995 Onwards

The Movement for Multi-Party Democracy (MMD) government, under the leadership of Frederick Chiluba, came to power with a programme of wide-spread economic reform centred on the privatisation of the mines. After a lengthy debate over whether the mines should be sold and, if so, whether as a whole or broken up in parts, the mines were eventually offered as "unbun-dled" units that roughly coincided with mining operations in each mining town. Thus, the sale of mining divisions of the ZCCM commenced in 1995 with the sale of the Luanshya mines to the Binani Group. This was not a trans-parent process and was dogged with allegations of corruption that, in the end, besieged Chiluba's administration (Van Donge 2008). In the case of the sale of the Luanshya mines, these dodgy dealings in subsequent years served to obscure ownership of the mines and had a devastating and destabilising effect on the residents of the town (Gewald and Soeters 2010).

During this time, an estimated two-thirds of the ZCCM workforce was laid off. Without enough money to pay retrenchment benefits, the state opted to sell the mine housing stock to sitting tenants, most of them mine employ-ees. A cash benefit package for retrenched miners was, in most cases, paid after a delay of three years. Many Luanshya residents remember this period as one of extreme suffering, with families resorting to eating mangoes, foraging for wild fruit in the nearby forests, and turning to the "bush" to cultivate.

Fraser and Lungu (2007) recount the effect that the sale of the mines had on the mining industry in Zambia. They point to the casualisation of labour and the resultant weakening of the mineworkers' union. Larmer's (2007) in-depth historical study demonstrates how the union had hitherto played a central role in lobbying continually for better wages and living conditions on the Copperbelt. Fraser and Lungu (2007) point to the inability of the Zambian state to monitor and regulate the mining industry, a failing that Haglund (2010) notes resulted in numerous abuses, including violations in health and safety practices and an incoherent investment culture that encouraged patronage. This inability had serious repercussions for the collection of mining revenue.

By way of illustration, *The Post* on 9 February 2011 reported allegations of irregularities in Mopani Copper Mines tax remittances with the falsification of copper revenue to avoid taxes. This was deemed especially underhanded given that mine privatisation had, it emerged, involved secret development agreements that had offered very generous benefits to the mines. Corporate tax had been offered at 25% and mineral royalties at 0.6%, zero taxes on customs duties, and up to twenty-year tax breaks. With rising copper prices from 2004, this tax rate began to seem extremely unfair to the Zambian populace, and under pressure from civil society and the urban-supported opposition party, the Patriotic Front (PF), the government—led by Levy Mwanawasa—was forced to engage in a re-negotiation of the development agreements, which resulted in the introduction of a windfall tax in 2008.

Unfortunately for the country, just as this new tax was being put in place, copper prices that, in the early half of 2008, had been approximately US\$8,000[8] a tonne plummeted to US\$3,000 a tonne. In response, the mines laid off workers, many of whom were just beginning to feel confident about the economy. In Luanshya, the mines, which had been taken over by JW & Enya in 2004, were placed under care and maintenance, sending the town's residents into a wave of economic despondency. Around this same time, Levy Mwanawasa died. Following an election held in October 2008, which was strongly contested by the PF, Mwanawasa's vice president, Rupiah Banda, running on the MMD ticket, was ushered into office, albeit amidst election irregularities (*Mail and Guardian*, 5 November 2008). The PF had developed a strong following in urban Zambia for articulating social concerns, in contrast to the abstract rhetoric of economic growth of the MMD (Larmer and Fraser 2007).

Amidst fears that a windfall tax would further frighten investors out of the country, the state backed away from implementing the tax. But the government's 2009 decision was seen as misguided when copper prices rapidly rose to reach all-time highs of US$10,000 a tonne in the first half of 2011. Many advocated a reintroduction of the windfall tax. The country's rapid copper-fuelled growth led to an announcement in July 2011 of the country's fast journey to middle-income status. Many viewed the announcement as a cynical political ploy in an election year. Amidst signs of increased consumption amongst a "re-emerging" middle class, it cannot be argued that some sectors of the population have not benefited from this economic boost, and much of the population still struggles to earn a living. In neighbourhoods of Copperbelt towns such as Luanshya, the landscape still displays the ravages of the withdrawal of the mines in infrastructural maintenance.

PRESENT URBAN WELFARE ON THE COPPERBELT

The previous section has provided a historical account of Zambia's heavy reliance on copper production, the organisation of the copper industry, the capricious influence of the world copper price, and the rising success and later dismal plunge in urban welfare related to the state of the copper industry. The following section teases out the implications of this history for the here and now, drawing attention to how the urban population's welfare and social identity are faring, beginning with the effects of privatisation on people's urban way of life.

Privatisation's Impact on Housing

The privatisation of state industry went hand in hand with the privatisation of urban housing, which had mainly been tied to employment from the colonial period onwards. The sale of housing to private individuals was enacted in 1997 by a presidential decree that stated that parastatal and council housing would be sold to "sitting tenants." This shift in policy had a huge impact on settlement in urban areas and on the character of the Copperbelt. A formal job with the mines on the Copperbelt had previously meant a guarantee of shelter of a reasonable standard.

When the mines were privatised, beginning in 1997, the new owners were unwilling to take up these costly social responsibilities, and the administration of the mine townships was transferred in 2002 to the local authorities through a World Bank–funded programme. This meant that former mine employees, who had previously received free water and subsidised electricity, had to start paying bills. Many struggled to do so (Kazimbaya-Senkwe and Guy 2007). To meet the demand for water, residents of towns like Luanshya, which had been hardest hit by privatisation, initially drew water from an industrial supply that, during the mining period, had been used to water gardens. When this supply was closed, some dug wells in their backyards, and in the dry season, when the wells dried out, begged for water from neighbours who still had piped water. To meet their energy needs, many residents turned to charcoal-burning, chopping trees from the nearby forests and, occasionally, their yards and the residential streets of the town.

A lack of maintenance of neighbourhood infrastructure was readily visible in potholed roads and the disappearance of storm water drains that had filled with silt over the years; darkened roads at night that had once been lit by street lights; burst water-pipes that, it was speculated, were vandalised to allow the illegal drawing of water; and sewer overspills due to blockages, sometimes arising from an attempt to fertilise and water the acidic soils for commercial vegetable gardens. A garbage-disposal service, however, continued, though as many residents reported, there was little to dispose of as poverty had ensured that what some discarded was useful for others.

Crime was a major concern with the end of the mine-policing system, and poverty contributed to its increase. As the social realities on the Copperbelt changed, so too did residents' recreation activities. Grass sprouted in the cracks of the asphalt tennis courts of the mine recreation area in Luanshya. Fields of maize were planted here and there through the town. Anthills at the golf course were broken down to make building bricks. The local cinema was converted into a church since few could afford cinemagoing. The squash club was converted into a drinking place.

On the domestic front, residents who had previously competed to win a best-garden award, which the mines had put into place as an incentive to beautify the neighbourhood, no longer grew poinsettias, gardenias, and other flower-bed plants. Nor did many bother to tend to their lawns, and dry swept-up patches of earth appeared around houses, reminiscent of the dry-earth surroundings of village homesteads.

It was not only the impressions of the rural that gave rise to discussion of the Copperbelt becoming village-like; it was also the economic activities that residents engaged in. While women's social life in particular bears some resemblance to aspects of village life (as I describe later in the book), Copperbelt residents see themselves as modern. For this reason, they bemoan their

Figure 2. Street view of house with maize stalks in the front yard and smoke coming from the smokehouse for curing meat in the backyard visible. Photo by Mulemwa Mususa, December 2008.

Figure 3. Potholed road partially filled in with flux stone sourced from the mine dumps (see chapter 4 on economic activity at the mine dump sites). Photo by Mulemwa Mususa, December 2008.

Figure 4. Luanshya mine recreation centre with signage directing to sporting and recreational activities like tennis, soccer, rugby, ballroom dancing, swimming, and the former mine mess. Photo by Mulemwa Mususa, December 2008.

towns, which were "beginning to look like villages," pointing not only to the towns' changing physical appearance, but to forms of sociality and mutual support that were suppressed or discarded when mine administrations dealt with town infrastructure and welfare needs. As residents adopted new forms of livelihoods, material landscapes were being reconfigured, infusing social relations with altered needs and meanings reminiscent of village life.

Edward Casey (1997) argues that space should be seen in its "two-ness," one dimension that colours the temporal experience of being or dwelling in a "place," and the other that traces paths, from, to, and beyond this temporality. This means thinking about the Copperbelt not only as an extractive locale for copper whose activities are affected by the market, but also as a place where the residents' engagement with the reality of losing jobs, and struggling to earn a living amidst the withdrawal of mine welfare, is re-texturing simultaneously the material and social character of the place. What this implies is a blurring of boundaries in activities that connote the modern, and thus urban, for example, the formal copper-mining economy, and those implied by a subsistence livelihood, the village.

A term that well embodies this process of the urban becoming like a village is *villagisation*, defined by René Devisch (1996, 573) as "a process of psychic and social endogenisation of modern city life, that allows the migrant to surmount the schizophrenic split between traditional, rural and 'pagan' life as against the new urban Christian world." While Devisch is writing of Kinshasa in the 1970s, his description of a process that allows for several possibilities of living in the environment and that resists the tendency towards linearity of urban narratives remains apt. It enriches what Ferguson (1999, 221) observed to be a situational stylisation of social life on the Copperbelt that drew on idiomatic identification of persons as being *uwa kumushi*,[9] "from the village," or *uwa kutown*, "from the town," similar to Filip de Boeck's (1998) observations of the Aluund people and their pragmatic relationship to the environment in the context of hunger in the Democratic Republic of Congo. This view in relation to thinking about place regardless of how it is politically categorised (urban or rural) focuses much more on what a place affords its inhabitants, and the affective experiences it generates. For example, Copperbelt residents increasingly turned to foraging mushrooms, caterpillars, and fruit for food from the nearby forest. This pragmatism also enters Copperbelt residents' conception of themselves and their position within a changing world. It recalls Wim Van Binsbergen's (1998) concept of the virtual village that refers to people who avoid identifying solely with the town or the village. What had come to the fore as a key concern, despite the visual references to the loss of the aesthetic order of the town, was a pragmatics of engagement. As one informant asked me rhetorically, "What is the point of having a nice lawn when you can use your garden to grow food?" What all this illuminated was that the Copperbelt residents practice "converged" lifestyles with often internally discordant modes of social interactions, as described in this chapter.[10] This could be interpreted as going beyond Devisch's (1996) psychosocial notion of villagisation to encompass tangible lived experience. To cite just a couple of concrete, everyday examples, the tendency was manifested in more meals cooked on charcoal braziers and more water collected from wells or poached from neighbours. It also informed neighbourly interaction and forms of sociality people define as "rural-like," trespassing and conflicting with the Copperbelt's erstwhile nuclearizing family life and residents' sense of modernity.

Informalisation of Working Lives: Agriculture and Small-Scale Mining to the Fore

Before privatisation, the end of mine employment had necessitated moving out of one's urban house and retiring to one's home village, a rural resettlement scheme, or to some peri-urban area. With the sale of houses in the privatisation process, retrenchees and retirees could opt to stay in their urban home or, if not, generate a rental income from it (see Chapter 3). Many Copperbelt residents gained a house as part of their retrenchment packages at the time of the worst social economic depression between 1997 and 2003. The house and its yard became an important asset in sustaining urban livelihoods, with retrenched former miners staying in the lower-density former mine suburbs and carrying out agricultural activities that included growing vegetables, rearing chickens and pigs, and fish farming. Other residents in addition to backyard farming also had fields or farms.[11]

In Luanshya mine township, following the loss of jobs, many residents started growing food in an area designated for future mine development. When plans got underway to develop this area in 2004, the new mining company evicted the farmers and built an electric fence around the perimeter, forcing the cultivators to move their fields further into rural Luanshya and Mpongwe. Cultivation now entailed walking long distances and camping in the "bush" during busy farming periods. Some residents decided to settle in these areas, and either sold or rented out their town property. These moves explain why Luanshya's annual population growth rate between 2000–2010 was only 0.3%, while that of Mpongwe, the nearby farming block, grew by 3.6% (CSO 2011).

This movement to the rural outskirts and to forest reserve areas resulted in several land rights problems (Hansangule, Feeney, and Palmer 1998). Land contestation was not confined to agriculturalists, but also affected small-scale, mainly illegal, artisanal copper miners who emerged alongside the privatisation of the mines. Small-scale and illegal mining activity has contributed much to informal livelihoods of not only Copperbelt residents, and those of the new mining areas of North Western Province, but also members of the general Zambian public who were willing to migrate to exploit this opportunity (see Chapter 4). On what people call the "old Copperbelt," women and children work on the copper-mine dumps, trespassing on the larger mine company's property to retrieve flux stone, a by-product of copper processing, which is then sold as building aggregate in the manufacture of concrete blocks. This industry has thrived in tandem with the rise of the small-scale building industry, spurred on by expanding homeownership and the construction of out-buildings for small livestock, as well as the maintenance of potholed roads.

In the "new Copperbelt" in North Western Province, small-scale mining camps have emerged in the bush, either at older mine camps like that of Kalengwa mine, which was abandoned in the early 1980s, or, more commonly, in customary areas under traditional authority. The populations of these camps have fluctuated since 2004 corresponding to fluxes in world copper prices. The majority of these camps have no basic services due to their rural location, but nonetheless, socially, the camps have an urban character that contrasts with the surrounding countryside (see Chapter 4). They could also be described as "rurban slums," as they accommodate a densely concentrated migrant population who are squatting on rural customary land.

Global Mining Boom, Urban Resurgence, and the Expanding Poverty Gap

With Zambia named amongst the ten fastest growing economies in the world between 2011 and 2015 by *The Economist* (6 January 2011), there is increasing pressure on the state to tax copper-fuelled growth. The economic growth has sparked an increasing rate of urbanisation (CSO 2011). The urban/rural split of the population in the 2000 census was 35/65, moving to 39/61 in 2010. The average annual population growth rate in the 1990–2000 decade was 3.0% for rural and 1.5% for urban areas, contrasted with 2.4% for rural and 4.8% for urban areas during 2000–2010 (CSO 2011). On the Copperbelt, the drop was more radical, with the decade 1980–1990 measuring an average annual growth rate of 1.9%, which dropped to 0.1% in 1990–2000, recovering to 2.2% during the years 2000–2010 as a result of the copper boom.

The region with the highest growth was Lusaka, which had an average annual growth rate of 4.7% during 2000–2010 (CSO 2011), reflecting its continued status as the country's premier city. Lusaka's growth does not, however, reflect a decent standard of life for the majority, but rather the fact that the city offers diversified and better opportunities and services. The minimum cost of living per month for a family of six in December 2010 for Lusaka was calculated at ZMK 2,897,430.[12] The average monthly income for families in urban, low-cost settlements, which comprise 80% of all settlements in Lusaka, was ZMK 645,326, while civil servants like teachers and nurses earned from ZMK 1,300,000 to ZMK 3,450,000 (JCTR 2010).

In contrast, in the rural district of Mufumbwe in North Western Province, where there is a combination of informal and formal copper-mining activity, the residents of the area consumed on average 900 calories a day,[13] a deficiency of more than half the 2,400 calories required per day (JCTR 2009b). In comparison with the Copperbelt and Lusaka, there is little social infrastructure, with residents having to travel on average more than sixty kilometres to access the mission hospital at Kasempa. With these inequalities and deficiencies in income, many Zambians feel they are not benefiting from the copper boom.

Foreign Investment

Given the highly visible impact that changing foreign investment in copper has had on the welfare of the Zambian population, local perceptions and attitudes towards foreign investors in mining are continually expressed in people's everyday discourse on the Copperbelt. There is a general recognition of a major shift in responsibility for infrastructural and welfare provisions onto Copperbelt residents. A question often posed in local discussion is "What kind of investment is this, if they (foreign investors) can't build houses for us?" reflecting the still widely held expectation that mining investment will lead to modernisation for its employees.[14] Lumwana Mines, which is developing a greenfield site in the North Western Province is perceived by Copperbelt residents as a prime example of good investment because "they are building houses."[15] The construction of housing for many Copperbelt residents is also seen as a gauge of mine-investors' commitment, showing their willingness to accept responsibility for the workers' welfare, as had been the norm in the years of mine-welfare largesse. In Luanshya, people frequently commented that JW & Enya, which owned the Luanshya mine at the beginning of the copper boom in 2004, had made no signs of planning new housing. Apart from the rehabilitation of the public swimming pool and the former mine hospital, the company did not undertake any major infrastructural development. The temporary nature of its stay was further highlighted by the conversion of offices into residences for some expatriate staff. When, in 2008, the mine was placed under care and maintenance, it confirmed the dim view of Luanshya residents of the short-term nature of JW & Enya's investment.

In 2009, the Luanshya mine was purchased by the China Non-Ferrous Metal Mining Company (CNMC). Despite general resentment towards Chinese investment—stoked in large part by the xenophobic populist rhetoric of the then-opposition party, the Patriotic Front—on the Copperbelt, many residents of the town expressed relief because this purchase was perceived as more sustainable in the longer term, largely due to significant investment in developing the infrastructure of the mine and the well-publicised construction of what was to be the largest copper smelter in the Copperbelt. Others, though, were worried because there was no evidence that CNMC was building any large-scale housing development and the Chinese management were staying in the old general manager's residence, which had been subdivided into flats. One resident noted, "They like to stay together," a practice confirmed by Lee (2010) in her study of Chinese enclaves in Zambia and Tanzania. This mode of living contrasted with that of former British managers, who "wanted swimming pools immediately after they arrived."[16]

The Chinese mining company's spartan approach to settlement and willingness to work long hours alongside the Zambians are applauded as evidence of a strong work ethic. However, these are also problematic for Zambians because Chinese presence and work practices alter the playing field for labour negotiations, which were previously conceptualised in terms of the moral inequalities embedded in the disparity of labour and living conditions between African and European mineworkers, and later between African manual labourers compared to the managerial and political elite. According to Mr Hu, a Chinese citizen with business interests in Zambia, Zambians can no longer afford a work ethic and lifestyle inherited from the British; he extended his criticism further to observe that if Zambians learnt "not to spend on Coca-Cola," their incomes would go further. Though President Kaunda had made a similar argument in the years of the copper decline, it is one that does not sit well with a majority of Zambians, who point out that the majority are living below the poverty line and struggle just to meet their basic needs.

Emerging with new investment in the new mine areas of North Western Province, new mining activity, while welcome for many of the old Copperbelt residents who are taking up jobs there, is proving a major threat to the immediate livelihood of its rural dwellers. In Musele chiefdom, which lies in the district of Solwezi, where First Quantum Minerals (FQM) is developing its Trident Mines—a greenfield site—the people of the chiefdom have been involved in a dispute with the state and the mining company over the legitimacy of the land acquisition process for mining and surface rights.[17] While the Zambian state can issue prospecting and mining licences, as it has rights over minerals under the ground, to gain access to surface activities on customary tenure the state needs the consent of traditional authorities who are the custodians of this land. The majority of Zambia's land (prior to an ongoing land audit) falls under the aegis of customary tenure. The state and investors increasingly have to engage with traditional authorities and the people occupying this land in order to alienate land for development activities. Rohit Negi (2013), who conducted extensive research in the new mining areas of North Western Province, writes about how these relationships have come to be reconfigured with the emergence of mining activity, casting traditional authorities as some of the key purveyors of development in Zambia.

In northwestern Zambia, rural dwellers' fortunes, much like those of the older Copperbelt residents, have varied with the large injection of capital in these areas. Some rural residents (as described in Chapter 4) have "made it," while others have been dispossessed of their land in not very well executed resettlement programs. Zambia's resettlement guidelines provide only a paltry compensation for forced resettlement. The long-running absence of the state in rural affairs, as well as the often-repeated statement by urban dwellers and Zambian politicians that "chiefs are selfish people," has fed into the contemporary subversion of traditional authorities, many of whom rely on handouts from the state. This view has justified the state's position in casting itself as the fairest arbiter of rural peoples, and has limited traditional authorities' abilities to negotiate on behalf of their people. Though the Zambian state has long espoused decentralised governance, it never fully committed to it, and revenue collected from mining activity is centralised rather than managed by regional authorities. This has led to disaffection with the sharing of revenue particularly from high-growth areas and has fed into federalist impulses of regions like North Western Province and the other rural hinterlands. These are seen as a threat to the idea of a unitary Zambian state.[18] The process for the acquisition of land for investment activity and the negotiation and distribution of revenue collected from it are seen by many as unfair to rural residents, who, due to the long deprivation in investment in education, seem unlikely to benefit directly from mining activity through employment.

Diversification from Copper

Efforts are being made to attract new investment to diversify away from copper production, which disproportionately contributes 11% to gross domestic product and realised over 80% of the country's foreign exchange earnings in 2010. Regulations were put in place in 2009 to mine uranium in the North Western and Southern Provinces. The viability of oil production and diamond mining is being explored in the western part of the country that borders with Angola and Namibia. Gold is being mined by FQM at Kansanshi as a byproduct of copper-mining operations. However, a weak mining regulatory system and tax evasion[19] by multinationals beset these emergent extractive industries and raise questions amongst Zambians as to whose benefit was the re-privatisation of the mines.

The dramatic decline in living standards from the 1980s to the present day has renewed efforts both on the state level and the individual level to promote investment in agriculture. The Zambian state has been wooing displaced Zimbabwean commercial farmers and South African farmers worried about potential land redistribution to invest in the country. In the new mining areas of North Western Province, mines like FQM are beginning to experiment with supporting local out-grower schemes using high-yield techniques of conservation farming to supply the mines with fresh vegetables. Meat and grain production in close proximity to the mines is also encouraged to enhance food supply and provide alternative livelihoods for the long run. The state's support for large-scale commercial agriculture and its attendant favourable land and financial policy towards foreign investment in this sector have, however, led to accusations that the state is inhibiting prevalent and localised small- and medium-scale agricultural production.

At a household level, many Copperbelt residents carry out backyard and small-scale agricultural activities not only for subsistence but also as a way to earn an income (see Chapter 3). Civil society organisations, especially the Pentecostal churches that preach a prosperity gospel, have also been active in promoting farming as an alternative means of livelihood. One sermon entitled "Getting Back to God's Plan," prepared by a Luanshya pastor (Kasonka 2008), prescribes a formula for creating a Garden of Eden that would include livestock, birds, and fruit, and result in a "land flowing with milk and honey." This kind of plan characterises the experiments of many Copperbelt residents in self-sufficient, small-scale agriculture and livelihood diversification, which some argue creates villagers in the town.

WHEN THE TOWN BECOMES LIKE A VILLAGE

As the economy declined towards the end of the 1970s, the state increasingly called on people to become self-sufficient. On the Copperbelt in the 1980s, the mines promoted various schemes such as fish farming, sunflower cultivation and processing, poultry farming, and similar activities. While the latter activities might not have been adopted widely, many Copperbelt residents recount going *kuma bala*, "to the fields," in the 1980s. There they grew groundnuts, maize, pumpkins, and sweet potatoes, mainly for home consumption. Most of these farming activities were taken up by mine employees' wives, their children, and visiting relatives. While their relatives farmed, the men, as several of my interviewees readily admitted, were to be found at the various recreation clubs that the mines offered. Agricultural activities intensified in the more difficult years following the sale of the mines. A kind of pragmatism towards livelihoods set in as the number of waged labourers on the Copperbelt declined as a consequence of massive retrenchments. With reduced income, going to rural areas became less viable as progressive years of reduced remittances from those in wage labour in the towns increased the harshness of rural poverty. In addition, the movement of rural kin to the towns decreased, in part because the public transport sector was increasingly privatised and the previous benefits of a decent education in the towns became hard to support with the introduction of user fees.

The increase of urban poverty in the previously better-served Copperbelt towns resulted in shifting exploitative capitalist relations from the mine to the home. Several incidents during the period of my research indicated that extended-family members, who because of circumstances like the deaths of parents, were living with former mine employees on the Copperbelt, were made to work long hours, often without pay, in the small enterprises that emerged. Neighbourly relations also became more fractious, as families without access to running water siphoned water from their neighbours. This usually occurred in the dry season when the wells they had dug in their backyards were completely dry. In retaliation, their neighbours closed off outdoor water supplies. Such difficult relations concerning basic needs suggest that while the towns were increasingly like the village in visual and material terms, they were far from the ideal of convivial village life.

If this process of villagisation is conceived as people's pragmatic approach to the realities of their changing material environment, one that encompasses multiple possibilities of dwelling and livelihood, then it is hard to see the Copperbelt as a place that is either urban or rural. Rather than dichotomizing the Copperbelt as urban or rural, modern or rustic, or viewing it as in transition to becoming modern, it is best seen as textured by possibilities and constraints in an altered environment. In this way, places change, not because of an abstract structure that stylises an idea of the modern or urban, but because our rooted engagement and entanglement with the environment grounds our experience and leads to a reality that is readily discernible in what we do.

NOTES

1. A version of this chapter was originally published in the *Journal of Contemporary African Studies* 30 no. 4 (2012): 571–587, www.tandfonline.com

2. See Michael Faber's (1971) discussion of one of these concessions claimed by Joseph Thomson (an emissary of Rhodes) with the Lamba chief Msiri.

3. The mining towns on the Copperbelt resemble in form the idea of the "garden town," inspired by the vanguard town planner Ebenezer Howard's vision of open spaces and public parks. However, whereas Howard imagined the city as a socialist collective, the reality that emerged on the Copperbelt were towns closer in ideological principle to capitalist enclaves—spatially organised to be exclusive, drawing on the racial colonial hierarchies that still texture many African cities.

4. A larger portion of this income was allocated to developing commercial farming and infrastructure for white settlement in Southern Rhodesia (now Zimbabwe) connected with the 1953 formation of the Central African Federation consisting of Nyasaland (Malawi) and Northern Rhodesia (Zambia).

5. Robert Home (1996), Garth Myers (2003), and Ambe Njoh (2007) have written extensively about the underlying ideologies that influenced colonial-era planning, which were variously those of extending imperial control to the colonies, capitalist extraction, and a racially inflected utopian idea of creating a better society for European settlers in appropriated lands.

6. An increase in tensions between the minority white-run racist government of Rhodesia and independent Zambia, which was supporting the country's liberation movements, saw the closure of the rail export route down south through Rhodesia in January 1973, and thus increased the country's transportation costs for the export and import of goods. This persisted until the commissioning of the Tanzam railroad project, a rail route linking Zambia's Copperbelt to Tanzania's Dar es Salaam port, and built through Chinese cooperation.

7. Unless otherwise indicated, I have used pseudonyms throughout the book to protect the welfare of my informants.

8. Unless otherwise stated the USD is used.

9. Bemba is the lingua franca of the Copperbelt.

10. Bank (2011) documents analogous contested place-making between urban modernity and rurality in the suburbanisation of Duncan Village in the South African city of East London.

11. Out of one hundred households surveyed in August 2009 within a low-density former mine township in Luanshya, thirty-nine had fields or farms. These ranged in size from one hectare to fifty hectares, most of which were located on the periphery of the town.

12. On 1 January 2013, the Zambian kwacha was rebased to address the costs of often devaluing the currency as a result of years of high inflation. To this effect, the old currency was divided by a thousand, which meant that a billion kwacha in the old currency (which is used throughout the book to reflect practice then), would be one million in new currency, a million would be a thousand, and so on. The currency code also shifted from from ZMK (used in this book) to ZMW, reflecting that the currency has been rebased. Where necessary, I convert the kwacha amount to US dollar at the prevailing historical rate.

13. This average does not take into account the fluctuations in food consumption that vary seasonally between lean and bountiful months.

14. "N/Western Province Elders Urge FQM to Build Modern Structures," *The Post*, 8 February 2011.

15. However, the local rural populations living in the vicinity of the new mine are increasingly concerned about the potential degradation and pollution of their environment, in-migration from the old Copperbelt, and what the overall benefit to themselves will be from the mine.

16. In contrast, Lumwana Mines and First Quantum Minerals in the new mining area in North Western Province have planned golf courses.

17. An article published 17 October 2013 by Paul Carlucci highlights the challenges rural communities face with new mining development in North Western Province: 'When Companies Meet Communities: Copper Storm Brewing in North Western Zambia," at http://thinkafricapress.com/zambia/when-companies-meet-communities-copper-storm-brewing-north-western-fqm-actionaid (last accessed 10 December 2013).

18. The 2012–2013 constitution review process revealed that all the regions in the country opted for political devolution (email correspondence with Dr Rodger Chongwe, chairperson of the constitutional review process, 30 May 2013).

19. A report by War on Want written by Mark Curtis (2015) argues that Zambia is losing approximately US$3 billion per year through corporate tax dodging by mining multinationals and other industries.

CHAPTER 2

"You Can't Plan"

Dreams, Practice, and Order

Despite the continual decline of the mining industry through the 1980s, many Copperbelt residents, particularly those working for the mines, could not conceive of a time when the industry would come to a standstill. Many of my Copperbelt informants recounted their belief that even after receiving retrenchment benefits—in the first instance, a house, and much later, "lump sum cash"—there would be new, and possibly even better, jobs in the mines. This view, quite out of step with the social realities described in Chapter 1, nevertheless had taken hold, spurred in part by the notion that a more open economy, which people had agitated for against the United National Independence Party (UNIP) and Kenneth Kaunda, would deliver. Shopkeepers in Luanshya described how miners receiving cash benefits had, despite the uncertainty of their futures, embarked on short-lived extravagant spending and lifestyle choices.[1] Opinion was divided amongst them as to whether the spending sprees were a result of mineworkers' recklessness and inability to plan beyond the next pay cheque or a consequence of an inability to conceive of a future without the mines.[2] Rather they remembered the past with nostalgia.

Hope is an idea for the future. Does a life looking in a rear-view mirror[3] (Nyamnjoh 2001) preclude hope? If not, where would it lie? I found that life on the Copperbelt is not just one of getting by, or just a nostalgic look into the past, but also a place of "unrealistic" expectations and flights of fancy, where impossible dreams are dreamt. Later, I give examples of these forays, such as one instance in which a family planned an ice-cream parlour in a depressed neighbourhood where people struggled to have a meal, or the couple who borrowed close to a billion kwacha[4] to set up an oil-processing refinery.

These examples, I argue, are not unconnected to Edward Nkoloso's[5] vision of a Zambia entering the space age at the cusp of the country's independence in 1964, or Kenneth Kaunda's last desperate vision of a "Heaven on Earth"[6] in the waning moments of his power. While these journey's into "space" could be derided as millennial cults, I argue that these forays into the "impossible" are another iteration in the attempts for livelihood and a harmonious life that, like many religions, offer potentials of existence that stretch beyond the immediate environment and hint at a life that can emerge, maybe not in that place, but in another. However, these journeys, which could be described as hopeful, are at the same time pragmatic. Many Zambians say of the future, "We'll see when we get there." This view recognises the constraints of action and hurdles that might emerge, but does not preclude movement towards an uncertain future. It is an approach that requires "doing," even if, like Edward Nkoloso's vision of astronauts training for a trip to the moon, the prospects look crazy in the immediate context.

THEORIZING THROUGH DOING: A PHENOMENOLOGICAL ENGAGEMENT WITH THE COPPERBELT

In this chapter, I introduce the theories and methodology that underpin the whole book. These draw mainly from a phenomenological engagement with the Copperbelt. My concern, much as human geographers started to do in the 1970s, is to study the Copperbelt from a "man-in-the-world" (Tuan 1971, 191) perspective and not only a man standing apart from the world. As such, my approach mixes methods and theoretical discussions with practical examples, starting from the perspective that in order to understand people's experience of place, the researcher must engage in a process of "doing," a direct participant observation. This is line with the ethnographic tradition that is grounded in concrete examples rather than just abstract theory. In this approach, I am inspired by the work of Pierre Bourdieu, who sought to reconcile the tensions between knowing the world as we see it and as we experience it (Bourdieu 1977). However, drawing from the work of Tim Ingold (2000), which posits a material, phenomenological experience of the environment, and from Edward Casey (2001) and Gaston Bachelard (1969), who explore the imaginary of place as we experience it, I describe the Copperbelt as a *textured place*. Raymond Williams, in an influential essay, "Structures of Feeling," succinctly describes this approach as a concern "with meanings and values as they are actively lived and felt" (1977, 132). Thus, following on from James Ferguson's (1999) ethnography in the 1980s, which broke from the linear narratives of progress on the Copperbelt and drew on performance theories, I build on his work, not only by describing what happened later, but also by analysing it through an ontological approach embedded in the material environment. This, as others like Dennis Cosgrove (1988), and Williams (1977, 1980) himself have noted, is not divorced from the ways in which we assign meaning to the markers within the landscape that indicate what a place is, was meant to be, or has become.

My aim is to describe the texture and experience of life on the Zambian Copperbelt and not just offer, as prior anthropologists have done, an explanatory framework about social relations there. I borrow from cultural and human geography an approach to describe aspects of place that defy easy categorisation. For example, Adams, Hoelscher, and Till (2001) use the notion of textures of place to describe not only the "surfaces, processes, and structures" that characterise how we view certain places, but also those multiple experiences and situations that are constituted by the everyday practices and routines of living. In this regard, I build on Ferguson's theoretical departure from a mappable representation of the Copperbelt that characterised many of the earlier ethnographies of the region, to include "unintelligible" and "noisy" aspects of life (1999, 36). While Ferguson's work offered a brilliant critique of the myth of modernity and the teleological assumptions that underpinned the anthropology of the Copperbelt, I offer a view on how Copperbelt residents reconcile the myth, represented in the fantasy of the ability to plan their life, to the realities of living and dreaming in contexts of uncertainty.

I found that Copperbelt residents had not lost their capacity to dream. Rather, their dreams had taken a nostalgic turn, recounting a past within which the future could have been planned, and alternatively taken a fanciful turn that, on cursory observation, seems out of place. This "future imaginary" and the ways of being it invoked became both clearer to me and a site of reflection when I embarked on looking for a house to buy following my employment with Copperbelt University and the process of renovating it that began my fieldwork in Luanshya in August 2007. With this introduction of my entry into the field, I hope to set the context for a discussion on the methods and theories I draw on to think through what I observed during the course of fieldwork. They also situate my observations about the villagisation of the town (presented in Chapter 1) and the stories of how Copperbelt residents went about trying to make a life and "get on" with life in a place that many said had "lost its order."

THE SEARCH FOR A HOUSE ON THE COPPERBELT

I had started looking for a place to buy in the Zambia summer of 2006, a year and half after becoming a lecturer in the Department of Architecture at Copperbelt University, located in Kitwe.

Where on the Copperbelt?

I embarked on my search for a house the conventional way by looking in the property sections of the country's three main newspapers, the independent *Post* and the state-sponsored *Times* and *Daily Mail*. I initially looked for places located in Kitwe, but many of the places I saw were outside my budget.[7] In addition, in Kitwe, the commercial hub and most populous Copperbelt town with a more diverse economy than the region's other towns, I found it more difficult to establish both the validity of property sale offers and trust with the sellers. In one incident, when I went to view a property advertised in the papers, the supposed sellers turned out to have set up a scam in which they had contrived to have a gemstone dealer holding a little pouch of stones to wander onto the property, supposedly lost, asking for directions to the industrial area where he could polish the gems. The Copperbelt, known for producing high quality emeralds, has plenty a get rich story based on emerald mining and dealing. As a result, fake gemstone dealers abound, targeting those perceived to have large sums of money to spend, and lured by the prospects of lucrative returns. What alerted me to the scam was that the property seller's newspaper I had perused, while he futilely searched for the key to the house on sale had a section torn out that matched exactly the piece of paper on which the gemstone dealer had scrawled the address he was looking for. While this incident was more obviously an attempt to scam, in the other cases, especially where property was being sold following the death of the title deed holder, ownership and inheritance were often contested, as it was a widespread practice for the deceased not to leave wills.[8]

As a result of these issues, I widened my search to the other Copperbelt towns. Chingola, where the Konkola Copper Mines, owned by Vedanta, are located, was a possible option. Long known as one of the neatest towns of the Copperbelt, Chingola had weathered better the infrastructural decline following re-privatisation. However, the heavy machinery and traffic of trucks carrying copper ore coming from the Kanshanshi mines in Solwezi, the emergent new Copperbelt, from the mines in the Democratic Republic of Congo and KCM itself to the Mopani Copper Mines smelter in Kitwe meant that commuting to Kitwe from Chingola would be risky, as the road that connected the two towns was considered one of the most dangerous on the Copperbelt. Mufulira, the Copperbelt town whose mine had been part of the Rhodesian Selection Trust mines and where my father was born, was out of question, not only because the shortest route to Kitwe still connected one to the dangerous Chingola-Kitwe road, but also because it is known to have poor air quality.[9] Ndola, the administrative centre and former industrial hub of the Copperbelt, like Kitwe, had higher property prices. Kalulushi, the most recent of the mine company towns on the old Copperbelt and in closest proximity to Kitwe, was also outside my budget. That left Luanshya, whose economy was hardest hit following privatisation and whose property prices as a result were the most depressed.

In the end, I found the place in Luanshya through a property agent who had advertised it and several other properties in the newspapers. The agent, a former civil servant who had retired from Lusaka to Luanshya because the cost of living was cheaper, had been selling the house on behalf of a former ZCCM employee, Mr Mumba, who wished to use the revenue from the sale to finance the building of a house in Ndola, where he planned to relocate. The house was located in the former low-density mine suburb that used to be administered by the mines. It was Mr Mumba's second property. In 2006, he had been leasing it out for rental income of ZMK 300,000 (about US$60) a month. Mr Mumba had another home in Luanshya, where he and his family lived, located in the high-cost council area, the part of town previously managed by the local authorities. In contrast to many of the other town's residents, Mr Mumba, an engineer, was doing quite well financially, as he had established several work contracts with the new mines on the Copperbelt. I bought the house from him for ZMK 55,000,000 (about US$11,000), with the aid of a lawyer to draw up contracts.

The house was a bargain, as most properties were at that time in the town. Luanshya was then considered likely to turn in a ghost town,[10] with little hope of reviving the copper industry that had been the backbone of the town's economy. Pragmatic reasons justified why I bought a place there. It was one of the few places I could afford to buy a house. Also, Luanshya was a forty-five-minute commute to work in Kitwe. While its depressed economy did not make it the best place to invest in property, it offered the security of a home. My father, a casualty of the retrenchments in 1995 during the privatisation of ZCCM assets, unlike other Copperbelt-based former employees, had not gained a house as part of his retrenchment package.[11] The months of anxiety about where we would move following the loss of his job made me seek to ensure that I never found myself in a similar situation.

Not Clear-Cut Aspirations

Like other Copperbelt residents I had met, I was also prone to fanciful ideas. Several of my Zambian colleagues had asked me why I had done the foolish thing of buying property in Luanshya when I could have invested in a piece of land in Kitwe or Lusaka, where, over the course of my service at the university, I could have built my own house. It was not uncommon in the urban areas of Zambia for people to spend upward of half a decade building a house, financing the construction according to variable revenue streams. This often placed persons in confrontation with the local authorities, who were mandated to repossess land that lay idle, especially in the capital, Lusaka, where the demand for land was high.[12] In addition, the slow and highly centralised land administration meant many miners, including my seller, Mr Mumba, did not yet have title deeds, other than a letter of sale from the mines, and the house at the point of sale was in the name of the former mining company, ZCCM. This was baffling to my European friends, who asked why I would take such a legal risk. The only surety was a contract of sale drawn up by my lawyer and signed by myself, the seller, the agent, and two other witnesses. In 2010, Mr Mumba did eventually get title deeds and contacted me to begin the process of transferring the deeds to my name, but several things could have gone wrong in between.

Like many other Copperbelt residents, even those in stable jobs such as the one I had at the Copperbelt University, I explored other livelihood options. I was influenced in large part—like others—by the need to maintain multiple options and not to rely on only one stream of revenue. This need to maintain a range of options reflected people's increasing sense of precariousness of life, an aspect I explore in greater depth in Chapter 6. With a good friend and colleague, also an architect at the university, I set about a number of economic forays. In 2005, we tried to open a tearoom on the main university campus, but this idea failed because the union that managed the property we planned to rent stalled and did not reach a decision to lease it to us. A year later an ill-advised venture to Lubumbashi, the centre of the copper-mining region Katanga in the Democratic Republic of Congo, in the quest of establishing links to manufacturers and suppliers of woven raffia fabric for interior design commissions, was curtailed by our being quickly distracted by the city's buildings and architecture. Temporarily forgetting we were in a war-torn country, we took photographs that resulted in our apprehension by the city's plainclothes secret police and resulted in us losing half the money we budgeted to buy the fabric. Our more successful work was in small architectural consultancy commissions, often by clients who approached the university.

One venture that my colleague and I engaged in made me aware of the shifting economy of the Copperbelt. After years of low prices, the price of copper began to pick up in 2004. This brought the entry of international venture capitalists and other opportunists looking to cash in on the copper boom. I met one such venture capitalist, who pointed out the Copperbelt forest[13] and its reforestation potential to create a green economy for the region. At the time, he envisioned that in view of the push towards a green economy, mining companies, especially copper mines, which are great polluters and cause significant destruction of trees and the ground, would want to offset these negative effects by replanting indigenous forests.[14] Unfortunately, he said, the country then did not have the regulations in place to create a carbon market. In a utopian view,[15] I imagined that the implementation of this mechanism would result in jobs in agro-forestry, especially for a town like Luanshya that is completely surrounded by forest, and hence the revival of the town. My colleague and I had drafted a position paper to be tabled at parliament outlining how Zambia could participate in a green economy. However, a member of parliament who had seemed keen on this initiative during the initial meeting had in a follow-up meeting been more eager to tell us that he had been offered a position on the board of a copper-trading company. He conveyed his reluctance to talk about the position paper by urging us to have a drink with his coterie of male party cadres at his parliamentary accommodations, a situation that my colleague and I read as open to ambiguous interpretation, and accordingly we abandoned our pursuit of this avenue.

During fieldwork, I realised that there were other people like myself who had set out on a particular course in the hope that at some point something might change to shift the game in our favour. While my colleague and I had set out on a course that had little chance of success, the fact that we went as far as we did on a chance encounter highlighted the flexibility and permeability of the social context. This made me realise, early on in my fieldwork, that I should look at how overly ambitious dreams, and a call to religious symbolisms, for example through prayer, play out in practice.[16] Accordingly, my approach to fieldwork overall was grounded in bodily material practices that owe to a spatial framework that emphasises what people do and their perceptual engagement with place and situations. This approach has been used by anthropologists and human geographers (Tuan 1977; Rodaway 1994; Ingold 2000; Escobar 2001) who elaborate on cultural and political economic variations not as inherent traits of peoples and their environments but as contingent and emergent from both social and material relations. Departing from the idea that skills, as embodied, and societal structures are not fixed, these scholars see the body as interactional and in continuous transformative movement, engaging people and environment in a process of becoming. As I show, this prior work was useful in thinking through how Copperbelt residents conceptualise the practice of living—as Ingold (2000) describes it, a "wayfaring" movement towards an uncertain future.

The renovation of the house that I summarise in what follows enmeshed me in a process that allowed me to engage quite intensively with the broader macroeconomic issues affecting Copperbelt residents. This account sets the context for the chapter on the informal copper economy. As a "making" activity that was both material and social, it provided me with insight into how people navigate practical life in an informalising economy where capital is scarce. Very much like the options and variation in business ideas, I found that people's interactions were improvised within the possibilities of what they could manage within the given social and material constraints, which in themselves were also unstable. The here and now of the Copperbelt within which people acted was not divorced from the broader macroeconomic forces driving the copper economy, such as increased demand for the commodity from China. Nor was it detached from the actions of locally and globally dispersed policymakers who variously proposed, sometimes at odds with one another, measures to increase or reduce taxation in the extractive sector. These intangible aspects to everyday living nevertheless affected Copperbelt residents' livelihood options in ways that could not always be neatly described or connected. For my part, the renovation of the house that was to be my fieldwork home was an opportunity for me to reflect on the nature of this practice.

The Renovation of the House

The house, one bedroom with a generous-sized living room and dining room and a closed veranda, was structurally sound but in a bad state of repair and needed much work. It sat on a large plot, thirty by sixty metres, that characterised the low-density former mine suburb, and which, like most other yards in the area, was not maintained. After drawing up a schedule of works and costs, I set about looking for tradespeople who could help me execute the repair work. I was uncertain about where to begin my inquiries.

As a start, for the more urgent plumbing work I opted to contract a plumber from Kitwe recommended by a colleague. While he did reasonable work in installing new pipes, as the old ones had rusted through, it was not entirely satisfactory, as there were leaks due to the pipes not being laid precisely to gradient. I knew, however, that this did not reflect on the work ethic of the plumber but rather showed that, in addition to not having a good set of tools and well-calibrated measuring equipment, he, like many of the region's young tradesmen, had been inadequately trained in some of the abridged courses that had been offered by well-meaning non-governmental organisations following the closure of mining company trades schools on the Copperbelt. Also, the contraction of the region's economy meant that many received little experience on the job due to the dearth of construction work.[17] This knowledge and my awareness of the changing political economy directed my attention towards older tradespersons who had gained a more solid technical education and experience in the heyday of the mines.

A few weeks after getting the plumbing done, I was in Lusaka visiting my parents when I happened to spy through the window of the minibus I was riding in a banner outside a hotel announcing a meeting on traditional authorities' views on the country's 1995 Land Act.[18] Exiting the taxi before my intended destination, I decided to attend the meeting, despite not having been invited, to learn more about how chiefs felt about an aspect of the law that allowed—for the first time in the Zambian state—a conversion of land on customary tenure to state leasehold. During the lunch break I struck up a conversation with Mr Banda, the maître d'hôtel where the meeting was taking place. Mr Banda, who was in his late forties, happened to be a former resident of Luanshya and had worked as a mineworker for the Luanshya mines under ZCCM and RAMCOZ before they were liquidated and he was laid off. Mr Banda, who had gained a house as part of his retrenchment package, had left his family in Luanshya to look for a job in Lusaka. He had found one running the restaurant of the three-star hotel. His family was unable to join him in Lusaka because, combined with household expenses for his family and school fees for his children, he could only afford to rent in a nearby informal settlement. He also said he did not wish to subject his children to the difficulties and "morals" of "compound" life in Lusaka. By this comment, Mr Banda was referring to the villagisation of life in the informal settlements of Lusaka, where the expectations of convivial social relations more akin to ideas of village life fostered by material constraints such as poor sanitation[19] and the need to share communal taps, intermingled with city life where all-night bars blared music until the early hours of the morning. This was unlike the small town of Luanshya, where Mr Banda's family still lived in the low-density former mine suburb where I had purchased a house.

Such chance encounters, and the opportunities they presented, were not uncommon and highlighted the fluidity of urban Zambian social experience. There was a tendency for people to "step outside of themselves" and take chances. This "stepping out" could be seen as a willingness to trespass social and material boundaries and, as the encounters in my research suggested, seemed to characterise a strategy that my Copperbelt informants drew upon to cope with the end of the certainties of the ZCCM system. This "wayfaring" beyond the established paths allowed people to perceive new opportunities. It was these very actions that led me to meeting Mr Lackson Mwale.

Creating Kinship: Mr Lackson Mwale

Mr Banda happened to have a close friend, Mr Lackson Mwale, who had worked in the mines' property maintenance department. Following retrenchment, Mr Mwale had set up a small construction and building works firm in Luanshya. Mr Banda gave me the contact details. When I called Mr Mwale to set up a meeting to conduct a preliminary assessment of the work that needed to be done on the house, he came over to my place within thirty minutes, with one of his assistants, Mr Zulu, a former mineworker who had been retired in the mid-1990s. After the social niceties of greetings, Mr Mwale asked me where I was from, saying I sounded Indian on the phone. I knew this was a query about my "home village" and a way of establishing ethnic relations that went some way to setting the context for the social, communicative strategies we were to engage in. Mr Mwale said he was from the Eastern Province of Zambia. This established me as "kin," as my paternal grandparents had hailed from the eastern part of the country. Establishing that I came from the same "home" region allowed for a play of kin relations that extended the relationship beyond a straightforward business transaction and also allowed for breaking the alienation of capital. I became Mr Mwale's "sister." However, Mr Mwale had found a system that worked to reduce some of the liabilities that came with creating such familiarity. After looking around the property himself and going over the schedule of works, Mr Mwale told me that he usually preferred his customers to buy their own materials, though he could advise on the quality, the cost, and where to get them. This, he said, was because he did not want to be accused of cheating, for example, buying lower-quality materials and charging higher prices for them. Also, this way, he said, he would only charge and be responsible for the labour costs.

Mr Lackson Mwale also became a valuable point of entry to my fieldwork in Luanshya, introducing me to his family and colleagues. His wife Rosemary and I were able to establish a common link, as she was an "auntie" (again, a relationship anthropologists characterise as "fictive kin") to a young woman she worked with in Kitwe who was at the time dating my cousin. Through similar entry, by establishing relationships with family members of my key informants, most of whom adopted me as fictive kin, I was allowed a reasonable degree of freedom to conduct my research and was easily able to explore how women, men, and young people experienced life on the Copperbelt.

I met many of the people who became my key informants in the early days of renovating the house, and the services they supplied and advice they offered indicated the informalisation of the Copperbelt economy. For example, when looking for aggregate to make a cement mixture for setting a new feeder sewer pipe to replace the one that had burst in my yard, I was referred to a woman who sold flux stone that was being dug from the copper dump sites by women and children who were trespassing onto mine property to collect the flux. The sewer pipe itself was purchased in the hardware section of Chisokone market in Kitwe, the largest outdoor market of the Copperbelt. There, pipes such as the one I bought were manufactured in someone's backyard, and as they were not tested by recognised testing bodies, I employed my own methods of strength testing. When I had the misfortune of an attempted robbery, having been resistant to installing burglar bars for aesthetic reasons and cost, I relented, and the metal bars were purchased for a fraction of the prices found in the stores through an introduction by Mr Mwale to a wholesale supplier of steel bars. I found out later that the bars had been part of a large consignment destined for the mines and as such were tax-exempt, thus enabling the supplier to sell quietly on the wider market at a lower price, thereby undercutting local competition.

Informalisation and the inevitability of trespass characterised how most people lived on the Copperbelt. Limited access to capital meant that many people were looking for cheaper goods so they could afford to "get on." For example, when Mr Mubita, whose activities I present in greater length in the next chapter, on the improvised nature of Copperbelt livelihoods, decided to build his front-yard store, he could not afford even locally sold flux stone to use as a cement aggregate. Rather than abandon the construction of the store, he made several long trips with his wheelbarrow in the early mornings, sweeping the little stones off a major road whose potholes were being patched.

Lack of access to money and credit did not stop people from carrying on with their plans. Bank loans were available mainly to salaried employees and larger, more established businesses. This allowed banks, such as the one from which I had borrowed money, to make monthly deductions directly through employers. Interest rates were high, ranging between 20% and 25%, and loan repayment periods were short, averaging two years at the most. This meant that many people borrowed from family members and friends; from microlending institutions, whose interest rates were even higher (often above 35%) with even shorter repayment periods; and from loan sharks, who charged over 100% on loans for the shortest repayment periods. For some of my informants who tended to bigger plans and had a corresponding need for credit, such the pastor and his wife I present below, the high cost of credit had serious consequences. However, those many whose financial circumstances made it difficult even to borrow money from friends and family had to rely on other means, like Mr Mubita, to get things done without using money. How this section of the Luanshya population got on was hinted to me shortly after moving to the house.

On the day that I met Mr Mwale to assess what work needed to be done on the house, I met some of my immediate neighbours. They sat under a tree and I could see them through the scraggly lantana hedge that formed the boundary of the two properties. After Mr Mwale had left, the man who had been sitting on a stool near a mat where two women and a baby sat wandered through the hedge. He introduced himself as Lazarus Nsofu. Taking me to introduce me to the women, the one with the baby turning out to be his wife, he asked if his wife, Sandra, could work for me as a domestic worker in turn for accommodation in the "servants' quarters," a room at the bottom of my garden. I told them that I was not in need of a domestic worker and did not plan to lease the room at the bottom of the garden. However, when I moved into the house a few weeks later, I found that Mr Nsofu, his wife Sandra, their baby, as well as a Mr Nsofu's young niece had moved in. The family sat within a circle of mango trees at the bottom of the garden. Unsure what to tell them, whether to ask them to leave, I did not immediately approach them, and neither did they approach me. Eventually, loathing the task of having to ask them to leave, I resolved to employ Sandra for a couple of days' work a week and

Mr Nsofu a day for a week of gardening, and in return they could stay.[20] This was unplanned expenditure for work I did not need, but the greater costs lay later in the water bills I was to accrue. The Nsofus, being neighbourly, allowed nearby residents whose water supply had been cut off to draw water from an external tap, which, previously blocked by the former owners, I had unblocked to enable the watering of a vegetable garden. Mr Nsofu, I was also to learn, when I found a youth I did not know working in the garden, also occasionally subcontracted the gardening work for gifts in kind, the youth saying Mr Nsofu gave him things people did not want. During the period of Mr Nsofu and his wife's employment with me they did similar things that stretched the bounds of what I found acceptable and which inevitably resulted in me asking them to leave.

While what the Nsofus did was socially risky, I came to realise in my encounters with other Luanshya residents that it was these risks that allowed them to extend the possibilities of their existence beyond the formal conventions of what was feasible or deemed acceptable.

Copperbelt residents, including myself, learnt more about the vagaries of the place we inhabited not by rigidly following a plan of action but by casting ourselves out into the flows and rhythms of life on the Copperbelt. We increased our knowledge of life and the place by what was referred to in the Copperbelt's everyday speech as "trying." Through this process, and successes and failures, Copperbelt residents textured both themselves and their environments.[21] Drawing from Thorsten Geiser's (2008) work on apprenticeship learning, one might describe me as having become an apprentice to life in Luanshya, increasing my knowledge by continuous improvised attempts. This learning process was not detached from that of other Copperbelt residents, as I learnt from people like Mr Lackson Mwale and others, as they did in turn. A mutual learning of how to get on with life was fostered by what Geiser describes as an empathetic "reciprocity of view points" as well as the sharing of "similar kinaesthetic experiences" (2008, 300).

Although Geiser's approach is useful in thinking about phenomena experienced in the more immediate environment, it requires elaboration for those that seem to exceed or escape it.

COPPERBELT DREAMS AND ASPIRATIONS

Despite the difficult and uncertain realities, many Copperbelt residents still had dreams for their futures. Some were fantastical and some, as Ferguson

(1999) noted in his research, seemed to have an air of desperation. However, what appeared to be the millennial nature of these aspirations was based not only on disaffected or delusional fantasies, but in belief that one could not know what lay in the horizon.

Jean and John Comaroff's ideas about "millennial capitalism" (2000) offer a useful starting point for thinking about things that seem to escape the present. In their work on contemporary capitalism they narrate how production, as a tangible expression of the making of things in the temporality of here and now, has given way to consumption, lending a spectral quality to the emergence of things that have been produced through processes invisible and intangible to those consuming them. This unknown aspect of the production of desirable goods has been of interest in anthropology in the study of cargo cults (see Lawrence 1971; Linstrom 1993); however, these studies have often tended to focus on identitarian discourse and power relations, seeing people who have cast their time and resources on improbable dreams and aspirations as marginal and their activities as expressions of disaffection with capitalism and modernity. My intention here is not to depoliticise the disjuncture that arises out of the inequalities of access to resources, but to draw attention to the ways in which they are localised and how persons try to bridge them and maybe move beyond the constraints of their circumstances. It is a view the Comaroffs espouse in looking at how the abstract properties of capitalism happen in situ (1999, 295).

This view resonates with the recent work of Lisa Cligget et al. (2007) on the Gwembe Valley, which reviews longitudinally how its residents have coped and made their lives in times of uncertainty and crisis, and how they have taken advantage of momentary economic booms. It contributes to the questions that anthropologists are increasingly asking, that is, how to make sense of human experience and explain it in times of crisis, instability, and rapidly fluctuating social change. Many of these questions arose with the triumph of neoliberalism that saw the fall of state capitalism and welfare in countries that had adopted socialist or communist orientations with political affinities with the former Soviet Union. Neoliberalism and the attendant structural adjustment policies that reduced social welfare, as described earlier, have created a paradoxical mix of hope and despair: hope in the promise of prosperity seen in the few who have "made it," and despair as a result of the erosion of people's social safety support and the abject poverty into which many have fallen. This paradox, I argue, has been key in contemporary anthropological studies in rethinking the concept of agency. The problem has been that if one takes an analytical approach to agency that sees people as willing action towards a goal, then when they fail to achieve their goals, are we to assume they have no agency and are fatalistically circumscribed by their circumstances and those "more" powerful with agency, or can we think about it another way? Anthropologists working in other African countries that have experienced similar socioeconomic stress are thinking through such issues through the lens of seeing people's actions as continuous attempts to seize opportunities or chances (Johnson-Hanks 2005; Piot 2010). For example, Charles Piot's (2010) study of post–Cold War biopolitics in Togo illuminates how "nostalgia for the future" shifts the hopes and aspirations of Togolese from the uncertainty of the present to the future. In his presentation of American Green Card aspirants, Piot shows, through the case of Kodjo (2010, 82), how a visa aspirant becomes an immigration consultant entrepreneur for those wishing entry to the United States. Piot demonstrates how Togolese are willing to draw on what they had in hand to increase their chances and options. He gives an example of a man who was willing to use his disability as a strategy to gain a visa after hearing of someone who had gained one on the grounds of his need for a hip replacement (2010, 4). For the Togolese presented in Piot's study, one did not know when one's luck might change (2010, 164). This is a view shared by my informants on the Copperbelt, a view that explains their engagement in less than feasible livelihood and economic ventures, as I describe below.

Waiting for Formal Re-employment

There were a number of former ZCCM employees who had appointed themselves as caretakers of former ZCCM recreational infrastructure. This included several who looked after the former ZCCM golf club, the pony club, and the recreation centre. These appointments involved no remuneration. This employment was not just a voluntary activity but also a way to occupy time productively in a familiar setting. Former mineworkers at these places waited in the hope of being rehired should the establishments they were looking after were to reopen under a paying employer. In my discussions with them, they all had indicated that they had failed to become the entrepreneurs that the new market economy expected.

One such person was a Mr Kabemba, who had held a supervisory clerical role in the ZCCM mines and had enjoyed playing golf in his spare time. When Mr Kabemba was laid off the mines, he used to his generous retrenchment package from the mines (when he eventually received it) to send his two sons abroad to study golf, one to Scotland, and the other with a scholarship to the United States. With most of the retrenchment spent, Mr Kabemba tried to raise chickens, but was no good at it, and said he had come to the realisation that he was no good at manual labour, nor trade, and that his wife, the more entrepreneurial of the two of them, was now supporting them by offering a tailoring service. Mr Kabemba was part of an unpaid board managing the golf club, a job he did full-time, and one he said he could do well. The job involved providing a presence to prevent the encroachment of subsistence farming and other activities onto the greens, and trying to host occasional tournaments—although there was hardly anyone playing golf at the time of my research. There was a sense from Mr Kabemba and others like him that they were expecting a return to "normal" (by which they meant the order that had characterised paid employment on the mines) and would keep vigil till that time came, if it ever did. Their circumstance brought to mind Miss Haversham from Charles Dickens's (1890) *Great Expectations*, living their lives in the decaying cocoon of yesterday and waiting, living in a place that is a tangible reminder of a time when leisure fell into the smooth rhythms of a planned workday.

An Ice-Cream Parlour

There were other dreams that seemed to hark back to a past when ice cream was an expected treat for children, such as Mr and Mrs Spaita's idea for an ice-cream parlour. One afternoon in early 2008 I sat on a porch that was part of a storefront for a shop selling an assortment of household groceries in one of the most depressed neighbourhoods of Luanshya's former mine suburbs. This space was where Mrs Spaita and her husband were selling ice cream in cones. It was also where they had previously run a second-hand clothes store that had eventually been burnt down by jealous neighbours.[22] That afternoon, other than an ice cream cone sold to me, they only sold one other. Despite what seemed to be a dismal business, the Spaita's had a dream of setting up an ice-cream parlour. Mr Spaita, who was then working for Luanshya Copper Mines, had already undergone training in making ice cream, and the couple, who had two children under the age of ten, were saving to buy a few more ice-cream-making machines and find premises to rent. Mr Mwanja, a former workmate of Mr Spaita, was incredulous that they could even consider such a business. The question was, who could afford ice cream when it was a struggle to have a meal a day?

A Business Processing Used Oil

While the Spaita's business ideas were located in and based on a lifestyle of the past, others, like the Mwenyas, were anticipating a future industry, but one that unfortunately was overly ambitious, as they did not have access to affordable capital, nor had they properly assessed the viability of the business in the prevailing economic climate.

Mr and Mrs Mwenya, who ran a charismatic Pentecostal church, one among many that had sprung up to fill the spaces vacated by former mining company recreational activities, had a grand plan to set up a large used-oil refinery to service the entire Copperbelt. With the re-emergence of the copper industry, they envisioned that mining machinery and trucks would have a lot of used oil to dispose of that could be recycled. With a business proposal and using the revenue from the church and its tax-exempt status, they had secured a loan with the banks to purchase an old disused factory, the detritus of the region's former significant manufacturing industry. They had approached me informally for an assessment of what it would take to make the factory habitable. It was a significant cost that entailed their seeking another loan from the bank. Later they approached me to ask whether I would have the money to loan them, telling me that the bank had denied them the extra finance until they covered their existing loan, which amounted to close to one billion kwacha (about $200,000). One evening when I dropped by to visit them, I found out that they also owed money to a loan shark, who that very evening had threatened Mr Mwenya with a gun. Had it not been for his wife's intervention and passers-by's curiosity, the loan shark would have probably shot him. Outwardly successful, the Mwenyas, who owned two luxury cars and lived in a house furnished with glitzy heavy furniture in an aesthetic commonly seen in the Nigerian movies that had become popular in Zambia, had, towards the end of my fieldwork, lost most of these assets. Mrs Mwenya told me they had resorted to borrowing money from microcredit lenders for daily expenses.

The Mwenyas were characteristic of the highly ambitious business people who had emerged following the liberalisation of the country's economy. Their exhibition of wealth was, as I had been persuaded by several business people, an important aspect of the performance of building confidence amongst potential investment partners. To be a successful business person, you had to be seen as already wealthy, what Zambians refer to as *kulibonesha ta* (to show yourself). As I show in Chapter 3, this view also related to Copperbelt residents' views of class, which had shifted from status based on occupation and rank to perceptions of wealth and ability to get by.

The stories presented here provide a micro-understanding of the ways in which hope is crafted and experimented with in times of great uncertainty and the future is imagined. They highlight that where hope for the planning and expected outcomes may not be readily visible in the immediate environment, nevertheless it is thought of as lying "out there," on the horizon. The troubled side of this "out there" is reflected on in Chapter 6, on young people's conception of the future and their ability to steer their lives. It responds to Ferguson's (1992) article "The Country and the City on the Copperbelt," where he writes, speaking of his Zambian informants' apparent lack of "any morally positive images at all of a Zambian-made future" (1992, 85–86), that people's conception of the future may not lie in a mirror view back to the past (see Nyamnjoh 2001). While the bleak narratives of self and the future that Ferguson recounts are still encountered in contemporary Zambia, they need to be placed within the context of Copperbelt residents' dreams and aspirations, as in the examples I have given in this chapter. My informant's dreams indicate that in times of trouble, Copperbelt residents are willing to speculate, even wildly, in the hope that something might change. This indicated not a lack of hope, but a hope that is cast way beyond the difficulties and hardship of the immediate present or even immediate future, and a belief that an iteration of activities within the present and the environment they inhabit may open up possibilities leading towards realising those dreams.

René Devisch's (2006) use of "borderlinking," a concept borrowed from Bracha Ettinger, offers a useful concept for looking at how Copperbelt residents work towards efforts that look improbable from a cursory examination of their circumstances. Borderlinking, in Devisch's work, is the bridge that transverses varying temporalities of becoming in the flow of persons and things, an intersubjective and intercorporeal experience that resonates from the past in the present and the future. I pursue his insights in the chapters that follow.

PUTTING IDEAS AND DOING THINGS "OUT THERE"

My informants frequently told me that *teti u planne*,[23] "You can't plan," and indeed it seemed that their activities involved placing ideas and doing things "out there" and seeing what happened next, with the expectation that the most unrealistic might bear fruit, because the most realistic ones often came with crushing disappointment. This "putting things out there," is what Copperbelt residents often referred to as *ukwesha*, "to try." Trying is what created the possibility for things to emerge. Jennifer Johnson-Hanks (2005) provides a good description of what kind of action trying is. She writes of the uncertain perception of the future young Beti women from Cameroon highlighted by their argument that one could not plan for reproduction or marriage . According to Johnson-Hanks (2005, 363), in the context of uncertainty that characterises much of life in Africa, "Effective social action is based not on the fulfilment of prior intentions but on a judicious opportunism" whereby "the actor seizes promising chances." This action, Johnson-Hanks argues, is not based on a utilitarian and Weberian notion of rational choice but rather involves the ability to "respond effectively to the contingent, sudden, and surprising offers that life can make" (2005, 376). Accordingly, young Beti women, like Copperbelt residents, tended to cast their lines wide in the hope of something concrete taking hold. This type of action requires responsiveness, I argue, a tuning in to one's own conscious and unconscious abilities, and also to what the environment affords.

Johnson-Hanks further observes that "actors take advantage of whatever means are available and thus settle on a specific end out of many that would have been acceptable" (2005, 376). This point is applicable to Copperbelt residents as they address living in crisis. The experience is also akin to what Lisa Cligett et al. (2007) write of the Gwembe Tonga in southern Zambia, who, ever since the construction of the Kariba Dam in 1958, have lived uncertainly. Cligett et al. observe that the Tonga have responded to this uncertainty by making use of "whatever opportunities present themselves, and the uncertainty of the duration of those opportunities, in order to grasp what security they can at a given moment in time" (2007, 20).

What I observed of how Copperbelt residents went about living their lives amidst the crisis that followed the reprivatisation of the mines and job layoffs, and their frequently offered statement, "You can't plan," challenged my ideas of agency. Prior to my engagement in fieldwork, my notion of agency was strongly influenced by my architectural training and the anthropological work of Alfred Gell (1998), the idea that if one can impose order and establish patterns, then in turn one can trace out a network of patterns and relationships.[24]

Order, Objectification, and Structure

Anthropology, like architecture, has been trapped in the practice of giving precedence to form rather than to the processes that give rise to the conglomerations of things we perceive. Both draw on a notion of predictability and routine, anthropology in its focus on regularities in thought and action and architecture in form and function. Both are a practice of abstraction, a reduction of experience in order to communicate something of the world.

In my study, the environment within which Copperbelt residents do things is not an abstract place. While Ferguson's use of performativity in characterising the Copperbelt demonstrates dynamism and movement without getting trapped in a teleological framework, it does not address how the landscape itself provides the surface and volume to study a connected world. In this way, partial understandings of the world within which we live are not disconnects (Ferguson 2006), but rather a partial knowledge premised on a largely unconscious engagement with a wider, unstable, always changing whole.[25]

While much structuralist theory flirts with wholeness, in this work the structure of the world is imagined as a web of influence—I am thinking here of the work of Claude Lévi-Strauss (1963) and that of poststructuralists Michel Foucault (1975) and Pierre Bourdieu (1977)—with people acting with various degrees of intentionality on a spectrum that ranges from fully constrained or entrapped within their position in the web to actors fighting the constraints of their position. In this world view, the world is prescribed. It does not give rise to much surprise; the unexpected only arises due to someone not knowing the field, and this can be remedied by looking for the underlying rules and patterns. In Lévi-Strauss's work, the way to knowing the rules is to look for hierarchy, rank, taboos, and so on. For Foucault, it is to look at how history gave rise to these formations such that even when people rally against their constraints, they struggle to extricate themselves.[26] Bourdieu looks at the clusters of influences that give rise to the different ways in which people act within a structure that is loosely determined by the characteristics of the powerful, as well as from their own learnt dispositions. What is imagined in this view of wholeness is a map with people only able to move along predetermined paths. This cartographic notion of wholeness does not give way to much surprise. As I was warned by a colleague on the Copperbelt, "It is not good to pin things down," as it limits the possibilities of perceiving what could emerge.

Systems theorists (Bateson 1972; Bohm 2002; Oyama 2000) have argued that to study a part as separate from its whole simplifies and closes off understanding of the workings of wider phenomena, and results in circular reasoning that does little to advance what we know about the world. Drawing from an example by David Bohm, this would be like approaching a person with a stereotype of who they are, relating to them as such and in effect reproducing the stereotype (2002, 7–8). This, Bohm argues, limits our vision because "theories are ever-changing forms of insight, giving shape and form to experience in general" 2002, 7). As such, our movements in the world are guided by an illusory perception (2002, 9) that I would say involves an improvisory repetition of actions to order our always partial understandings and increase our knowledge about our fragmentary and unstable notions of the world and how to navigate it.

Rather than abandon structural explanations of the modern world, it may be useful to see them as like an architect's initial thoughts, as sketches, unstable idealisations. This, as Friedrich (1988, 442) suggests, would be a precarious position between the classical and the romantic, the classical representing a clear traceable path to an ideal of harmony and the romantic an exploratory path that grows into an unknown. As Ingold suggests in *Lines* (2007), drawing and writing as inscriptive practices of objectification could be seen as learning processes in the skilling of telling a story. Thus, those with sufficient skill are able to indicate traces that open up the mind, as experienced through their own knowledge of the world, to others. But within the modernising project, as in the classical, which places precedence on form (and here my own training as an architect resonates), the skill is related to attempts to "finalise," close off and have a final say on what the world is.

A presentation on the quest for European excellence in research by the anthropologist Rane Willerslev (n.d.) highlights the contradiction between the classical and the romantic. For example, Willerslev begins his talk by saying that a good theory is one that wipes out all other explanations, but then goes on to make a strong case for the importance of fostering the "free spirit" which allows for those things that cannot be predicted to emerge. The idea of a grand theory that explains everything would not have sat well with many Copperbelt residents who, as I will show in Chapter 6's exploration of their reflections of life and death through popular music, viewed life as an exploratory journey where outcomes were unknown and options encountered were to be mixed together to try to chance upon new conglomerations for living. This did not mean that they did not seek to make a somewhat orderly life, a desire reflected in their nostalgia for the heyday of mining company welfare largesse, where the mine administration sought to order all aspects of mine-worker's lives, but that they were alert to the need to take advantage of emergent possibilities in their social and material environments.

It Is Difficult to Contain the Environment

The Luanshya Township monthly report for October 1978[27] illuminates how the administrators of the mine township tried to contain the environment. I reproduce some of their concerns here.

1. DANGEROUS TREES

Dangerous trees were found at 58 "Z" and 116 "I" Avenue and were reported to the Engineering Department (T) for cutting and action was taken.

2. RE DISTURBING NOISE—MONGRELS

It was reported that mongrels at 66 "E," 77 "E" and 45 "D" Avenue were disturbing neighbours by making noise. Owners of the mongrels were warned to keep them under control at night and that was followed up.

How does one account for the things that spill outside the plan? My study, like Ferguson's, draws on performance and iterative practices, but departs from a discourse-centred approach to employ an ecological one, which takes into consideration Copperbelt residents' perceptions of their environment and their interactions within it.

The ecological approach employed here differs from the urban ecology of the Chicago school, which, when looking for patterns in the processes of urban ways of life, used a scaled analysis that saw places as progressing from simple to complex and accordingly tended to posit interactions that were functional rather than generative. Rather, it draws from what is in the environment, which means acknowledging the perception of difference rather than emphasizing the exclusions that make for a neat fit. For example, while the anthropologist Hortense Powdermaker, an outlier of the Manchester school, cannot be said to have used an explicitly ecological approach, like Gregory Bateson (1972), her work on the Copperbelt and other areas employed an eclectic range of ethnographic and methodological perspectives in looking at society, in particular popular culture. Powdermaker's *Copper*

Town (1962) describes the various transformations that were happening on the Copperbelt, offering detailed descriptions that, while they address social change, do not make a strong attempt to identify neat categories. This may have been because of her use of different ethnographic vantage points; she looked at not only African sociality (as was the case for many of the Manchester school anthropologists), but also European lifestyles within the same context. In describing the activities and aspirations of various research subjects, from the aspirations of schoolchildren, to cinema watching, domestic life and disputes, the variations in life and aspirations amongst the Copperbelt's European workers, the labour contests, Powdermaker (1962) presents a setting that is hard to contain within the boundaries of mechanistic or even categorical analysis. Whereas Epstein (1958) and Mitchell (1969) can be argued to have worked like the Lévi-Strauss "engineer" in attempting to "pin" down as precisely as possible the social setting on the Copperbelt, Powdermaker (1962) resembles the Straussian "bricoleur," making do with a patchwork of what was available and going on, thus hinting at the complexity of life that went beyond mere categorisation of urban or rural.

In this way, my study of the Copperbelt relates to contemporary urban studies that emphasise the dynamics and texture of place. An exemplar of these works includes Ato Quayson's (2014) *Oxford Street, Accra*, which describes sensitively the itineraries, activities, and social relations of the city's local and transnational residents in a particular place, and amidst a varied and changing built landscape. Quayson's book is part of a growing study of African cities that engages scholars and built-environment practitioners to consider the characteristics of places, rather than view them only through a developmental lens, a perspective that Jennifer Robinson (2006) has criticised earlier urban studies of the Copperbelt for doing. This consideration, Robinson (2006) argues, is key to locating the dynamics of what goes on in African cities in a global perspective, and lays regions like the Copperbelt open to potentially interesting comparisons. Stephen Marr (2016) in his comparative work of Lagos and Detroit has made a similar point, urging us to understand how the forces of global capitalisms and neoliberalisms play out in different places. This is important because some of the changes that Copperbelt residents described after the re-privatisation of the mines are akin to the reflections on life, past and present, in post-socialist Eastern Europe (Hann 2002; Pitcher and Askew 2006). Accordingly, there is scope for relational comparative studies to look at the experiences of the effects of urban deindustrialisation, decline, and austerity policies from the Copperbelt to the

American Rust Belt (Dandaneau 1996) and the Greek economic crisis (Rako-poulos 2013). To do so, however, requires using analytical framings as a tool rather than as an end—to open up a conversation rather than close it. In the following sections, I describe the mixed analytical lens I use.

AFFECT AND TEXTURE

Text, as a discursive, semiological practice, has been of interest to anthropologists looking to understand people's spatial engagements. A good example of this is Henrietta's Moore's (1986) *Space, Text and Gender*, an ethnography of the Marakwet of Kenya. Moore reads the practice of social actors in the built environment using the idea of cultural text. She uses it not to look for meaning in the symbols in the environment but to look for social strategy and strategic interpretation or translations in the everyday use of the environment that are found in how social actors use space and act in it, and in how they tell their stories (1986, 75). Her approach relies on local translations or interpretations of action that are gendered and self-interested, and as such enact and reproduce relations of power. Power, as an underlying cultural text comes to the "surface" in everyday practical action, is told not in ordinary language (because of its elusiveness to straightforward description), but in metaphor. Moore draws on the work of Lakoff and Johnson to describe metaphor as a work of poetic imagination (1986, 76). Gaston Bachelard (1969), a phenomenologist, emphasised the importance of imagination in the understanding of space as experienced, and argues that metaphors become useful in the rhetorical manifestation of this experience. For Bachelard, the experience of space is poetic, and as such, the experience is an affective one. It is through poetry that text moves beyond the lingual domain to capture essences that are varied, nuanced, and textured. Tim Cresswell's (2013) work on poetry of urban landscapes and Raymond Williams's (1980) reflections on the Welsh industrial novel respectively draw on the strength of poetry and metaphor to narrate the aspects of place that elude easy description. Overall, these narratives create a textural quality that Williams (1977, 132) refers to as structures of feeling, describing "the palpable" aspects of lived experience from which persons infer meanings and values.

Henri Lefebvre (1992) notes that it is texture rather than text that allows for the theoretical integration of the senses within spatial experience. Texture is an experience in which the things encountered by persons in the environment are not mere objects, but things that have resonances, linked to the rhythms in the continual production of space. I illustrate this in Chapter 6 in exploring how the rhythms and sounds of popular music create a communitas of shared experiences. I show that Copperbelt residents' exploratory engagements with the world do not occur in a vacuum devoid of affect. The phenomenological basis from which I draw is underpinned by perceptual engagement and dwelling within the environment. This implies a sensory engagement. And, as Fiona Ross (2010), drawing on the experience of getting lost, demonstrates, our perceptual engagement of the world is premised not just on a kind of detached spatial geography of a place, but also on our emotional and intersubjective engagements with place. This implies a sensory engagement with the world that is not only temporal but interconnected to other experiences through which we have learnt the world.

Edward Casey (2001a) provides a concept for understanding this type of dwelling. He has argued that space, the abstract notion that makes us part of a wider world, and place, as that which we inhabit and experience, do not need to be mutually exclusive, that the two can coexist in what he calls the "place-world." He draws from Bourdieu's notion of habitus[28] to describe the "place-world" as that which provides "an indispensable dimension of the body's role in emplacing human beings" (Casey 2001b, 716). Unlike Bourdieu, whose concept of habits is embodied and offers a dispositional modus operandi for action in the world, for Casey "habits are movements in space even as the amassments of their own repetition and deployment," and as such, he argues, they "dilate" rather than limit our being in the world. Indeed, they "are the very basis for our inhabiting the world" (1984, 54). For Casey, place is "open-textured, ever-altering, always challenging, never fixed" (2001b, 719). Casey uses the term "implacing" to denote an active ongoing movement, a navigational process that is both objectifying in its search for signs, and exploratory in its employment of the experiential. He argues that "place" is also one of the main ways in which we leave traces of ourselves in the landscape as the "world's felt texture" (1983, 87). Casey further notes that "place is the congealing of this texture into discrete here/there arenas of possible action" (1983, 87). As an experience of here and there, place is both somatic, felt on the skin, and visceral, in the depth of feeling that manifests itself in memories and affects like nostalgia.

As Filip De Boeck's description of Kinshasa (2006) has shown, places have many invisible facets. On the Copperbelt, one of these is nostalgia, which provides a weave between the visible and invisible traces of the past.

Some of these are the archaeological fragments of a planned garden city and a way of life, which despite the evidence of urban decay still lend themselves to this vision in the tree-lined roads and the overgrown recreational centres. Nostalgia as encountered on the Copperbelt is about both loss and a romanticisation of the past. As Casey, writing on the general aspects of nostalgia, notes, it is a "baffling combination of the sweet and the bitter, the personal and the impersonal, distance and proximity, presence and absence, place and no-place, imagination and memory, memory and non-memory" (Casey 1987, 379). Nostalgia is also a layered experience that, as Ferguson (1992) shows, in the Zambian post-independence political and moral discourses of the village expressed a romanticised vision that was intended to counter the selfishness perceived in town life. As a moral discourse, it was meant to serve as a mode of redistribution. In the contemporary period, reference to a home village, as I have shown through the example of my initial encounter with Mr Mwale, is a way to turn potentially alienating urban interactions into meaningful ones by means of linking to a place of a past origin. In this way nostalgia also serves as "a cultural practice that hinges on position and perspective; it should be seen as part of a social imaginary—that is, as expressive and creative activity grounded in the dynamics of everyday life" (Bissell 2005, 215).

However, as Ferguson observed, Copperbelt residents during the years of decline increasingly struggled to reconcile the romanticised idea of a home village to the loss and decay in the towns that made the reciprocal relations fostered in the moral discourse of the village come to be seen as parasitic. As the economy worsened, Ferguson notes, the village became a real option for those struggling in the towns. At the same time, particularly for urbanites who had not cultivated rural ties, the village had also become "an object of intense fear, often articulated as fear of witchcraft" (Ferguson 1992, 89–90).

What Ferguson's observations bring to light is that when nostalgia as a fantasy of a place out there or distant past becomes more immediate, it does not always sit easily with the realities of that imagined place. For example, while the state and mining companies lauded self-sufficiency, the reality is that, for many, self-sufficiency also meant uncertainty and precariousness, and the back-to-the-land policy, when put into practice, meant a real confrontation with fears associated with the village. As I show in Chapter 4, working on one's own with one's own hands also meant risky work and working even when unwell. The fear of witchcraft is not to be trivialised either. When conducting research in the rural districts of North Western Province in Kasempa in 2008, I encountered an investigation by the police force into twenty-one murders tied to witchcraft accusations committed over the year.[29] Rather than focus only on a nostalgia of loss and regret, I prefer, like Dlamini (2009) writing on everyday life in a South African township during apartheid, to draw also on those aspects of Copperbelt life that lend multiple perspectives and texture to the sense of place during a period of decline.

Many of my informants' nostalgic fantasies were tempered by real anxieties that coated their experiences of the present. These manifested in various ways. One was in their aspirations for a harmonious life, a nostalgia for a maternal, caring type of love similar to that encountered by Mark Hunter (2010) in his research in South Africa on love in a time of AIDS. This was elaborate in the love songs of Copperbelt popular artists Dandy Krazy and Macky 2, and in the complex domestic arrangements people sought. Karen Tranberg Hansen (1997) describes similar desires in her ethnography of women's lives and their aspirations for homemaking in an informal settlement in Lusaka. Another way it manifested was in the loosening of the strictures of formality. There was the view that one had to wander outside formal boundaries in order to survive and maybe "make it" in an increasingly uncertain world.

Informality and Trespass

The increasing spheres of informality offer a helpful place from which to look at these multiple ways of life. If informality connotes a propensity for trespassing (as I show in Chapter 4), it well describes Copperbelt residents' "open textured," exploratory, and improvisational way of being. One might describe this mode of life as being like foraging. Indeed, a study conducted in 2005–2006 by Manyewu Mutamba (2007) on two communities, one on the outskirts of Mufulira and another in Kabompo, North Western Province, shows that foraging (of forest products) forms an important part of livelihood. Foraging as an activity requires searching over a wide area for food and provisions. Within urban settings often characterised by rules of private property, foraging as a way of inhabiting place is bound to lead to trespass. But it is also likely to open up new possibilities for livelihood.

The options of less formal types of livelihood existed even during the tightly administered period of the mines. As Karen Tranberg Hansen and Mariken Vaa note, informal activities, even when falling outside legal frameworks, were not always seen as illegitimate by those involved (2004, 7–8). On the Copperbelt, where mining activity employed few women, the informal economy was an important aspect of women's work, and occasionally the mining company sought to bring it within the fold of formal livelihood strategies by allowing women to sell their produce, usually agriculture, in designated markets. However, women's more lucrative ventures, such as brewing beer, were discouraged (Hansen 1984, 227). In the contemporary Copperbelt, women's economic activities have expanded to include mining, albeit informal mining.

As the spheres of life governed by a state weakened by the adoption of free market policies expand, the informal economy, as Keith Hart (2009) notes, becomes the real economy. Out of informality has emerged the invisible city, where, in the spaces where the formal modes of life have departed, one finds the hidden and not so hidden possibilities that sustain these places. In Luanshya, where the decay of town infrastructure has been in progress from the end of the period of state-run ZCCM mines, the town, as De Boeck (2011) observed of Kinshasa, has increasing been "banalized and reduced to its most basic function, that of a shelter. The built form is generated by a more real, living city which exists as a heterogeneous urban conglomeration through the bodies, movements, practices, and discourses of urban dwellers" (2011, 271). It is within such a landscape that Luanshya residents, like those of Kinshasa, some more skilfully than others, discover new itineraries and generate options where none seemed possible (De Boeck 2011, 272).

For many Copperbelt residents, the end of ZCCM was also an end to the mine township administrators' almost obsessive compulsions to try to maintain order in the mine areas and in turn smooth the texture of the Copperbelt landscape. Copperbelt residents staying in the former mine township, especially male former mine employees whose lives had been more in tune with the work rhythms of the mine, lost their bearings, resulting in an affect of uncertainty akin to that which Ross (2010) describes regarding getting lost. This sense of losing one's bearings can also be related to the uncertainty in the process of giving form to things. As I demonstrate in the remainder of the book, Copperbelt residents "tried"; that is, they were not always sure and indeed maintained a kind of scepticism about what might emerge from the livelihood enterprises they embarked on.

Making a Living

"Just try" was an expression I frequently heard people when people encouraged their colleagues. As I describe in Chapter 3, some people were more successful than others in their enterprises. The variations in relative success coloured Copperbelt residents' perceptions of class, which was increasingly connected to consumption. In the ZCCM past, former mineworkers could track each other's social climb, as it was connected to career progression within the mine company hierarchy. In the post-reprivatisation period, former mineworkers are engaged in multiple livelihood strategies. Their neighbours in the former mine suburbs now have more difficulty establishing how they are doing relative to others. Those who became successful in contemporary Copperbelt were often accused of having drawn from dark, magical sources to secure their success. There was a sense of awe and also suspicion, a perplexity over how persons made a success of their lives, much like what Alfred Gell (1988), in his article "Technology and Magic," describes in relation to how the work of a particularly skilled craftsperson is perceived, as somewhat mystical or enchanted. What this means in relation to how Copperbelt residents see each other's livelihood activities is that what people do to become successful goes beyond the skilful execution of tasks at hand to encompass something beyond what can be readily seen. Gell (1998) illustrates this in his reference to Malinowski's ethnography of Trobriand Island coral gardens to describe how Trobriand Islanders try through magic to harness nature, using metaphorical evocations of the ideal garden. In these magical chants of the ideal garden, pests leave the soil and plants swiftly take root. Rather than seeing, as Gell does, the chants as a template from which the ideal garden is drawn, they can also be seen as poetry, an evocation of feeling, and hence energy in the attempt to harness the uncertainty of nature's flows and the intangibilities that wreak havoc with any process of giving form. This implies an affective engagement with doing. In this way, as in the case presented in the next chapter of Mr Mubita's call to his wife to share his vision for his backyard projects, they can also be seen as a call for an emotional engagement, what Geiser (2008) would describe as a call for empathy.[30] In looking at how people make a living in places where they are experiencing great psychosocial stress, it is important, as I show in the later chapters, to explore the areas from which they draw the "energy" to keep going and trying.

Making Things

Early on in fieldwork, I met informants like Mr Mubita and his colleague Mr Mulenga (see Chapter 3) whose livelihoods, like many other Copperbelt residents', had embraced self-sufficiency and using one's hands, for example in the building of a water well. How do we learn to dig and build a well? Asking this question highlighted those aspects of life, such as tasks and techniques of the body, that rely little on the spoken word. These drew me to one of Ingold's central questions: if we come to know the world by dwelling[31] in it and through our engagement in it, how do we increase our perceptual knowledge of certain aspects of it, so as to be able to give form within it?

Studies of livelihood in anthropology and other disciplines such as sociology and the new development studies have often tended to focus on the social relations of making a livelihood. What has been less of a focus are the material aspects of livelihood, and the skills and tools people draw on to sustain themselves. I explore these here, contributing to the growing interest in anthropology in re-engaging the issues that had fascinated the early discipline: tools and skills. While Ferguson was generally correct in what he observed on the Copperbelt, by focussing on the linguistic pragmatics of performance, such as the stylistic variations in Copperbelt identities, he omitted a realm that too is crucial in describing a process of becoming. To illustrate this point, when Copperbelt residents talk about the place becoming like a village, it is not just in its appearance, as I outline in Chapter 1, but also in the broader sensory realm. When people regularly rather than occasionally use firewood to cook, they begin to smell in ways people associate with the countryside, even though they may not reside there. Also, when people engage in more strenuous activity in the process of generating a livelihood in a depleted context, their bodies begin to take on the form and appearance that reflects the characteristics of a rural lifestyle, where the body is nourished according to the seasonality of food available and shaped by production's regimes of labour. Accordingly, Copperbelt residents' view of the village is perceived too in the changed physical appearances: leaner faces, darker complexions—sunburn from working out in the sun.

This extra-sensual perspective, in which people are engaged, not in a conscious reshaping of themselves and the landscape, but in an unintentional co-shaping, goes beyond Bourdieu's (1977) notion of habitus as an embodied realm of socially influenced dispositions. Copperbelt residents are not only shaping their identities and environment, but being shaped by the things they do. The cumulative effect of their social and material experiences is not just internally inscribed but spills beyond their bodies as they go about giving form to the things that sustain them as living organisms. This way of being can be seen as giving form to the "unconscious" of our interaction with the world. The unconscious I refer to here is not the object but the flow of mind as entangled with other organisms (Bateson 1972) and the world. It is complex, difficult to grasp, in that it often eludes our objectifying attempts know the grain of the world.

However, in order to make things or create forms, we try to conceptualise stable objects that guide our attempts to increase knowledge. For example, conceptualising categories like social, cultural, and economic capital as embodied offers Bourdieu a model that separates and distils within the body, a prototype for the workings of society. In an ethnographic study of the engineering firm ARUP, Penny Harvey (2009) observed that engineers use models as a predictive tool to try to understand the uncertain outcomes of giving form. Harvey looks at the model as a "point of contact between different ways of knowing, [which] could operate as a site of provocative overlap, drawing out what does not fit rather than simply looking for neat accommodation" (2009, 272). In this way methods or theoretical engagements operate very much like tools that guide our points of entry, that distil and separate the complexities of the things we work with.

If we had to draw from Ingold's conception that life flows and is not static, the point of contact that Harvey refers to becomes like a fisherman's line. To cast, one needs minute improvisations that are influenced not only by the line, but by the drag of water, the wind, the musculature of our bodies, the heat of the sun, and the many intangible things we cannot always readily describe or may not be aware are factors in our casting. Thus, these places of contact are where one tries to harness, distil, and separate, sometimes successfully, other times not, the variables we perceive or anticipate. This is a common approach in scientific experiments. The variables are numerous and uncertain, as are the interactions, so the model is continuously adjusted to try to harness these flows better. Tryings, or experiments, then, are knowledge seeking, aimed at getting to know the complexities of the world in our attempts to create forms within it.

GETTING BY: TRYING AND PLANNING

In the cases presented through the rest of the book, it becomes clear that my informants were engaged in a continuous process of trying to "get on" and live. This was not detached from what their bodies could physically do or from the skills and tools employed. As I found out myself, it was difficult to "order" the field, but I argue that rather than giving up entirely any attempt to do so, life—like fieldwork—should be approached as a continual process of "trying," experimentation. In turn, agency should be seen as a "blob" of blurred signifiers that indicates an ever-moving intent that is entangled within the ever-changing environment and our histories. Accordingly, my application of Ingold to thinking through the Copperbelt is heavily influenced by a pragmatic engagement with the environment that draws on an experimental approach to getting things done.[32]

Ingold's approach is useful for understanding the on-the-ground constraints of fieldwork that can only be appreciated by engaging in the physical and social tasks of the research process where as researcher I become an active participant. This demanded an exploratory approach, one in which the wayfarer revisits a place she had been to before with the open expectation that the environment will reveal something new (Hallam and Ingold 2007). It resonates with a view of agency that was more fitting within an uncertain and textured world. In the renovation of my house in Luanshya, I learnt, like other Copperbelt residents, that in a context of uncertainty it was better to look out for possibilities beyond one's initial plans, and to try, that is, maintain a hopeful stance toward the future.

NOTES

1. Critique from the 1980s against IMF economic restructuring policies argued that liberalisation would see production and investment oriented much more towards consumption for high earners, and for luxury goods (see Makgetla 1986). The proliferation of shops and malls across the country selling high-priced consumer goods has in some sense created Guy Debord's (1967) society of the spectacle, with residents desiring goods they could ill afford given their low and sporadic earning.

2. There was an awareness amongst many of the residents of Luanshya following temporary closure of the mines in 2000 that there were still copper mineral deposits, such as the Muliashi deposits. As of 2010 these were being developed by the new mine owners, the Chinese mining company NFC Africa.

3. An aspect of Ferguson's book that Francis Nyamnjoh (2001) takes up in his review is how Copperbelt residents conceptualise their future amidst hardship. Ferguson notes that it was not only commentators on the Copperbelt industrialisation that bought into the myth of modernity but also its own residents, such that a description of a hard life in the present could only elicit a nostalgic look to the past, where a prosperous modern future had seemed a reality. Nyamnjoh draws on a vehicular metaphor in his reading of Ferguson, writing that "like a driver with little prospect of advancing, their [that is Copperbelt residents] only chance of pulling out appears to be looking in the rear-view mirror" (see Chapter 6 for a discussion on how Copperbelt residents perceive their lives).

4. This translated to about US$200,000.

5. At the time of Northern Rhodesia's (Zambia's) independence from British

colonial rule, Time-Warner circulated a story that today still does the rounds online. It reported that Edward Mukuka Nkoloso, a science teacher, had set up a space program called the Zambia National Academy of Science, Space Research and Philosophy in the outskirts of Zambia's capital. There, using swings and rolling drums to simulate the conditions of space, he trained a youthful team of astronauts who, with a cat, were to compete with the United States and former Soviet Union in the race to the moon (see http://en.wikipedia.org/wiki/Edward_Makuka_Nkoloso, last accessed 10 December 2013).

6. During the 1991 campaign for his and his party's UNIP re-election, Kenneth Kaunda, who had then ruled the country for twenty-seven years (since 1972 as a one-party state), had proposed turning over one-quarter of the country's land mass to a yogic Maharishi group who were to have helped turn the country into an earth-friendly agrarian paradise in addition to encouraging meditation amongst the country's populace as a practice to promote calm and peace. Kaunda subsequently lost the elections, and the scheme (which was seen as odd by the majority of the populace) was never implemented.

7. My budget, including cost of renovations, which I knew were very likely, was ZMK 65 million (approximately US$13,000), to be financed by some savings, an employment-attached loan from a commercial bank, and a long-term loan from a friend.

8. In the absence of a will the intestate succession act of 1994 proposes the division of property between children, spouse, and dependants, as well as parents of the deceased if still living. There are frequent disputations over the distribution of resources.

9. Glencore's Mopani Copper Mines located in Mufulira had been cautioned in 2012 by the Zambia environmental agency over air quality pollution, particularly acid mist. See the *Mail and Guardian* newspaper article, "Zambia Halts Copper Treatment Plant's Operations," 6 March 2012.

10. Joe Kaunda, "Luanshya Risks Turning into a Ghost Town," *The Post*, 4 November 1999

11. Unlike many other ZCCM employees who occupied ZCCM housing and had thus gained a house as part of their retrenchment package, the subsidiary company located in Lusaka had not owned its own property and had rented from the private market.

12. Land for which building permission had been obtained had to be developed within a period of five years.

13. Copperbelt towns like Luanshya had been established in the middle of *miombo* woodland. Some of this woodland had been cleared to establish pine and eucalyptus forests that, following the sale of the mines in the mid-1990s, were being settled by retired and retrenched urban Copperbelt residents seeking agricultural livelihoods. See Hansangule, Feeney, and Palmer 1998.

14. There are growing markets where you can exchange carbon-offset activities for "credits" then sold on special markets.

15. I learnt several years later, when doing research on the development of new mines in Zambia in areas adjacent to nature reserves, that mining companies were lobbying to remove environmental protections as a means to allow mineral exploration in protected conservation areas.

16. Noami Haynes (2012), writing on Pentecostalism on the Copperbelt, for example, looks beyond the "spectral" qualities of prosperity gospel to how its fosters social relationships and exchange by promoting visible displays of material wealth that in turn play into expectations of moral obligations and reciprocity based on the hierarchies signified for those who are living well and not so well.

17. The award-winning architect Walter Dobkins, who had designed the building that now houses the COMESA headquarters in Lusaka, whom I had interviewed for my master's thesis, had taken these factors into account in the design of the building, which used a more organic form that, in contrast to a linear design, allowed for the concealment of errors for builders not adept at setting out straight lines, and the use of familiar, low-tech building materials.

18. The 1995 Land Act allowed the conversion of land on customary tenure to state leasehold land, but not vice versa, as well as vesting all land under the president of the country. As most of the country's land mass was under customary tenure, this act was criticised by both traditional authorities and by activists as potentially dispossessing the rural poor by, in effect, privatising land.

19. Tembo, Nyirenda, and Nyambe (2017) estimate that about 90%, of residents living in Lusaka's informal settlements use pit latrines, which pose a serious health concern given that untreated faecal matter remains in the environments where people live.

20. I found out later that a number of residents had been offering work for board in former "servants' quarters."

21. Texture connotes the movement and the sensing of things, place, and persons as they transform, shift, change, allowing for both "smooth" movements (here drawing from the notion of smooth space as that which allows for movement that drifts or wanders) and the nitty-gritty of place (as the movements that place the body in the immediacy of experience) (Casey 1997).

22. I was surprised that they would set up again in the same place after this experience, but this was characteristic of what I encountered—trying again (see Chapter 6).

23. All vernacular quotations in this work are in Bemba, the lingua franca of the Copperbelt, or a slang version of it, unless indicated otherwise; translations have been provided by myself and my key research assistants, Hendrick Kapepa and Kasonde Mwenda.

24. Gell's (1998) approach is to treat objects and humans as agents, and he sees both participating in social interaction and the making of form, both social and material. However, in Gell's work, affect is not taken into consideration. By this I mean the affordances that are perceived in the environment in the process of going about living.

25. By "whole" I am not referring to a notion of holism as a container of life, but as a medium through which our activities resonate and co-shape us and our place.

26. An entrapment of rules and norms whereby people within the web imagine they are watched and therefore self-regulate.

27. Ndola Mining Archives document WM/EC/pcm 31/10/78 box reference 300.60.4.

28. Habitus as the embodied sets of beliefs and dispositions of a person that give limitless options for action, or possibilities that in turn offer options for the shifting of this set of dispositions and beliefs (Bourdieu 1977).

29. A personal example: in 2012 when running a workshop on community mine engagements in North Western Zambia, my colleagues and I encountered a man running for his life from a mob who wanted him to answer to an accusation of witchcraft.

30. For Geiser, empathy is the tuning in to another person's perceptual engagement with the world (2008, 310–311) that forms a crucial part of apprenticeship learning. I would also say that it involves tuning in to the texture of place and exploring what it affords us. This is clear for those who work with their hands, as it is an engagement that traverses the mind/body split, which as Fisher notes, "allows us to resolve the tension between the cultural and the physical in our interaction with objects" (2004, 5). But in interactions that are less obviously physical and material, the affordances are less visible and may inhabit the more ephemeral aspects of life, like music, dance, poetry, and other energetic/vital sources that imbue places with invisible qualities or texture.

31. For Martin Heidegger (1962), to whom a phenomenological approach is widely attributed, the nature of human experience is a concern of man's situatedness in the world—what he calls dwelling—and revealing or making accessible that which is hidden in this experience.

32. Ingold (2000) argues that we come to know the world by physically engaging with it through practice and through a constantly adjusted perception of it in relation to our bodies.

CHAPTER 3

"Getting By"

"Improvising a Life" on the Post-privatisation Copperbelt

Prior to the privatisation of ZCCM, large sections of Copperbelt towns had been under the direct control of the mining company, which provided social infrastructure, basic housing, and services, and oversaw general urban management (see Mutale 2004; Kazimbaya-Senkwe and Guy 2007).[1] ZCCM-owned housing and other physical infrastructure were allocated to employees to occupy or use, according to employment rank and family space requirements. Other mine employees lived in neighbourhoods known as *ku maini*, divided into low-, medium-, and high-cost (or high-, medium-, and low-density) areas. These divisions also indicated employee rankings within the company hierarchy. A promotion often meant relocation to higher-cost housing. Privatisation of ZCCM and the sale of its assets spelt the end of this clearly demarcated social hierarchy. When wholesale privatisation took off, miners[2] were offered the houses they occupied at a subsidised price that was to be deducted from their terminal benefits in retirement packages. The subsidised sale of houses allowed ZCCM to make up for its inability to pay terminal benefits in full. With the economic hardships that ensued for most miners and the success for a lucky few in the liberalised market economy, some Luanshya residents moved up and some moved down these social scales and the physical spaces that corresponded to them. Wide variations in the physical infrastructure of houses became clearly visible in the varying degrees of dilapidation and renovation, indicating inequalities amongst residents in the same neighbourhood, residents who had once been of a single social class.

In Luanshya, as in the rest of the Copperbelt, the privatisation of the mines and the ensuing major downsizing of the workforce marked the start of an unprecedented economic crisis, with drastic effects on the local population.[3] Many leased out their houses and left to seek employment elsewhere. The vast majority of those who stayed behind initiated an array of economic activities to "get by,"[4] including subsistence agriculture in their backyards[5] and on the outskirts[6] of Luanshya. Despite the enormous difficulties of the economic transition period, the result was an impressive outburst of small-scale enterprises cutting across spatial divisions and class groupings in the local socioeconomic landscape.

This chapter focuses on the lived experiences of former miners from Luanshya living in the high-cost neighbourhood (*kuma yard*, in local parlance). The "European area," as it had been known, was built in the 1930s just after copper production began at the Roan Antelope Mine in 1931. The first black families moved into these houses in 1963. By the 1980s, the high-cost neighbourhood comprised predominantly higher-ranking black mine employees.[7] More specifically, the chapter explores the role that former miners' newly acquired houses play in their livelihoods and the small-scale economic activities carried out in their backyards. The first part tackles the local perceptions of the relationship between the past (during ZCCM administration) and the present (marked by wholesale privatisation). This is followed by three brief accounts of local informants' life trajectories after privatisation. The emerging features of these lived experiences will be dwelt upon in more detail in an extended case study of a former miner's experience of housing and of the innovative, small-scale economic activities carried out in his backyard. These cases are indicative, but not necessarily prescriptive, of the social situation on the Copperbelt. They suggest the conditions that create variations in socially observable data, such as perceptions of suffering and assessments of who is "doing okay" and who is "doing well." These observations, as Max Gluckman (1961, 9) noted, can also indicate how a particular social system operates, for example, by illuminating the micro-political economy of the context. While it may be possible to map out particular individual trajectories from case studies and quantitative data from surveys, I intend to demonstrate, drawing on work by Elizabeth Hallam and Tim Ingold (2007), that living is a series of improvisations. "Scripting social life misses the processual aspects of living" (Hallam and Ingold 2007, 1) and, I argue, theoretically trivialises the temporal praxis of "getting by." This chapter describes improvisations in the livelihood practices of Luanshya's former mine employees and demonstrates the different directions they have taken after the homogenising influence of ZCCM. The overall aim is to show how structure, from a micro-political perspective, is woven. It also describes how the disappearance of the old ZCCM system and its de facto control of socioeconomic differentiation sparked new processes of "class" formation.

CLASS ON THE COPPERBELT

Class formation and social mobility on the Copperbelt have been of interest to social scientists studying the region ever since the establishment of the copper- mining industry at the turn of the twentieth century. From studies of the proletarisation of African rural migrants to the copper towns, and the transformation of their lives in the urban spaces, that characterised the Manchester school's urban anthropology to those that looked at the configuration of labour from the workplace to the household, this anthropology has been formative in methodological, descriptive, and theoretical terms. For example, Michael Burawoy's (1972) seminal workplace ethnography looked at the Zambianisation policies that were meant to indigenise the workforce, make local and expatriate pay scales equitable, and wean the country from a reliance on expatriate technical expertise. Jane Parpart's study of gender, class, and the household illuminated women's roles and their stake in labour and class struggles in the Copperbelt's mine towns. In many of these studies, as Ferguson (1999) notes, the idea of progress that fed into expectations of upward mobility was central. And as Ferguson points out in his critique of the modernisation narrative, an account that Copperbelt residents too bought into—was that this modernity failed to materialise. What residents were left with, as Ferguson observed, was a sense of downward mobility characterised by a nostalgic backward-looking gaze to the country's modern past.

A more recent study of class and social mobility on the Copperbelt after re-privatisation is Monisha Bajaj's (2009) study of the notion of transformative agency amongst former and current school pupils of an alternative school in the Copperbelt town of Ndola. Drawing on pupil diaries and interviews, the study revealed that the idealised notion of transformative change that formed a key component of the school's pedagogy ill-equipped its former pupils to deal with the much harsher social and economic realities that characterised Copperbelt and Zambian life more generally. Bajaj found that the former pupils who coped and adapted better to the changed circumstances of the Copperbelt were those who adopted a more pragmatic approach to life. Bajaj demonstrates this pragmatism in the presentation of the case of Christopher, a former pupil of the school whom she interviewed in 2004. After graduating from Copperbelt University, Christopher expected to get a job, but when he failed to do so went on to create opportunities for himself, making money from tutoring, a service he had already been providing to other students (2009, 563). A similar type of pragmatism characterised my informants' engagements with what they could do to get by. This, I argue, points towards an "improvisory agency." I illustrate this type of agency through the case of Mr Mubita, whose experimental engagement with opportunities not only involved being aware of the possibilities of enterprise in the social environment but also, as I will show in the case of his water-well-building colleague, Vincent, involved learning about the materiality of the environment they occupied. Accordingly, in this chapter, rather than seeing class as embodied or inscribed within a "habitus" of learned dispositions, as Bourdieu (1993) suggests, I argue that class on the Copperbelt is emergent within fluctuating political, social, and economic conditions, and also through multiple strands of remembering the past, and that varying conditions and skilled practice make for the social distinctions perceived by Copperbelt residents. These differences are perceived not only in material or symbolic goods, but also in contrast to the recent past.

Akale twale ikala bwino ("In the past we lived well"): Life in Luanshya before Privatisation

It is hard to talk about one's current situation or way of life without contrasting it with the past. Following Gillian Feeley-Harnik (1996), I argue that the past is narrated as the "interactive" experience we have with the environment and others premised both on our memories and on markers of our memories. In this case, the markers are the phrases used to talk about space in Bemba, the lingua franca of the Copperbelt. *Kuma yard* ("at the yards") refers to the low-density housing areas, like the one under study. *Ku komboni* ("at the compounds") usually refers to low-cost housing areas. As I show, these expressions can mark the separation and sometimes opposition between particular spaces and lifestyles. They can also hint at movements across these symbolic and concrete spaces. For example, one of my interlocutors, Grace, remembered that when her husband was promoted in the mid-1980s, the family moved from Roan Township (a high-density mine area) to the low-density mine area under study. Shortly after moving to her new home, Grace was preparing a meal of dry fish when her husband "advised" her to cook the fish outside because it would make the house smell like *ku komboni*. This reprimand, based on an alertness to social markers of distinction, echoed the high level of social control that the mining company exercised over the social practices of the residents of the mine neighbourhood. One former mine employee staying in the area told me that in the mid-1980s he and his wife had kept over five hundred chickens in their backyard for sale. Even though neighbours bought chickens from them, someone from the neighbourhood reported their activities to a white manager who, while applauding their entrepreneurial spirit, insisted that they remove the chickens from their yard as the mines differentiated leisure and productive space in such a way that gardens were deemed inappropriate for production and entrepreneurship.

Despite the company's attempts to control social life, my informants look back to the "good life" before the privatisation of the mines with more than a hint of nostalgia. As one informant, a black Zambian miner living in *kuma yard* before the privatisation of the mines put it, he had "lived a good life" (*bale ikala bwino*). He had lived in a three-bedroom bungalow with a garden of expansive lawns bounded by a hedge of bougainvillaea. His wife did not have to work. If she did, she too worked for the mining company. In her leisure hours, she relaxed with other women at the recreation centre, learning how to knit or bake Victoria sponges. The miner's children attended the mine's trust schools, staffed by a predominantly white expatriate staff, where the language of instruction was English and where every November they celebrated Guy Fawkes night with a bonfire and fireworks. After a day of work, the miner headed to the mine club for a drink, usually the Zambian-brewed lager, Mosi. At the weekend, he played golf and occasionally took his family out to one of the Copperbelt dams for a swim and a picnic. From an outsider's perspective, these aspects of Copperbelt life closely evoke middle-class aspirations and a European colonial lifestyle.

However, a number of disjunctures hinted at a very different reality. To return to the miner I describe above: a number of extended family members frequently paid visits and at times established themselves for longer periods. His wife travelled to Luapula, a rural province of Zambia bordering the Congo, to buy fish. On return she sold some of it from her home or through her husband's workmates. This income supplemented the leisurely lifestyle of the family and became crucial during the economic decline in the 1980s and throughout the 1990s. After a day practising for the school play, *Oliver Twist*, the children roamed around the surrounding forest to gather wild fruit, to fish, or to trap birds, all the while chatting in Bemba. During the rainy season, the family went out to fields (*kuma bala*) allocated by the mining company on the outskirts of town to plant groundnuts, maize, or pumpkins for home consumption.

In the words of Victor, one of my informants, "ZCCM looked after our world. Things were okay. They did not look like this, and we had time for lots of recreation. We did not suffer." This summarises the feelings of most of my informants. Some attribute the decline of ZCCM to the Zambian state's increased interference in the mining industry through nationalisation. One informant, Mr Mubita, put it succinctly: "There was too much politicking."

Twali cula ("We suffered"): Catastrophe and Resurgence after Privatisation

The contrast between the "golden era" of the nationalised mines and the immediate aftermath of re-privatisation could not be more striking. Retrenched, waiting for their terminal benefits, and with no other avenue for a stable income, miners and their families went through an intense period of financial and socio-psychological struggle. In informal interviews and conversations, I heard how families had gone without food or had lived on one meal a day, and how children who attended fee-paying private schools dropped out because parents could not afford to pay the fees.[8] Luanshya informants described the crisis experienced between 1997 (the privatisation of Luanshya mines) and 2003 (the year when most retrenched workers received their terminal benefits) with the simple and straightforward expression: *twali cula* ("We suffered"). Hardship was not confined to the mining area's residents. Most businesses that relied on the incomes of miners closed, affecting the livelihoods of residents living in other areas too.

People used a number of different strategies to get through the crisis. A small survey of fifty-six households, which I conducted in the high-cost mine suburb of Luanshya in July to August 2008, revealed that only half of the households had one member employed in the formal sector (either in the mines or in other jobs), whereas, in 1997, all the households in this area had at least one member working for the mines. Most people ended up in self-employed economic activities. As one informant put it, "We suffered, but we have learnt how to use our hands." "Using one's hands" became a frequently heard expression, hinting at the new opportunities opened up by the crisis. On the one hand, it is reminiscent of idealised notions of rural self-sufficiency;[9] on the other, it describes the concrete experience of engaging in productive activities independent of any formal economic system. It also draws attention to increased scepticism about the positive effects of working for the privatised mines. As one informant put it, "The president said [to an investor], 'Come to mine for cheap labour.' . . . It is better to work for yourself than to be treated as a slave in your own country."

My data also demonstrate the central role that the house plays in the microeconomics of coping in the aftermath of privatisation. Of the fifty-six households in my sample, only four had sold their houses. Sixteen heads of household had left Luanshya to seek employment opportunities elsewhere and currently rented out their houses. Their tenants include self-employed business people from other Copperbelt towns; formal sector employees, such as bankers and civil servants; and, in three cases, long-term Luanshya residents involved in business, who moved from the high-density, local-authority-administered neighbourhoods of Luanshya. Of the sixteen who rented out their houses, six left for other Copperbelt towns, two lived in Lusaka, and four left the country (three for the United Kingdom and one for Botswana). Other owners remained in Luanshya, using the house as a source of income in different ways. Four owners rented out rooms as resident land-lords; some even moved into the servants' quarters and rented out the main house. Another three moved to the informal settlements on the periphery of the town and rented out their houses. In sum, half of my respondents earned rental income from their houses. Rentals are on average 500,000 Zambian kwacha (ZMK) (approximately US$100) per month for a relatively rundown house. Large houses in good condition may fetch as much as ZMK 2 million per month (about US$400) in rent from successful business people. Demand for housing is likely to rise with the recent entry of professional and managerial workers coming to Luanshya in connection with the prospects of increased mining operations. Such rentals constitute a considerable source of income, given the harsh economic conditions. In October 2008, the Jesuit Centre for Theological Reflection (JCTR), which carries out a monthly basic needs basket survey, estimated that a family of six in Luanshya needed ZMK 1,203,330 to purchase a basic basket of goods. A miner employed in the now-closed Luanshya Copper Mines could, at that time, earn as little as ZMK 800,000 per month, and a supermarket cashier earned around ZMK 300,000 per month.

In addition, the house provides, through the backyard, an important source of subsistence. Out of the fifty-six households surveyed, thirty-seven have a vegetable garden in their backyards. In most cases, the produce of these gardens is intended for subsistence. Twenty-four houses in the sample also carry out agricultural activities on larger plots located elsewhere, pre-dominantly in the peri-urban areas of Luanshya. Half of these households sell most of their produce, while the other half use it for subsistence. Many of those who sell their produce have a stall at their home. Others sell maize to the Food Reserve Agency (a parastatal agency that buys maize from local farmers). Produce is also often sold to marketers, and trading is a common informal economic activity. Also common is the rearing of poultry in backyards, while livestock farming, such as of pigs, can occasionally be found in the neighbourhood. One of my informants attempted to establish a fish farm in his backyard.

During "the ZCCM times," residents experienced similar working conditions and received comparable salaries. For the most part, this inhibited major socioeconomic differentiation. Now, the unstable economic conditions, the inherent risks involved in the new wave of informal activities, and the differing degrees of ingeniousness and luck have all contributed to a significant widening of socioeconomic inequalities and a general process of socioeconomic differentiation. These differences are clearly perceived by people living in Luanshya. In the eyes of my informants, some people are seen as *abale ikala bwino* ("those who are living well"), some as *abali fye* ("those who are just okay"), and others as *abale cula* ("those who are suffering"). Drawing on these local categories, I offer three short accounts of the differing trajectories of informants who faced the transition from the privatisation of ZCCM to the present day. To varying degree, they capture local ideas about "trying," that is, continued attempts to earn a livelihood, and *kulibonesha* ("showing off"). A common response to the question "How are you?" is "We are trying," while *kulibonesha ta'*, a performative way for people to express that they have "arrived," involves practices intended to show the value of consumer goods, such as driving—and frequently changing—expensive cars, wearing flashy clothes, being seen at expensive establishments, and throwing ostentatious parties. What is being evidenced in Luanshya may be the emergence of new "class" categories based on conspicuous consumption and its performance. "Class," here, is understood more in terms of perceptions of wealth and material goods than in terms of structural economic positions defined by relations of production.

In Lusaka, the capital of Zambia, according to Karen Tranberg Hansen (2005), tightening socioeconomic constraints are significantly limiting young people's social mobility, their ability to secure a house and a job and raise a family. This trend is evident in Luanshya, though unlike in Lusaka, it cuts across the spatially defined territories of *kuma yard* and *ku komboni*. Accordingly, it is worth noting that in the high-cost neighbourhood of Luanshya, a desperately poor family will reside next to a very well-off one. Drawing on Ingold (2000), I argue that the relative levels of success evidenced amongst the residents of this neighbourhood are due to the varying abilities of residents to adjust themselves skilfully to ever-changing conditions. These skills, as Ingold argues, are not embodied as some prior knowledge, but are learnt in the process of engaging through practice with the social and physical world. An example of this engagement is evidenced in the extended case of Mr Mubita and his colleague Vincent, presented later in this chapter, which highlights how Copperbelt residents have come to rely on exploiting small windows of opportunity. However, Luanshya residents generally hold that very few people are doing very "well." In the following accounts, we witness the extent of this in the livelihood activities of Gibson, generally considered to be "doing well," Lackson who is "doing okay," and Theresa, who can only be described as "suffering."

Abale ikala bwino ("Those who are living well")

Gibson Musonda, a former mine employee in his early forties, whose rank within ZCCM was equivalent to that of a shift boss, has managed to exploit new avenues brought about by crisis. Close associates and other people outside his network of relations identified him as a clear example of a successful businessman. Before joining the mines in 1993, Gibson had tried his hand—unsuccessfully—in small-scale trade, leaving this to join the mines to work as a "timber man," with a trade certificate in carpentry. During the ZCCM era and through the Binani administration of the mines, he had stayed employed and had lived in the high-density neighbourhood of the mines. When RAM-COZ liquidated, its assets were stripped in a process described by a miner working for the company:

> We were surprised to see the new mine owners, the Indians, selling every-thing. They sold the copper that was waiting on the belts, they sold machines, and they even sold the cars. The next thing we were not getting paid, some-times for four months. We even heard that they had *inkongole* [debt] every-where, even with ZESCO [the state-owned electricity company].

While Binani was selling off its assets, Gibson was "helping" himself to small items the investors "would not want." When the other mines on the Copperbelt were privatised shortly afterwards and started buying mining equipment from private suppliers, Gibson established himself as a mine sup-plier from the "small things" he had purloined. When RAMCOZ was liqui-dated in 2000, Gibson continued his business by supplying other mines out-side Luanshya and had by then accumulated enough capital to set up various other businesses, including transport and grocery stores. Gibson now lives in a large, well-kept house with an expansive green garden and owns three "big" cars. He furnished his living room and veranda with heavy leather seats and glass-topped side tables, all clear markers of status. He is married and has three young children. His wife wears expensive clothing and keeps up to date with the latest Nigerian fashion (increasingly, a major status marker among emerging economic elites). Some, baffled by his "unexplained" wealth in a context where most people are struggling to get by, call him a satanist. Gibson is a clear example of *kulibonesha ta'*.

Abali fye ("Those who are okay")

Lackson Mwale, a former miner in his early forties, was considered by my informants to be one of "those who are okay." Lackson's experience is similar to that of most residents in the high-cost area under study. He had worked for the mines as a supervisor, a position he had risen to after joining the mines in 1989 with only a secondary school certificate in hand. Lackson had made use of the mines' in-house skills-training facilities and had trained in metal fabrication, timber work, and general construction. When he was retrenched, he left his family in town and moved to the "bush"[10] on the outskirts of town to farm. He stayed there for a year until his wife asked him to move back, as she had taken a job as a clerk in the formal economy in Kitwe and would be able to support him and their three children. Several of my male informants had talked about how their wives had supported them in the worst of the crisis through small-scale enterprise. Many of these women started their activities during the 1980s, in response to the worsening economic conditions of the mine sector.

When Lackson moved back to the family home, bought as part of his retrenchment package, he took a loan from his wife and established a small construction company doing building maintenance and small-scale road works. He was very thankful to his wife; as he put it, "If it was another woman she would have left me, [but] my wife supported me." Despite the economic difficulties, Lackson invested a considerable amount of time and resources in modifying his house. He added an extra bedroom, made the main bedroom self-contained, and expanded the living room. Even though the furnishings in his house were old and in some instances worn, Lackson had a large-screen television, a DVD player, and a music system, all placed on a steel and glass display cabinet. Technological gadgets are perceived by most people as markers of high status. Another sign of the aspirations to "make it up" is the considerable investment Lackson and his wife made to send one of their children to a private primary school (a former mine trust school, recently privatised).

Alongside the aspirations of social advancement, Lackson is aware that he needs to secure a material base that is not dependent on external economic conditions. With his family, he continues to grow maize in the outskirts of town. In his words, "It is important to be self-sufficient." He also uses his backyard to increase the family's subsistence base. He grows maize during the rainy season, as well as tomatoes, spinach, and onions. While these backyard activities started during the ZCCM period, they intensified from 1997 onwards.

Abale chula ("Those who suffer")

Theresa Miti is in her fifties and is the wife of a former ZCCM mine employee who had worked for the company from 1983 and had risen to the rank of mine captain after joining the mines as a trainee engineer. Theresa has little formal training, having left school halfway through secondary education. During the ZCCM era, she had carried out small-scale economic activities, such as knitting jerseys for sale, a skill she had learnt from her friends. She had also engaged in the sale of agricultural produce, travelling to North Western Zambia to buy beans for sale in Luanshya. When I met her, her husband was working on short-term contract in one of the privatised mines under a subcontractor in Kitwe and had not visited the family in three months. Kitwe is an hour away by bus and bus fare costs ZMK 24,000 (approx. US$5) for a return journey. Theresa hinted that he might have established another household in Kitwe. Theresa was staying with her six children, the youngest of whom was sixteen, and two grandchildren in the house her husband purchased as part of his retrenchment package.

Theresa's family is having a hard time "getting by." As Theresa puts it, "My husband does not make enough to send home." To supplement her husband's remittances, Theresa, like many other women in Luanshya, makes a meagre income digging flux stone from the huge mine dumps left from the ZCCM era. Her youngest son and one of her grandchildren help her. She sells the flux stone to other locals, who use it for construction work on their plots. The incredible burst of economic activity (often bordering on the illegal) concentrated around the mine dumps is a clear example of the creative strategies employed by Luanshya residents to get through the crisis. In Theresa's yard, where her children usually sit braiding each other's hair or cutting vegetables in preparation for the evening meal, stones from the dumps are piled high for sale. Theresa is HIV-positive and so are two of her children.[11] She is on anti-retroviral medications but struggles to get the appropriate nutrition to deal with the medication and the illness's side effects.

Despite living in a high-cost, low-density area, Theresa's house has no electricity or running water. These services were cut in 2003 and 2004, respectively, after the household failed to pay arrears. The lack of access to a stable water supply makes it difficult for Theresa to engage even in those so-called subsistence activities that have been booming in Luanshya since the privatisation of the mines. Theresa grows maize during the rainy season but cannot sustain other forms of vegetable production during the rest of the year. The limited income base also made this household vulnerable to other changes that came with the privatisation. As a result of the privatisation process, the everyday maintenance and administration of this high-cost area was transferred from ZCCM to the local municipal authorities. This meant that residents started paying "land rates" to the local authorities, an additional cost in an already tight economic situation. Theresa now fears that the local authorities might "grab" the house for failure to pay land rates.

The interior of Theresa's house, though very neat and homely, with doilies to cover the worn seats, has none of the usual electronic goods that are social indicators of material status, the kind of goods bailiffs usually pounce on. Theresa's fear for the house being grabbed also reflects wider social practices where women often lose out on property after the death of a spouse (Catell 2003), and indicates the difficult economic circumstances of women who have been left alone. My 2009 survey of one hundred households in one section of a former mine housing area in Luanshya,[12] revealed that of twelve households that were living on less than ZMK 500,000[13] (about US$100) per month, the lowest income bracket in the area, six of them were headed by women whose husbands had passed away after 1999.

"TRYING": LIFE AS JOURNEY OF ATTEMPTS AND IMPROVISATIONS

The three case studies portray the skewed and uncertain places in which people find themselves in the present. They also indicate the ways in which gender, choice of production activity, marital status, moralities, household composition, and situation make the steering of a life journey differ from one informant to another. Gibson tries, Lackson tries, and Theresa tries, and the distinctions among them are not for a lack of effort.

Unlike development discourse with its teleological understanding of transition, Copperbelt residents see life in the transition as a journey undertaken in the midst of an ideological "pothole" without a clear map. This can make steering difficult and has consequences both various and unforeseeable. Indeed, the metaphor of a precarious journey has been taken up in contemporary popular music in Zambia and has become a way of portraying suffering and crisis. For example, the lyrics of the popular song "Oh No" by the artist Petersen from his 2005 album *Munyaule* encapsulate this notion of a journey that is too frightening to contemplate, suggesting that it is better not to look (*sinifuna nakulanga*, "I don't even want to look") and that all one can do is "try." The themes of Petersen's music are to be found in other popular Zambian songs, such as "Kaya" ("I Don't Know") by the artist Danny (2005), who sings about the uncertainty of the future and the fear of a young death. (I explore this theme further in Chapter 6.) The notion of suffering is also seen in the dramaturgical moments of the popular dance songs of the musician Mozegater, in which Zambian partygoers dance in a moving circle in a parody of suffering. Mozegater's songs combine the style of morale songs heard at football games with funeral songs to create what he calls *chiunda* ("noise") music. He, like Petersen, sings of the attempts to make a livelihood and the precariousness of these ventures. His lyrics from the song "Chikokoshi" include statements such as *yali survival* ("It was survival"), *business ya nwena* ("The business sinks"), *ala boyz cali bipile* ("Oh, boys, it was bad"). Like other Zambian artists, he links suffering, death, and livelihood strategies as a social commentary on life in Zambia. Some people make it, others don't—what happens in between is a series of improvisations to extend life, *uku topinga* (literally "to add on," popular Bemba slang in reference to extending life using HIV/AIDS anti-retroviral medication).

Improvisation implies that effort, circumstance, relations, possibilities, and materials coincide in ways that make things possible. The case study of Mr Mubita, whose story I draw on in the next section, attempts to show the experimental nature of improvisation. His case embodies the notion of trying. Following on from the three cases above, his demonstrates that structure and agency do not exist at two poles but are lived out in continuous practice.

"EXPERIMENTING" IN THE BACKYARD: HOUSEHOLD ECONOMICS IN THE NEOLIBERAL COPPERBELT

Mr Nathan Mubita, who is in his mid-fifties, lives with his second wife, Susan, and their two children in a large, two-bedroom house in *kuma yard*, having divorced his first wife, with whom he had two children. Mr Mubita joined the mines in 1979 with an incomplete secondary education to work first as a pump attendant, then rising swiftly through the employment ranks. Despite his limited schooling, Mr Mubita approached his livelihood challenges scientifically—by which I mean experimentally. Of particular interest to me was the array of activities in Mr Mubita's yard. At a first meeting at his *kantemba* (street-side store), on entering his yard I noticed the orchard of orange trees, banana plants, dried maize stalks, a water tank, a partially completed chicken run, and a rundown house and unkempt lawn. The contrast between the lawn and the agricultural setup was striking. A complex network of irrigation pipes differentiated Mr Mubita's yard from any other I had seen. As I got to know him better, I gradually realised that his yard is an excellent example of the recent wave of informal economic activities sparked by the privatisation process. His activities not only represented wider trends in the area, but also showed a distinctive mark of creativity and innovation.

Hardship and Innovation: Mr Mubita's Informal Activities in His Backyard

Mr Mubita refers to his several activities as "experiments" and "pilots." The first was the construction of a *kantemba* in early 2003, before he received his terminal benefits from the liquidation of ZCCM. This is how he started out:

> You see, a few houses away from mine down the road, there used to be a small *kantemba*. One day I went there asking for some sugar, you know, these small units packed in plastic bags by *kantemba* owners, yes? So I asked [the store owner] if he would loan me some on credit and some buns for my kids. Now I had gone there whilst he was packing these units from a new packet of sugar. He said that he could only give me the goods after somebody had bought at least one of the plastics, as it was bad luck to loan . . . without having sold anything first. He was very superstitious. So I waited for two hours before any one bought the packet of sugar and was allowed the credit facility. So as I was there I observed the little boy run the business and said to myself, if this boy can do it, why can't I? It seemed profitable enough. So I went to a loan shark and borrowed ZMK 100,000. I was expected to pay back with 50% interest. This was in 2003.

Mr Mubita then constructed a store out of timber off-cuts and some nails he had bought with the help of his son. He stocked the shop with sugar, painkillers, a "pan" of buns, ten packets of tea, some pencils, and biscuits. With these, he opened for business.

When he received his terminal benefits late in 2003, he spent the money on his son's college education, a water tank with stand, a well, tomato seedlings, and orange trees. He planted a batch of Israeli-origin tomatoes in his backyard from which he yielded a return of ZMK 10 million from an initial investment of ZMK 600,000. Within the current economic context, this is a considerable sum of money, more than enough to kick-start other small-scale entrepreneurial activities. Mr Mubita used the proceeds to start the construction of a chicken run. He obtained the plan for this from Yielding Tree, an agricultural shop that held a stand at the agricultural and commercial show in Kitwe, which he had attended on invitation from a friend. The chicken run is situated in the backyard and its walls are at roof level. To date, the construction is still incomplete.

Another successful project is the orange tree orchard that takes up almost the whole large front yard. Another experiment is visible on one side of the house, where Mr Mubita planted two varieties of banana, one indigenous and the other exotic. The indigenous variety is more successful in agricultural terms, and it has higher resistance to disease; however, its value on the market is lower. He considered the possibility of establishing a vaster banana plantation, but later abandoned this idea, because the cost of water needed for it would have offset the yields.

In the backyard, maize stalks lay drying from the recent harvest. Mr Mubita said that he would soon start planting another batch of tomatoes and onions for home consumption and sale. There are also a costly water tank and the incomplete rectangular concrete block building intended for the chicken run. In a little room at one end of the chicken run is a concrete-lined well that he had designed and built with a help of a young man, Vincent, who worked as a gardener in the neighbourhood. His entire yard is crossed by a series of pipes, his "irrigation experiment." Mr Mubita created his own DIY version of a drip irrigation system, as he could not afford to buy a standard one. His modifications were intended to save on water bills,[14] which would have been higher with a standard drip irrigation system. Mr Mubita's activities well encapsulated what was increasingly valued, that is self-sufficiency and working with one's hands.

TO WORK WITH ONE'S OWN HANDS

Self-sufficiency was promoted as a policy by the Zambian state and on the Copperbelt by the then-nationalised mines, especially during the 1980s, in the early years of the country's economic decline. However, on the Copper-belt, it only came to the fore during the worst of the economic crisis that followed the sale of the mines. Then the residents of town like Luanshya were forced to draw on a range of social and materials skills to get by, as well as the dexterity of their bodies, as they were required to work more with their hands. Drawing on the case of Vincent, who helped Mr Mubita construct his backyard well, as well as the activity of digging the well, I aim to show how social life, like the practice of making things, comprises a continuous series of improvisations. I also demonstrate how the sensory aspects involved in a process of improvisation play a role in how we learn and try. Vincent's and Mubita's "experiments" also point to pliability and the notion of mutual per-meability, or *ukusankaya*, the process of mixing ideas, things, and oneself in the practice of trying to make things work.

Vincent and the Construction of the Well

I interviewed Vincent when I found out that he had helped Mr. Mubita con-struct his well and that he had dug wells for quite a few people in the mine area under study. Vincent Bwalya was born in Luanshya in 1978 and grew up in the mine township of Mpatamatu in Luanshya. Vincent described him-self as self-employed, with his work involving *ukulima amabala* (cultivating fields), cutting grass and hedges *muma yard* (in the yards), and digging and repairing wells, as well as the odd jobs in construction such as plastering.

His father worked for the mines as a shorer of excavated pits and tunnels until he retired in 1989 and moved to Mufulira. Vincent, then a young boy, moved with the rest of his family—his mother, three sisters, and four broth-ers—to Mufulira. There the family set themselves up in Chibolya, a council-run township where other retired miners unwilling to return to their rural "homes" had settled. The family's main source of livelihood was farming on land they had acquired on the outskirts of Mufulira. There they grew maize, sweet potatoes, and groundnuts for home consumption and for sale locally and in Lusaka.

When Vincent married Sheila, they stayed in the mine's former low-density suburb in a "servants' quarters," one room with detached ablutions. They met the cost of their accommodations by working in lieu of cash pay-ment, Sheila working as a maid and Vincent doing the gardening. In 2000, he moved back to Luanshya, where he had procured a job as a casual labourer with the RAMCOZ mines, though, because of the low pay, he quit this job shortly after joining and started doing agricultural "piecework." Following the liquidation of the RAMCOZ mines and associated job layoffs, many min-

ers turned to farming. This was fortuitous for Vincent, as there was significant demand for casual labour for agricultural work. Other than clearing and
cultivation of fields, Vincent also started sinking wells at some of the farms
he worked, charging in 2000 and 2001 about ZMK 150,000 (or US$30). Fol-
lowing the privatisation of water utility services in the mine township that
necessitated former mineworkers paying for water supply, Vincent's activities
extended to sinking wells in the backyards of mine township residents. This
is how he met Mr Mubita, who, Vincent had heard from one of his customers,
wanted to sink a well.

How Vincent Learnt to Build Wells

When Vincent's parents moved to Mufulira and started farming on the outskirts of the town, they decided to sink a well in order to grow vegetables
outside the rainy season, which was from November to early May. Vincent
says he learnt how to sink wells from the man whom his father had hired to
dig the well. The man had asked Vincent to help him by hauling the earth he
dug up from the well via a bucket attached to a rope. Vincent had watched the
man and tried the digging himself. Following this experience, when he had
heard that his parents' neighbours were looking to sink a well, he offered to
do it for them because felt he could do the job, but did not request payment.
These were unlined wells. Later Vincent learnt how to make lined wells from
Mr Mubita.

Vincent says he gained the most experience in sinking wells in 2001, when
he had a lot of clients wanting to sink wells at their backyards and farms. He
charged ZMK 300,000 (about US$60) in 2008 for sinking an unlined well,
a job that took approximately four days of work to complete. He charged
around ZMK 500,000 (US$100) for a lined well, excluding the cost of mate-
rials like cement and wire reinforcement that the client had to buy. The job
usually took six days. Though Vincent says his well-sinking rates varied for
abaya kaya (his kinsmen), denoting real and fictive kin, on further query I
had found that his rates did not vary much, but modes of payment did, as
he extended longer repayment terms to "kin." I also found that he used the
notion of kin as way of establishing a convivial client relationship.

The first thing Vincent did when he was approached for a well was to
make a query about his potential client's reliability when it came to paying for
the job. As many of the commissions he got were in the low-density suburb
where he lived, he was easily able to find out by asking other pieceworkers
in the area who might have previously done a job for the person, or making

queries at the *katembas* (little front-of-house stores) where they might have shopped. He opted not to risk working for those he heard were unreliable payers, because, he said, *teti ubombe fya mahala* ("You cannot work for nothing"), as *abantu balishupa ukulipila ikongole* ("People are a problem when it comes to paying back a debt"). Vincent informed me that he was especially careful not to take on jobs that might not be paid for because many of his clients were unable to pay the full sum of the job, and paid in instalments, with a negotiated retainer that ranged from a tenth to half the full amount, and the rest paid on completion of the job. Sometimes he says, some clients had struggled to pay the outstanding amount on completion, and this payment was then further broken up in two payments. He did not mind being paid in instalments as long as he was informed prior to taking on the job. He had, however, had problems with clients who made him go back to collect small payments over long periods of time and those who he says never intended to pay the full amount. These jobs he treated as a loss.

Vincent did not differentiate the cost of a well based on its depth but on its type. Most wells around the mine area were 8.5 to 9 metres in depth, but, because of the topography, were in some cases deeper or shallower. These variations sometimes created problems with regard to payment. He gave one example where he was commissioned to sink a well for a woman who sold plants from her back garden. Vincent told me that when she had contracted him to sink a well, they had agreed on a price of ZMK 300,000. He says he had explained to her the general specifications for a well, telling her that it was likely to be a depth of 8 metres. However, Vincent says that when he dug the well, he found water at a depth of 5.5 metres and dug an extra metre as usual, for a total depth of 6.5 metres. Vincent told me that despite the fact he found water at that depth, his client was dissatisfied and would have preferred that he dig deeper to the depth of 8 metres. He told me that she had been adamant despite the technical difficulties, not to mention the danger to himself that digging further would have entailed, arguing that she would only pay a third of the agreed price. Vincent decided not to push her for the rest of his money. He read his client's insistence on a deeper well despite the fact that they had found water as a strategy to avoid paying for it. "If only she had told me she did not have the money," he said. Such incidents, though not frequent, were not uncommon, and caused Vincent inconvenience, especially for jobs where he contracted a colleague to help him with the construction of a well.

Explaining the division of labour when he sank wells with a colleague, Vincent said that when he did all the digging and his colleague did the work of hauling the dirt out, he got two-thirds of the payment and his colleague a third. If they shared the digging and hauling dirt, then the payment was split in two. The biggest risk in the job, according to Vincent, was to the person inside the well digging, and the understanding was that that person was paid more. Sometimes clients opted to take on the responsibility of hauling the dirt out themselves or getting someone else, like their gardener, to do it to reduce the fee. In reference to Mr Mubita, Vincent said, *for example bamudala balikosa, so bale ibombela* ("For example, the old man is strong. so he did the work himself"), whereas referring to another client he said, *bamudala abe ikala pa number three bali bonfya aba bombi* ("The old man who stays three houses down used his worker"). These observations by Vincent not only indicated which clients were willing to literally work with their hands, but also pointed to the type of working relationship. I had observed Vincent work with Mr Mubita on his other backyard project and seen that they appeared to share a collegial working environment. Vincent too appeared to take great pride in this garden, in contrast to others that he had worked on.

In explaining the details of payment in Vincent's well-sinking business, my aim is to highlight some of the factors that newly self-employed business persons encountered on the Copperbelt. One of the key issues many small businesses faced were delays or nonpayment for goods and services, and this played a key role in whether a business succeeded or not. Whereas people like Vincent, operating in a relatively small geographical area, were able to make queries about whether or not a client was likely to pay, those doing business with strangers and dealing with large amounts of money in the absence of collateral were sometimes forced to come up with creative ways of getting payment. One such way was the threat of cosmological violence, as reported in the story "Copperbelt Tortoise Shocker!" on 22 November 2007 in the *Times of Zambia*.

> Residents of the Copperbelt have in the past few months been awakened to a rude shock as incidences of animals and birds descended on some unsuspecting families with warning messages in letters strapped on their backs.
>
> Some shrewd businessmen who have found this phenomenon as the best and quickest way to retrieve their monies from people who owe them have perpetuated this bizarre practice.
>
> In history, it is pigeons that were known as the best senders of mail in far-flung areas to communities. Dogs have also been known, if well trained, to send parcels and messages to others.

But the stories coming out of the Copperbelt in the past two months have been rather odd. Letters delivered on tortoise backs and pigeons to a number of people who allegedly owe large amounts of money and apparently fail to pay on agreed dates have rather unsettled many, including those that may not be superstitious.

Because it is strange for anyone to see a tortoise strapped in clothes and beads and an envelope on its shell addressed to them, some people who have been owing tortoise senders have been quick to pay back what they owe because of fear of being killed through witchcraft.

During the course of my fieldwork, three persons in the former mine suburb in Luanshya had encountered such threats; and in one case, the monies owed were paid back with help from extended family members who feared the threat of witchcraft would also befall them.

I return now to the physical, practical aspects of making the well in Mr Mubita's backyard to draw attention to the affordances of the environment and the modes of Vincent's and Mr Mubita's engagement with it. This is crucial in thinking through how people get by. Anthropologists, apart from those who study material culture, tend to focus much more on the social, cultural, political, and abstractly economic possibilities that a place affords, and often tend to forget what the phenomenologically experienced lived world affords (this includes not just the earth, flora, and fauna, but things like weather). How do people improvise within all these contingent variables?

The Techniques of Sinking a Well

Vincent sank lined and unlined wells for his clients. Unlined, unprotected wells are not considered safe for producing water for domestic consumption. Nevertheless, in addition to being used by the residents of Luanshya to water their backyard gardens, they were also used for cooking, cleaning vegetables, washing dishes, and bathing. Those residents who relied on them as their main source of water collected drinking water from neighbours who had running tap water. In these cases, children were usually sent to ask for water from neighbours and, for the few who had outdoor taps like myself, the children sometimes just wandered into the yard to draw water without asking. Vincent was usually commissioned to dig unlined wells because many of his clients could not afford a concrete-lined well. Unlined wells provided Vincent with follow-on maintenance work, as walls were prone to collapsing, especially during the region's rainy season from November to early May.

The first lined well that Vincent had ever built was with Mr Mubita, who had initially explored the option of sinking a borehole in his backyard but had been deterred by the cost, more than twenty times the cost of a lined well. Mr Mubita had, however, looked at the technical specifications of a borehole and figured that he could make the concrete-lined casting of the hole himself. He commissioned Vincent to dig the well, and together they set about building a lined well, learning in the process as they went along. According to Vincent, "Mr Mubita had the idea, *elyo ifwe twa landa po, twa nsakanya* [then I had a say, we mixed ideas]." In what follows, I describe how Vincent and Mr Mubita built the well so to give a sense of the skills and techniques they learned and some of the difficulty they encountered in building it. What follows takes the form of instructions on building a well.

Digging the Well

Set out the perimeter of the well, usually 80 to 100 cm in diameter, and dig a hole till you find water and a further metre beyond the point where you find water.

The well is dug using a short spade or shovel; a solid, pitched bar known locally as *umungwala*; and a chisel. The *umungwala* is used to soften the ground around and within the perimeter of the well, using stabbing motions. After this has been done, the short shovel is used to dig and shovel the dirt out. The chisel is used break up rock when it is found when digging inside the well.

One man digs inside the well, and the other man stands outside to haul dirt out via a bucket attached to a rope. Vincent advised digging a well during the country's dry season, not only to avert the threat of being buried should the rain-softened side walls collapse in the absence of shoring but also to reach dry-season groundwater, making the well usable for during the dry season.

When breaking sharp stones, in particular white, crystallised stones that were very sharp and often encountered in the Luanshya mine suburb, Vincent advised wearing leather gloves to avoid cutting one's hands.

Vincent also cautioned that the person hauling the buckets of dirt had to be careful not to spill any of its contents onto the person digging inside the well. Even small stones falling on the body could cause excruciating pain, because *umu bili ulakaba, noku piba sana* ("the body gets hot and very sweaty"). He also noted that wearing shoes when digging inside the well was very uncomfortable because feet tended to get uncomfortably hot and swell.

Preparing Mould for the Lining for the Well

Prepare two drums, oil drums that are about one metre in height and 80 cm in diameter for making the mould for the concrete lining. (Mr Mubita had bought the oil drums from a vendor who sold second-hand hardware products.) The bottoms of the drums need to be cut out and one drum has to slightly bigger than the other in diameter so the concrete mixture can be poured into the space between the two drums. The space between the two drums should be about two and a half inches. Making one drum bigger than the other can be done by cutting out a longitudinal section out of the second drum and cutting the first drum length-wise, then welding the cut longitudinal section from the second drum to the first drum to make it wider.

Place reinforcement wire in the space between the two drums. Mr Mubita used the interlinking wire normally used to make fences and used a section from his own boundary fence.

Make two pairs of opposite holes to go through the oil drums, approximately 15 cm from the top. The holes should be about 15 mm in diameter. The holes are used to insert two steel rods that will make a central cross to which a chain will be attached and used to lower the set concrete mould into the hole. These holes should be sealed with sticks before the concrete mixture is poured into the mould and allowed to set.

Other holes, randomly placed, should be made. Sticks too should be placed in these before pouring the concrete mixture. These holes are created as weep holes for when water is poured into the space between the drums in the concrete curing process.

Making the Lining

Vincent and Mr Mubita mixed half a pocket of cement with two wheelbarrows of flux stone (a crushed stone obtained from the mine dumpsites with a powder-like, sandy texture) and small stones of about 5 mm (which had been sourced by a night-time sweep of roads that were being rehabilitated in the town). They mixed this on ground cleared of organic matter with about forty litres of water.

The concrete mixture was poured into space between drums and allowed to cure for eight days, with water being poured over it twice a day to aid in the curing process. When it was cured, the oil drums were removed to create the next mould.

Mr Mubita and Vincent made concrete moulds to line the entire length of the 8.5-metre well. This required ten concrete moulds.

Making a Chain Block and Frame

Create a sturdy frame to place centred over the well to which a chain block will be connected. The chain will be hooked to the crossed rods centred in the mould, and the mould be lowered into the well. Mr. Mubita's sturdy frame was a hollow steel pipe about 10 cm in diameter (scavenged from waste near the mine plant area) cantilevered from the concrete block wall of his chicken run. The chain block was supported from the steel pipe.

Lowering the Mould into the Hole

Pass two steel rods through the holes at the top of the mould. Vincent advised that the rods must not extend beyond the holes as they would stop the descent of the mould into the well by getting stuck to the sides of it. Vincent noted that this technique also allowed their removal by chiselling around them to prise the rods out for reuse.

Making the Well Cover

Vincent and Mr Mubita made a precast concrete cover for the well. It comprised two half leaves of metal from the cut bottoms of the oil drums and was made using a method similar to that used with the concrete lining; that is, they reinforced it with wire, created weep holes, and used the same concrete mixture. When the cover was cured, they passed a strong synthetic rope through the weep holes of the precast concrete cover to make lifting it easier.

It is for this well that Mr Mubita installed a water pump and devised a drip irrigation system for watering his garden.

When Vincent was contracted to build a lined well for one of Mr Mubita's neighbours, Mr Shona, who was planning a fish pond, both Vincent and Mr Mubita worked on the job, sharing the payment equally. Mr Mubita made the lining, and Vincent did the digging of the well. Mr Shona's gardener hauled the dirt up from the well. Mr Mubita and Vincent revised the technique they had developed for the well by changing the way in which the concrete mould was lowered in the well. They did away with the chain block that had caused them problems in centring, which had required the construction of a sturdy frame to support it, and which had caused the loss of several moulds that had dropped and broken in the process of lowering them. The following is a variation of the building of a lined well in the absence of a chain block that they had heard of by hearsay.

Variation on the Lined Well

Set out the perimeter of the well, a diameter of about 80–100 cm.

Place the precast concrete mould to sit on the outline of the well's perimeter.

Dig the hole within the confines of the mould. Once you dig to a depth of half a meter, dig around the outer wall of the mould to create space for it to slide down to that depth.

Continue digging, and once the top of the first mould is at ground level, place the second one to sit on the outline of the perimeter of the well.

Dig to the next half metre, then dig around the edges of the well to allow the moulds to slide down to that depth.

Repeat the procedure to the required depth of the well, which is the point plus a metre below where water is found.

The advantage of the variation they used for Mr Shona's well was that it minimised the use of other tools such as the chain block and reduced wastage of materials like cement, because concrete mould was unlikely to break in this process of lowering it.

In describing in detail some of the technicalities in building a well, I aim to indicate some of the skill employed in construction and the innovations and variations employed in their making, as well as what the makers learnt from the process. Much of the material used in the construction of the wells Vincent worked on, other than the cement, were salvaged recycled materials. This required an alertness to what was lying around in the environment. It also inserted the enterprise of building the well into the wider informal economy, as evidenced in the aggregate used to bind the cement—flux stone that was sourced from the copper mine dumps characteristic of the Copperbelt landscape.

INDIVIDUAL AGENCY IN A FLUID ENVIRONMENT: THE "INFORMAL" AS PRIMARY SITE OF ANALYSIS

The innovative ways in which Mr Mubita turned his backyard into an economically productive site that guaranteed his family's livelihood provide a useful gateway into the lived experience of the transitions on the Copperbelt. Mr Mubita's "pilots" and "experiments" provide an excellent example of the improvisations involved in the process of earning a livelihood and capture the essence of the Zambian expression of "trying." This case links to the earlier three accounts in showing that the story of the liberalisation of the Zambian mining industry and the ensuing economic crisis is not only about winners and losers (see Fraser and Lungu 2007). It is also about the creative process of trying to earn a livelihood through ongoing effort, the ability to take advantage of and manipulate social situations, and the development of new moralities to justify and explain economic activities that fall outside the remit of the formally legal. The cases presented in this chapter also show that in the self-sufficient livelihoods that have come to the fore on the Copperbelt, skill, the body, social life, and the physical environment are indissoluble in the process of making a living and sustaining life, and that each of these has to be taken into account in the analysis of the micro-political economy and social mobility. However, they also illuminate that none of these factors are fixed; that skill can be learnt and improved on; that the strength of the body is variable, both in its extension through the labour of other people and in its ability to carry out certain tasks; that social relations can be manipulated; and that the physical environment is pliable.

The cases presented in this chapter show people who are attempting to carve out a livelihood independent of formally structured employment. This reflects the practice of most Luanshya residents, even those with formal jobs. What the cases also suggest is that opportunities are largely perceived in situ, commonly expressed as *twala mona inga twa fika* ("We shall see when we get there"). Mr Mubita perceived he could run a little store by his home after observing a young man sell his goods. Gibson observed the opportunities available in supplying the mines with goods from the stripping of the liquidated RAMCOZ. Vincent learnt how to sink wells by observing and helping out the man who had come to sink a well by his parents' farm and learnt with Mr Mubita how to construct lined wells. While this may seem like a simplistic observation, I would argue that perception plays an important part in the process of making a livelihood in a context where anxieties about the future make forward planning difficult. This kind of perception highlights the possibilities that could be obscured in the volatility of the transition period. From this perspective, while the harsh material and psychological realities of the ensuing economic crisis have tinged the experiences of former miners living in *kuma yard* with more than a hint of nostalgia for a "golden" past, when the mining system provided a stable economic base and a wide range of social services, the crisis has also opened up new opportunities and has stimulated people's creative agency in devising survival strategies to make it through this difficult transition.

NOTES

1. A version of this chapter was originally published in *Social Dynamics* 46, no. 2 (2010): 380–394. www.tandfonline.com. The term "improvising a life" is a play on the title of Mary Catherine Bateson's (2001) book *Composing a Life*, which explores the creative potential of lives in complex times.

2. Reflecting local usage, I use the term "miner" to refer to any ZCCM employee, regardless of the actual job role or management position.

3. As I have already described, the residents of Luanshya arguably experienced the worst effects of the ZCCM privatisation process. The mines in the town were the first to be privatised. They were sold to Binani, an Indian company, and were renamed Roan Antelope Mining Company (RAMCOZ). RAMCOZ was liquidated in 2000, and the mines were later bought by JW & Enya and renamed Luanshya Copper Mines (LCM), during a wave of higher international copper prices from 2004 onwards. Most retrenched ZCCM miners received their terminal benefits only in 2003, three years after RAMCOZ went into liquidation. Former miners were left with a house, some cash (the remainder of their terminal benefits), and uncertain employment prospects.

4. In a survey I conducted in August 2009, forty-five out of one hundred households had run a business from their residential premises in the previous year, with the most common activity being rearing poultry (twenty-four out of the forty-five), followed by running a little grocery store (fourteen), and moulding bricks for sale (five).

5. Seventy-seven out of one hundred households surveyed had a garden on their residential premises, used for subsistence agriculture.

6. Thirty-nine out of one hundred households surveyed had a field or farm on the outskirts of Luanshya, or in another district adjacent to Luanshya, e.g., Mpongwe and Masaiti. Only four farms/fields were over 70 km away from Luanshya (200 km, 140 km, 120 km, and 70 km). The largest farm mentioned in the survey was 150 hectares, and the smallest 1 hectare.

7. Despite African advancement policies being widely adopted after independence, as well as the 1969 Matero Declaration that advanced Zambianisation as a policy to

replace white expatriate labour with black Zambian employees, a colour bar was still very evident in the workplace. White employees occupied higher employment ranks in the mines as a result of the shortage of black skilled labour (see Burawoy 1972). This colour bar was reflected in the social and spatial geography of the Copperbelt. It was only in the mid-1970s that more black Zambians took up management positions in the mines. Arguably, it was the country's protracted economic recession, from the mid-1970s and lasting well into the 1990s, that forced mines to reduce their expatriate wage bill, freeing up higher-ranking jobs and thus housing in the high-cost neighbourhood for blacks.

8. The mine trust school started charging market rate fees, but offered a grace period for the children of former mine employees in view of the crisis. State schools too showed leniency in pressing for fee payments.

9. Declining living standards, a growing external debt, and declining copper revenues on which the state depended for foreign exchange increasingly directed Zambian government policies, beginning in the late 1970s, towards self-sufficiency in order to reduce import costs. Throughout the 1980s and 1990s, ZCCM supported agricultural skills training among its employees, as part of the country's "Back to the Land" policies, intended for retirees (see Ferguson 1999), and also to increase the economic self-sufficiency of its employees and their families. In a personal communication, David Phiri, former chairperson of Roan Copper Mines, noted that few miners had then been willing to take up farming, despite the incentives offered by the mines, including land, inputs, and skills training. Such initiatives by a mining company were not new. During the colonial period, the mines had allocated plots on land on the outskirts of mine neighbourhoods to encourage food production amongst miners' families (see Wilson 1968).

10. The town of Luanshya is surrounded by indigenous forest, forest plantation, and small- to large-scale farming activities. Residents farming on the outskirts of the town often say they are going into the bush to farm.

11. About 14.3% of Zambia's population is HIV-positive, according to the Central Statistical Office of Zambia (2007).

12. The two former mine high-cost (or low-density) housing areas, Old Town and New Town, comprise about 1,123 houses. The survey in August 2009 was conducted in Old Town.

13. The Jesuit Centre for Theological Reflection, which carries out a monthly basic needs basket in Zambia, indicated that a family of six in Luanshya in August 2009 required ZMK 1,462,850 for their monthly household needs. My survey of August 2009 revealed that 37% of the households surveyed were living on less than this amount, while the rest (9% of whom were living on the higher monthly income of more than ZMK 5 million—about US$1,000) were living above it.

14. Kazimbaya-Senkwe and Guy (2007) detail the domestication of water in Luanshya after the privatisation of the mines. Mine employees did not pay water bills during the ZCCM era.

CHAPTER 4

Contesting Illegality

Women in the Informal Copper Business

The extent of the expulsion from Eden experienced since the ZCCM period is clearly captured by the striking view of copper waste dumps, a common feature of the Copperbelt landscape. On one side of the dumps, large excavators scoop out chunks of flux stone that will later be reprocessed in local plants to extract copper. On the other side of the dumps, it is not unusual to see small groups of women and children busy digging and sorting out flux stone and copper ore with only the support of sieves, picks, hoes, and shovels. The result of the work of these small gangs fuels the informal trade in copper ore to foreign buyers and of building materials to local residents.

This chapter draws on ethnographic research carried out in July and August 2008 in two copper dump sites, one located in the Copperbelt town of Luanshya, an urban setting, the other in the North Western Province (increasingly referred to as the New Copperbelt) district of Mufumbwe, a rural setting. There I observed women and children working on the sites and carried out informal interviews with informants both on-site and at their homes. This chapter asks: Why are women and children involved in these activities? What does their involvement tell us about the drastic restructuring of the local economy? How do these activities change the way people talk about the "free market"? How is illegality justified and pursued as a legitimate moral strategy? My aim is to provide some answers to these questions and to contribute to a deeper understanding of the informal economy of the Zambian Copperbelt and the body politic of neoliberalism in this context.

The chapter suggests that the dual economy of the copper dump sites highlights important features of the experience of boom and bust on the Copperbelt and in Zambia and Africa more widely. First, the formal and the informal, legal and illegal economies are increasingly coming together under an unspoken social contract where cunning local entrepreneurs (named by some as "copper thieves") "redistribute" the wealth produced by the mines through kinship and other local networks. The Organized Crime Watch of the Southern African Institute for Security Studies describes these processes as generating criminal networks on the Copperbelt (Institute for Security Studies 2009). Locally, understandings are less black and white. While this trade is illegal and the mining companies that own the dump sites prohibit informal digging and mining, mine employees and policemen routinely turn a blind eye in implicit recognition of the dump site workers' basic needs. This chapter suggests that illegality has become a legitimate survival strategy in the eyes of many living within the economic context of a failure to meet local needs and a political context featuring an ever-diminishing state intervention. The elaboration of an alternative morality to justify illegality should thus be seen as part of the creation of a narrative to explain the growing importance of informality as a way of inhabiting the world and making a living, as demonstrated in the previous chapter. Informality connotes a propensity for trespass that, in the context of improvisational livelihood-making, casts people outside formal legal systems, and in turn leads to contestations over ownership and control.

Within a discussion of power, the chapter contributes to an understanding of the body politic of neoliberalism in this context. This may be understood in a Foucauldian sense as the forces, emanating from the ideological and material structures of society, that impact the negotiating body of the actor, in this case women and children working at the mine dumps. However, rather than seeing structure as stable, it can be seen—like neoliberalism—as an ideological sketch that allows us to engage with it as a theme that emerges through various stories of the attempt to create a free market. As I show through the engagement of informal miners at sites that were once under the formal control of mining companies, the assertion of free market ideology and private property is not a given thing or object but is entangled with various contestations for economic action, giving rise in turn to the emergence of varying interests.

Second, economic shifts are driving changes in gender relations on the Copperbelt. The chapter shows how the "spirit" of neoliberalism's "free market" has co-opted women's and children's bodies into modes of labour in what are clearly recognised as unequal circumstances by the subjects themselves. While the more lucrative aspects of the informal trade in copper is dominated by men who operate as middlemen to copper ore buyers and organise labour gangs, women and children are an increasingly significant feature in this trade. They are perceived by some as harder working, less likely to cause trouble, more likely to escape prosecution for trespass, and more willing to work for smaller profit margins. While these perceptions often hold true, the dump sites are also spaces in which the distinctive moral and political voices that women have long constructed and defended on the Copperbelt find new articulations.[1]

THE SITES OF STUDY

As discussed in Chapter 1, between 1997 to 2000 the massive state-owned conglomerate Zambia Consolidated Copper Mines (ZCCM) was broken up and transferred into the ownership of a range of international private-sector investors. The mines in Luanshya were amongst the first to be broken off from the vast ZCCM and sold as a package as the Roan Antelope Mining Company of Zambia (RAMCOZ). The deal also included the Baluba mines and a greenfield site at Mulyashi. The initial purchaser was Binani, a consortium of Indian investors, who, although acknowledged as metal traders, did not have the same extensive experience running mines as the preferred bidders, the mine company First Quantum.[2] RAMCOZ initially retained all 6,294 of the former ZCCM workers (Mwaba 2004), but the inexperienced management of the company struggled from the very beginning to raise capital, run the mine, and pay employees and suppliers.[3] In Luanshya, suspicions were rife that the investors asset-stripped the company, and, in 2000, the liquidation of RAMCOZ represented the first major setback of the Zambian privatisation process. The company laid off all but a few care and maintenance staff. The failure of the company to provide even redundancy packages, known as "terminal benefits," let alone secure pensions, meant many residents of a town built in the "bush" in order to service the mine experienced immediate and profound material and psychosocial difficulties (see Chapter 6). In 2003, many people's hopes were briefly raised when a severance benefit package was agreed to by the mines, including an option to purchase the company houses still occupied by former miners, and a considerable sum in cash. This short-lived injection of cash caused an outburst of informal economic activities, often the only hope for most to make a living, as I have described in earlier chapters. It also facilitated a glut in spending, as the predominantly male former mine workforce lived a short "high life."

Mr Sanga, a Luanshya general dealer, described miners as "big spenders" and "careless with money," saying that during that period it had not been unusual for a mineworker to spend up to ZMK 10 million (in some cases a third of the cash benefit) in a single shopping spree; and a Mrs Muleya, a hairdresser, mentioned in passing that she had to obtain an injunction to prevent her husband from selling the family house, the only asset remaining, after her husband had spent his entire cash benefit. These stories were not unusual, or historically unprecedented. The lack of fiscal discipline among male mineworkers on the early Copperbelt was noted by colonial anthropologists such as Epstein (1992) and was a concern that ZCCM took up in workshops for retrenched and retiring workers. The perceived unreliability of men was one of the factors that Copperbelt women (and men too) told me drove women to seek an income, usually in the informal sector.

Expectations of a return of modernity to Luanshya were raised again in 2004, when a new wave of foreign investment started to flow into the Copperbelt to finance a rapid expansion of copper mining, due to the rapidly rising copper prices caused by the dramatic economic growth of China and India and the resulting demand for raw materials. In practice, however, formal employment did not increase much, and where jobs were created, the conditions of employment were considerably worse than during the ZCCM period. On the other hand, what the new boom did was to sustain and expand the fast-growing informal economy that replaced the increasingly diminished arena of formal wage labour on the Copperbelt. Neo Simutanyi (2008) and Alastair Fraser and John Lungu (2006) provide a general picture of the negative effects of wholesale privatisation on the livelihoods of people living in the Copperbelt, even during the boom. However, the boom they document ended just as fast as it started, in the aftermath of the credit crunch in September 2008, increasing the prominence of the informal economy as the primary source of income for Copperbelt residents.

The residents of the rural mining site of Kalengwa in Mufumbwe district did not experience the radical changes that the residents of Luanshya did, as mining operations had ceased in the early 1980s. During that period, the mining staff was absorbed into the other mines of the newly formed ZCCM, and a few retired. Apart from a small indigenous population, this left a few civil servants, teachers who ran a school, and a few retirees who had decided to settle in the area. Until about 2004, Kalengwa attracted few outsiders, as it was not very conducive for settlement. Sixty kilometres away from the district centre of Mufumbwe, it can only be reached by a dirt road in very bad condition. The mining site and settlement in Kalengwa is surrounded by dense miombo woodland. The soil in the area is stony, making it unsuitable for agricultural activity. In addition, residents complain of a peculiar taste to the water from the wells, potentially hinting at some kind of contamination of the water table. The residents of Kalengwa before the copper boom had subsisted on fish, some hunting, and small-scale *chitemene*—slash and burn, or shifting cultivation. The large mounds of the waste copper ore left from the mining operations in the early 1980s remained largely ignored by the residents. It was not expected that these large mounds would again contribute to their livelihood, and they were little more than a backdrop where children played.

At the Luanshya copper mine dump site women tended to work relatively independently. In contrast, at the Kalengwa site, work at the dump site has increasingly been enmeshed in a gang labour system. This might be because of the looser controls the mine in Kalengwa exercised over the space, and its general remoteness, making it harder for the state and mining companies to scrutinise activities there.

THE EMERGENCE OF THE INFORMAL ECONOMY IN ZAMBIA

Since the transition to democracy and the free market in 1991, the regulatory forces of the Zambian state have contracted, diminishing the surveillance capacity of the state that characterised the country under Kenneth Kaunda. This contraction was partly chosen by a new government that declared itself committed to a "market-oriented economy" and partly imposed by the spending cuts of structural adjustment policies implemented under pressure from donors, which reduced the manpower of the civil service and its institutions. Regulatory aspects of the Kaunda-era government, characterised by a widespread paranoia about being watched, loosened. This was an important precondition for the emergence of increased informal economic activities in the country. It was not that unregulated economic activity did not occur previously, but it had been much more tightly constrained. During the colonial period women had engaged in the illegal brewing of beer and other informal economic activities and had gone to great lengths to conceal them (Chauncey 1981). In the Kaunda era, an operation known as the Special Investigation Team for Economy and Trade (SITET) investigated business transactions, including those in the informal sector, as part of the regime's aims to centrally control the economy. One of my informants, Mrs Mwaba, who had actively worked in informal cross-border trade during the Kaunda era, narrated how, on several occasions, she had been followed by officers of SITET and questioned about how she got access to foreign currency. The limitation placed on the procurement of foreign currency led to a black market in currency exchange, one that Mrs Mwaba participated in.[4]

In the 1990s, following the democratisation of political life and the adoption of market principles, informal economic activities became much more visible.[5] This visibility was also precipitated by the dramatically worsened economic conditions and the massive formal sector job losses that accompanied privatisation. Though the economic system "opened up" and there was a great spurt of entrepreneurial activity, there were several contradictions in the regulatory system that was supposed to institute the new free market ideology. These inconsistencies are revealed in Karen Tranberg Hansen's study on the eviction of street vendors from the city centre of the Zambian capital Lusaka and attempts to relocate them to a newly constructed market (Hansen 2004). Hansen describes how, on one hand, the central state promoted informal sector activity as part of the free market system, with informal trade institutionalised through a vendors' desk established at State House (the official residence of the Zambian presidency). On the other hand, the Lusaka local authorities—who after 1996 and particularly 2001 had gained relative independence through the increase in members of parliament and councillors from opposition parties—initiated forced removals of vendors and enacted a series of regulations and practices to keep them off the streets. The local authorities drew on public health discourses of law and order, highlighting the illegality of street vending. These actions, Hansen notes, all occurred when greater economic difficulty drove more people to informal sector activity. Hansen notes that marketeers, urged to move to the new markets, complained of the high rates and rentals being charged for trading space. In the context of great economic hardship, this was not surprising. Since Hansen's study, there has been gentrification of informal sector trade in the city centre of Lusaka. In 2008, the new markets charged higher rentals—of up to ZMK 1 million (about US$200) for a store per month. These were amounts that many street vendors could not afford. The promotion of gentrification by the state eager for tax revenue that could only be collected with a degree of formalisation is a far cry from the surveillance of the centralised economy of the Kaunda era. In the seemingly chaotic context of economic life in Zambia, the dispersal of market ideology through entanglement of both macro- and micro-political economic relationships significantly impacted ordinary people's efforts to get by in free market Zambia. Hansen (2004, 62) thus argues that, rather than treating the economy as an ideology or a function of the regulatory regime, we need to examine the "meaning and empirical realities" of particular markets.

Sebana wikute ("Get embarrassed but get full"): The Moral Economy of the Informal Sector

On the Copperbelt, the contrast between the "nationalised" past and the "privatised" present is clear: many people feel they are not benefiting from foreign investment and that the cause is the investors' greed. The nationalised ZCCM mines had operated as the financier of the socialist vision of Zambia under the Kaunda regime. According to the dominant account (see Adam and Simpasa, 2010), this is precisely what led to the failure of the company to set aside funds for the capitalisation of new mining investments, and thus to modernise production and provide a long-term developmental model. The moral economy of mining was not, however, simply a calculation of long-term business strategy. In the minds of many Copperbelt residents, the mines were theirs. This sense of ownership was fostered not only by an affective relation to labour but also in the ways in which the mine company permeated many other spheres of mineworkers' lives. For example, ZCCM provided nappies and formula for babies born to mine employees; issued subsidised food and toilet paper to the household; and provided recreational facilities at the mine clubs, where alcohol could be purchased on tab, and housekeeping lessons for mineworker's wives. While these social provisions were welcomed, people resented the control that the mine company exerted in family life. Bridget Bwembya, a former mineworker in the social welfare department of ZCCM, informed me that her department had authorised the disbursement of salaries to wives who had complained that their husbands neglected their financial responsibilities in the home. The entanglement of the mines with workers' families mirrored the early period of mining on the Copperbelt, when the mine company had relied on women's agricultural and other labour to minimise the costs of care and stabilise its male staff; it also created a platform where women could actively place their claims for a better livelihood and could be involved in politics (Chauncey 1981; Parpart 1986; Larmer 2007). Women still aim to make political claims about mine revenues and the gendered distribution of work and income in the deinstitutionalised, postprivatisation world. In 1998, for example, a year after the sale of the ZCCM Luanshya mine, the *Times of Zambia* reported that mineworkers, aided by women and children, rioted over the delays in the payment of housing allowance and the unfair dismissal of a mineworker's union official (Kayira 1998). As is discussed below, women and children working in the illegal mining sector have also rioted over the unfairness of the workings of the "free" market.

Complaints over livelihoods on the Zambian Copperbelt cannot be seen only as a struggle for resources between a proletariat and those who control the means of production. There is an affective dimension at play, which draws upon a discourse of selfishness that James Ferguson identified when he carried out fieldwork in Zambia in the 1980s. Ferguson (1992) noted that mineworkers increasingly directed their critique inwards, as a negative assessment of themselves. Rather than seeing this self-directed critique as only the rhetoric of an anxious imagined community, as reflected in the musings of a Zambian intelligentsia, this moral critique needs to be examined in relation to the corporeality of practices of livelihood and social proprieties (Ferguson 2003).

To describe this in practice in the contemporary period, I draw on the case of the Luanshya family of Mr and Mrs Phiri, who have had relative success in the post-privatisation economy of the Copperbelt. During the toughest period on the Copperbelt, following mineworkers' retrenchments after Binani's collapse and before workers received their cash benefits, Luanshya residents suffered, many said. They described a situation where they were lucky to have a meal; some said they subsisted at times on raw mangoes. The Phiri family, in contrast to many of their neighbours, did not go hungry even though their business in informal trade, established long before privatisation, suffered. Mrs Phiri narrated in various conversations how neighbours who, in better times, had been careful only occasionally to visit at mealtimes, took to visiting almost every single day during meals. While Mrs Phiri understood what drove her neighbours to flout social conventions, which she summed up as *sebana wikute* ("Get embarrassed but get full"), the awareness of their own potentially precarious economic situation led the Phiris to having meals at irregular times to avoid being perceived as selfish when they failed to offer their visitors a meal. The perception that they fared better than their neighbours still persisted. Their neighbours pointed out to me that the Phiris had never become thin like the rest of them. During the copper boom, which encompassed my fieldwork in Luanshya, the Phiri family's prosperity stood in stark contrast to their neighbours, whose circumstances, though slightly improved, were still mired in difficulty. This contrast led to accusations of Satanism levelled at the Phiris, who, despite their generosity in offering various sorts of assistance, of food, palliative care, time and money for the organ-isation of social events like marriages and funerals in their neighbourhood, were still perceived as selfish. This strained the relations between them and their neighbours, as they felt they were being fleeced. Several attempted thefts at their home intensified this feeling.

The incidence of theft in the former mine townships of Luanshya is widely perceived to have risen. In my first survey in 2008, all but three of the fifty-six households mentioned security and theft as a problem. During the year and half of my fieldwork in Luanshya, I experienced two attempted break-ins and in another instance found the external copper piping of my house sto-len. There were also other transgressions that Luanshya residents would not necessarily have frowned upon, such as the instance I described in Chapter 2 where Lazarus Nsofu and his family moved into the domestic quarters at the bottom of my garden in the expectation that I would employ his wife. When I mentioned that I had not consented to either employing his wife or their moving in, I was reasonably asked what I intended to do with the space. To have an unoccupied building would have been too selfish indeed. In another incident, on returning home, I found two women I had not met before helping themselves to some vegetables I had planted in the back gar-den. Upon seeing me, they cheerfully shouted, "We are just stealing some vegetables from your garden." Surely, living alone, I could not have eaten all the vegetables in the garden.

While such "helpings" were common and indeed deemed acceptable, many residents had become worried about what was seen as the raiding of the maize crop during the harvest season. Maize is largely grown as a sub-sistence and small-scale cash crop in Zambia. This was considered "theft," unlike the "helpings" described above, and it led many residents to camp out in their fields in the rural Copperbelt as a preventative measure. It also led to field owners adopting violently threatening behaviour, such as chasing off would be maize thieves with axes. By highlighting these practices of "theft," I do not mean to portray them as a new occurrence on the Zambian Copper-belt. Indeed, on 27 February 1981, the *Mining Mirror*—the mining industry newspaper on the Copperbelt—reported on the theft of explosives from the mines that resulted in cases of injury, like that of an elderly man who had been using explosives to catch fish in the Kafulafuta River, on the outskirts of Luanshya.[6] My research highlights the intensification of these activities amid worsening living conditions and loosening social regulations and proprieties, on one hand, and on the other, the protection of private property. As Fiona Ross (2010, 40) argued, proprieties, in this case, the obligation to respect private property, cannot always be thought of as positive.

The increasing informalisation of livelihoods across the social spectrum of actors on the Copperbelt also suggests the inevitability of trespass and the development of new moralities to justify economic activities of uncertain legality. This view is best expressed in the philosophical musings of Zambia's first president, Kenneth Kaunda, who said: "The hungry stranger, could, without penalty, enter the garden of a village and take, say a bunch of bananas or a mealie cob to satisfy his hunger. His action only became theft if he took more than was necessary to satisfy his needs. For then he was depriving others" (Kaunda and Morris 1966, 25). The tactical aspects of this morality, if one follows Michel de Certeau's (1988) concept of tactics, is one where actors are in the continuous action of creating new itineraries for moral action amidst dominant narratives, such as capitalism's demand for respect for private property.

Actions such as the eviction of vendors from Lusaka's streets or the prevention of poaching of resources of food and shelter may occasionally be seen as selfish and also violating the integrity of life. The commonly heard expressions *twali chula*, "We suffered," *ku toping'a*, "to extend life," and *twala mona inga twa fika*, "We shall see when we get there" underline these daily struggles of survival. Struggle and hardship characterise the fate of many in Zambia, and few are considered to have "arrived," an expression to describe those seen as successful.[7] Struggle and success are in Zambian linked on a continuum, represented by the image of the everyday, a shirtless, malnourished man, urged to tighten his belt, who struggles to survive amidst a rhetoric of fiscal restraint and free market ideology. On the other end is the corpulent image of the *apamwamba*, "those on top," who represent the excess, indolence, and violence of greed. These two images highlight the corporeality of the relations and realities of economic life in Zambia. They also contextualise the narratives presented below of women who work at copper dump sites. Before privatisation, these women would not have compelled to eke out a living in the harsh working conditions of these sites.

Ukumbomba ichipuba ("To work foolishly"): Exploitation and Informality

Residents report that informal activities in the ZCCM period saw women in Luanshya involved mostly in small-scale trade of goods such as second-hand clothes and vegetables. The children spent most of their time after school exploring the surrounding forests, playing sports at the Luanshya recreation centres, or reading in the local library. Most mineworkers and their families in Luanshya had, for most of their working life, been employed by the mines, as had their fathers and their grandfathers. Mineworkers and their families were ill-prepared for retrenchment; most assumed they would be re-employed after foreign investment took over. Their expectations were not met, and, before and during the privatisation era, many remained jobless.

While Binani's "asset stripping" was widely considered immoral and a symbol of the corrupt nature of both the privatisation process and foreign investors, it also represented a continuity with a process of decline. The collapse of RAMCOZ was a disaster for all involved in the sense that the company, government, and community all suffered. Nobody was getting fat. The moral economy of formal and informal work has been transformed by the copper boom, and the possibility of massive profits.

"These investors want to take everything, even the waste that ZCCM left." As she dug up flux stone with her shovel at one of the main dump sites of Luanshya, Rhoda reflected on the new wave of activity brought about by the copper boom. Rhoda's husband was a casualty of privatisation. Like many other miners, he passed away soon after losing his job. Rhoda was left to support six children on her own from the meagre income that she made digging flux stone.[8] Her fourteen-year-old son worked with her at the dump site, helping her ferry bags of flux stone using a wheelbarrow. These were emptied and piled in heaps by the side of the street. For Rhoda, foreign investment after privatisation clearly coincided with a marked worsening of living conditions. The sense that foreign investment has done little to improve the lives of Copperbelt residents can also be captured by a Bemba expression used to describe work at copper dump sites, *ukubomba ichipuba* ("to work foolishly").

The newly acquired houses have provided a temporary safety net. However, many Luanshya mineworkers only received their cash benefits several years after retrenchment, and many mineworkers were forced to rent out their house or sell and move to the peri-urban outskirts of the town. Women whose husbands died following the privatisation of the mines lost even the safety of the house. Cultural practices of property-grabbing by the relatives of the deceased and the Zambian state's intestate law (which distributes the inheritance to wife, children, and dependants) in many cases forced the sale or rental of the house, in order to facilitate the sharing of the inheritance amongst beneficiaries who did not always reside together. Take, for example, the experiences of Mrs Ziyembe, a widow with two young children. When her husband, a mine company medical officer, died in 2002, his relatives demanded she sell the house located in the low-density former mine suburb of Luanshya immediately after his burial in order for them to collect their share of the money. Mrs Ziyembe explained that, considering she had been a good wife and reluctant to attract the ire of her late husband's relatives, she sold the house through a dubious legal aid officer who, apart from addressing issues of inheritance, predominantly operated as an estate agent. He sold the house and duly gave Mrs Ziyembe's late husband's relatives their share, but retained hers and her children's, claiming to have found a smaller and cheaper house they could move into. The smaller house turned out to have been sold by the owner to two buyers other than Mrs Ziyembe. When she attempted to claim her money, the owner failed to pay it back and claimed it had already been spent. The absence of a written contract other than the word of the legal aid officer made it difficult to get back the entire amount, and she could only claim a small amount—the resale value of the sale of a few second-hand household items collected from the seller's home. Forced to rent in a high-density former mine suburb, but unable to afford utility bills, Mrs Ziyembe now draws water from her neighbours and sparingly uses charcoal for cooking. She, like many other Luanshya families, illegally occupied land belonging to the mines for farming in an area aptly named *Mai Lange* ("shown by myself"); much of this land has been recently reappropriated by foreign investors during the current copper boom (see also Hansangule, Feeney, and Palmer 1998).[9]

The stories of many women working at the Luanshya copper mine dump mirror the difficulties faced by Mrs Ziyembe. The women know that while their hard work is unlikely to bring success, it at least provides for the minimal household basics. It also provides for a small income to purchase other goods, such as agricultural produce and second-hand clothes for resale.

Ukuibombela ("To work for oneself"): Everyday Life at a Copper Dump Site

Despite the perceived exploitative nature of working informally on the copper dump sites, women are often pragmatic about the need for an income, no matter how meagre it may be. Mary, a digger at the Luanshya dump site, said she worked there because

> I need to feed my family. My husband got a job as a casual [worker] with a contractor at the mines in Chingola. He gets very little, not enough for him to share with us, so he has sent nothing since he went to work there six months

ago. I don't mind working; besides he looked after us when he worked for the [ZCCM] mines. You see, us women here, if we got jobs we would work, even for these new mines. We are working right now. You see over there, the woman with a shovel, she can dig, she can be a miner. These mines only want to employ *abwapwa umulopa mumishipa* ["those who have no blood running in their veins"].[10] Who will employ our children? They are still sleeping in our homes. So we come to work.

The current decline in formal employment has pushed more and more women into the informal economy. Whereas these informal activities supplemented household incomes during the ZCCM period, now they have become the main source of income for most. Women and children are now increasingly expected to produce income for the household. In many cases, they are forced to do so by the death of a male breadwinner.[11] In some cases, children are pushed into dump site work by the death of both parents.

An average working day at the Luanshya dump site lasts from sunrise to sunset, approximately twelve hours, with a short lunch break on the site of about thirty minutes. Women and children all complain of respiratory problems caused by the residual dust. Workers are also regularly harassed and beaten by the mining companies' security officials, who are instructed by mine management to discourage illegal digging. Several informants told me that the reason that women and children were normally the ones working on the dump sites is that they are less likely to be prosecuted than men. Media reports of young men being shot dead at private mine sites show that the threat to life is real and that locals take pragmatically dangerous decisions to earn a livelihood (*Times of Zambia* 2009).

Despite these difficulties, the women interviewed prefer to face these challenges rather than embark on transactional sex and sex work, other options open to them. As one informant put it, "It is easy to go with a man for ZMK 20,000 but what will happen to your children when you die? *Kukosa pa ku sheta* [You have to be strong to be able to eat]."[12] The reference here is to the risk of contracting HIV-AIDS through sexual intercourse.[13] Women also typically prefer dump site work to microfinance initiatives aimed at starting up other informal trades. The reasons given are that family responsibilities are at a high level, emergencies are a regular occurrence, and it would be difficult for them to repay the loans. All in all, dump site work offers an opportunity to earn an income with no start-up capital costs and a great degree of autonomy. Any group of women and children can join the Luanshya dump site and start digging and selling flux stone without the involvement of any formal or informal third party.

Pa illegal twali beula ("During illegal, we made good"): "Illegal" Livelihoods

The new ideology of entrepreneurship and market competition is now mixed with the anxiety of destitution in a world of scarce (and almost entirely privatised) resources and nonexistent public welfare intervention. These two factors together have led to the rise in informal and illegal activities. Many participants in these illegal activities clearly feel entitled to bypass westernised notions of private property in the name of survival and individual gain. My informants all show a pragmatic approach that values economic self-sufficiency above wage labour. Informants see wage labour as limiting creativity and the space of individual agency; they also see it as an exploitative form of labour, where the employer gains much more than the employee. The newly rediscovered valuation of individual agency through self-employment constitutes an important break from the past. At the same time, it also shows a deep distrust of any form of economic development connected to the recent wave of foreign investment. This distrust also constitutes the foundations of the implied moral legitimation of illegality; illegal activity is regarded as both a necessity for survival and a morally justified act of redistribution. If, as they see it, foreign investors are here to "take everything," then there is nothing wrong with taking some of these resources away from the investors. Informants often mention a Bemba proverb to make this point: *ubomba mwi bala alya mwi bala* ("One who works in a field eats from the field"). Peter Walker and Pauline Peters's (2001) work on land use in Malawi brings home similar arguments: when people illegally appropriate resources from private spaces, they are not actually putting forward a claim over the ownership of these resources, but rather are pointing out the unfair usage of the same resources by the legal owner.

TRYING TO MAKE IT ON THE NEW COPPERBELT

The case of Kalengwa mining dump site, in the rural "new" Copperbelt, shows what these contests for resources entail in practice and how privatisation is radically changing socioeconomic dynamics on the ground. The workforce on this dump site is mostly composed of women and children. Informal operations at the dump site involve scavenging flux stone for copper extraction

Figure 5. A street lined on its sides with tidy heaps of flux stone from nearby mining dump site. Photo by author, August 2008.

and surface mining of copper ore. Although the mine was sold to a group of local investors as far back as 1982, no formal mining took place until 2008, when a dispute about licences between two contending owners was resolved in favour of one of them. Since 2004, however, the mine dump site has been informally run by "illegal" miners who came from as far away as Lusaka to exploit the opportunity of selling flux stone and copper ore on the thriving local and international markets fuelled by rising copper prices. Formal operations resumed in April 2008, and the "illegal" workers rioted shortly afterwards to oppose the owner's decision to stop all informal mining on his site. A compromise was then reached, and informal miners were allowed to continue their operations, but could now sell only to the mine owner. In practice, the informal miners continue to sell part of their produce to other buyers. At the outpost, there is no state law enforcement; the mine employs its own private security that occasionally confiscates copper ore accumulated for sale to other buyers. What is clearly at stake here is the very notion of legality and illegality. Informal miners rioted both to claim their rights over what they saw as a precious material resource "abandoned" by the state and to make a point about the exploitative nature of "foreign" investment. According to my informants, the general feeling was that it was unfair for the owner to stop an activity that has become the primary source of subsistence for so many destitute people.

In practice, the recent copper boom and the absence of any control over the dump site created a mini-boom in itself for the dump site workers. Informants remember this period as *pa illegal* ("during illegal"). The relatively high profit margins were also the main reason behind the involvement of many men alongside the women and children. This also shows how unequal gender dynamics tend to structure informal markets as well as the formal economy. Women and children are now predominant in the dump site workforce following the resumption of formal control. The patriarchal family structures and their values put a cheaper price on women's and children's labour. Women, who feel more compelled than men to provide for the basic needs of the household, now undertake activities that are not seen as viable by men.

Sarah, a woman in her early thirties, moved to Kalengwa in 2006 from the Zambian capital with her husband and her four daughters. During the height of illegal activity, Sarah and her husband used the proceeds from the copper ore sales to establish other successful informal activities. Three of her children work on the dump site. Sarah herself makes and sells a powerful local brew called *lutuku* to the local male population. Her husband set up a pig trade and is now based in the capital. Sarah reminisces about the good times of *pa illegal* when she used to sell twenty containers of *lutuku* in a day:

> *Pa illegal twali beula* ["During illegal we made good"]. In a day, I sold twenty containers of brew. I would get people coming to buy drink very early in the morning. This place was like town; there were small businesses and minibuses. If you had to ask a young girl to collect water for you, they would answer you back saying, "Did you give birth to me?" Many people left this place with sexually transmitted diseases. We made money. You see the house over there? The woman there built herself a house of concrete blocks and iron sheets and bought herself two trucks. Those from the villages came here with no shoes and left the place with shoes on their feet. It was paradise for them. *Amahule* ["women involved in transactional sex"] from town came here with almost nothing and got copper from boys from the villages by sleeping with them. Other women had to buy ten tonnes [of copper] for 3.5 million.

Before the formal owner regained control of the mine, the copper boom created unprecedented wealth for people like Sarah, who would have otherwise had very few opportunities in the post-privatisation formal economy. In Sarah's words, there was a sense of liberation and excitement about the new opportunities afforded by the "free market." However, free market and legality are not complementary concepts in this new world view. Furthermore, the resumption of "legality," which coincided with the involvement of the mine owner in mining activities on the ground, is regarded by many as contrary to that very spirit of entrepreneurship and self-sufficiency.

Katherine, a woman in her early sixties, is still involved in the buying of copper ore from the informal miners, despite the new rules imposed by the mine owner. She arrived in Kalengwa in 2006 from a distant Copperbelt town. The first time I met her, she appeared distressed, talking to a small crowd outside her second-hand clothing store. The mine security staff had just confiscated 800 kilograms of copper ore that she had stashed in her shop. She spent ZMK 2 million on buying the copper and she would have made ZMK 2.8 million by reselling it. Katherine buys copper ore from children who scavenge and dig around the perimeter of the now- fenced mining area. She pays the children ZMK 2,500 per kilogram of copper ore, considerably more than the rates offered by the mine owner. He buys low-grade copper ore at ZMK 1,500 per kilogram, and on rare occasions he pays up to ZMK 2,000 per kilogram for higher-grade copper ore. Katherine perceives the interference of the mine owner in her business as unfair and against the values of market competition:

They told us not to buy copper. What do they expect us to do? The people here, they did not cultivate because they were mining; now one buffalo [two and half litres of ground maize] costs ZMK 5,000. People are now buying on credit. Where will they get the money? Me, I am a widow; my husband died because there was no work when the mines closed. I look after eight children; only three are mine. The others they are orphans I look after. Me, if I had to stop buying, what will happen to the children here? I buy at a fairer price than this European does.[14] I give them ZMK 2,500 per kilo; and because I am buying in small quantities, I give them clothes for copper. . . . The market for copper is open! The government is only allowing Europeans to buy. What about us? I can go to the customs office, borrow from the government, and do my own work. No, nothing for us Africans—we have no rights. They are taking gold, diamonds—what about us? We can organise ourselves into groups and get ourselves a license. We women can do it! . . . Here, my daughter, there is no government. We are the ones helping the people.

Katherine's words come full circle and echo Rhoda's concerns about the greed of foreign investors. They also indicate the perceived absence of government in everyday life. This, again, provides further legitimacy to "illegality." If government is not willing or able to intervene to remedy the imbalances of foreign investment, then in local eyes it is only fair that the "people" take it upon themselves to produce and redistribute wealth. For many, the people involved in the illegal trade of flux stone and copper ore are not undesirable outlaws, but popular heroes.

"A Man Cannot Work for This Small Money"

While some women who had travelled to the mining outpost in North Western Province had made their fortunes, others had not been so lucky. Matilda, a single mother who had been digging for copper in trenches six to eight metres deep, noted that if the state had been serious about investment, there would be no children, pregnant teenagers, and old women digging in the mines. Desperation, she said, is what drove them to work in such harsh condition for so little money: *abaume teti ba bombe fo tu piya utu, nomba umwanakashi teti amone abana balala ne nsala* ("A man cannot work for this small money, but a woman can't watch her children sleep with hunger"). Matilda and the other women and children who dug for copper in the main mine area were not employed by the mine owner but were allowed into the premises to dig for copper as long as they sold to the owner. During an interview, the mine manager informed me that he allowed the "illegals" into the mine premises because if he did not, there was likely to be trouble in the area (referring to riots that took place in April 2008). When I commented that I had noticed more women than men working at the mine, he said that women were more willing to work and "caused less trouble." One of the few men who worked at the mine told me that those who caused trouble or complained about how much they were paid were "tortured like we are al-Qaeda."

Bana Jane, an elderly woman in her late sixties, had returned to the mining outpost after three months away, arriving in April 2008, just after illegal mining activities had been curbed by the licensed mine owner. She had travelled with her grandchildren who dug for copper, but the lower prices paid for the commodity by the mine owner had made Bana Jane seriously contemplate returning to her village in the North Western district, Kabompo. Bana Jane provided childcare for mothers who were working in the mine, and she waited in the area because rumours abounded of the mine owners pulling out from the site, paving the way for another surge of illegal mining. However, she was also aware that she had to leave the place in time to prepare her land for cultivation before the rainy season (November to March). The little money she made in the outpost she planned to use to buy maize seed and fertiliser to avoid being destitute like the others who had failed to cultivate the previous season because of the "copper boom."

GROWTH OF INFORMAL MINING

The cases presented above describe illegal mining activity just before the end of the copper boom of 2004 to 2008. Illegal mining on the Copperbelt was not a livelihood activity that emerged only because of higher commodity prices for copper. The copper boom attracted more players eager not just to survive but "to make it." A *Post* newspaper article dated 24 July 2000, titled "Zambia Is on a Potential Volcano," anticipated the burgeoning informal mining on the Copperbelt by residents desperate to make a living in what was increasingly seen as a lawful activity. The article reports on a letter written in complaint by Patrick Chilufya Bowa, Inter-trade Institute director, to an inspector general of police, Silas Ngangula, over the arrest of twenty youths for illegal mining. The article cites Mr Bowa offering a solution to what he saw as the failure of the state to create alternative livelihoods for retrenched former ZCCM miners. He argues for bringing "bonafide small scale miners, illegal miners and retrenched miners into the mainstream small-scale mining commercial activity in line with Zambia's status as a mining nation." Later, on 16 July 2001, *The Post* reported that the Zambian government, in recognition of informal mining activity, would begin to issue artisanal mining licences to illegal miners in order to curb foreign investors' unfair advantage. By 2007, when the late Zambian president Mwanawasa suggested that investors should consider passing on mine dump sites and unused mine pits to former mine employees as a way of reducing illegal mining and helping sustain livelihoods, informal mining was an established economic activity on the Copperbelt.[15]

Those involved in the informal copper business may not openly welcome formalisation. The increasingly tougher stand taken against illegal mining activity, such as the reported strengthening of an anti-copper theft squad and the suggestion of measures to stop the activity, is not likely to stop illegal mining or the danger associated with this livelihood activity.[16] While the most severe dangers posed by informal mining activity are caused by an unsafe work environment, an increasing danger is the violence with which mine property is being protected.[17]

WOMEN'S PRESENCE IN INFORMAL MINING

Dwindling employment in the formal sector on the Copperbelt has pushed more women into informal economic activities that previously had served the purpose of complementing their husbands' wages. Retrenchment and death have been the main causes for the rapid decline of income from formal employment. The informal sector has now become the primary site of livelihood.

The dominant role of women in the informal sector is closely related to local social expectations that women provide for the household's basic needs (see also Schlyter 1999; Hansen 1997). The involvement of women in illegal labour under harsh working conditions at the mine dump sites also indicates the contradictory nature of local perceptions of women's bodies. Women are doing what was previously seen as men's work. The few men who still work as low-level mine labourers in the formal sector are witnessing the rapid casualisation of their employment. Paradoxically, women and children are strategically inserted into the dangerous flows of illegal labour because they are seen as "soft" legal entities, and therefore are unlikely to be prosecuted. Their bodies are physically disciplined by beatings and by the confiscation of the products of their labour by mine security.

However, women have had no trouble inserting themselves into mining work. Much of the work they carry out at the mine dumps adopts bodily techniques similar to those employed in agricultural work, and though dangerous, it is not physically dissimilar in activity. Women dig, they sift through dirt, they do heavy lifting and carrying. The tools employed are not very different from those that they carry with them to work their fields: shovels, hoes, and picks. Thus, when I encountered women and their children coming from working at the mine dumps, in the tools they carried and the attire they wore, they could have been coming from cultivating their fields. Thus, despite the unexpected presence of women and children in informal mining, their participation forms part of their everyday taskscapes,[18] similar in activity and bodily movements to cultivating the fields.

As I describe in the next chapter, the impetus for women to engage in informal mining is also the expectation of the industrious woman (a social expectation by men and women themselves). In their performance of gender, Copperbelt women not only cultivate bodily comportments that are variable and nuanced across multiple identities or ways of being in varied social situations, but also employ a similar traversing or trespassing into places along the realm of social, bodily, and material possibility. This does not mean that this trespass is minimally contested.

Gender inequalities, to women's disadvantage, are also reflected in subsequent trade relations once the copper ore is mined from the dump sites. At all stages of the supply chain after the initial digging, men control flows, prices, and access to informal and formal markets. Women's bodies and their work are thus made invisible, as Katharine's case study shows. These concerns cast a different light over local understandings of global capitalism and strongly affect women's negative perceptions of their power position vis-à-vis the (male-dominated) "free market." Women's awareness of global copper prices and of the very minimal share they manage to appropriate contributes to these perceptions. Women involved in the informal copper business are also aware of the unfair advantage foreign investors have over local entrepreneurs in appropriating the largest share of the profits.

My findings suggest the informal sector does not constitute a discrete sphere separate from the formal sector. Rather, the two are interdependent and interact in complex and non-obvious ways (Castells and Portes 1978). The inequalities of global capitalism reflected by the increasing casualisation of labour and the worsening living conditions on the Zambian Copperbelt are coupled with gendered dynamics that constrain women and children in precarious and dangerous illegal activities in order to guarantee some level of subsistence to themselves and their households.

Fear of destitution, the exploitative nature of capital, and the absence of the state in welfare interventions set the framework for illegality as an economic strategy that is locally perceived as legitimate in ensuring survival and small-scale capital accumulation. The justification for pursuing economic activity that violates the "rule of law" needs to be contextualised against the real possibility of starvation. The state also loses legitimacy in local eyes since it is seen as a constellation of factional interests pursuing their own perpetuation of wealth and power in close alliance with foreign investors, with little concern for local development. These perceptions lead to the paradox that a loss of legitimacy of legal action is what ultimately legitimates illegal action as a viable economic and political strategy.

The contestation for control of the Kalengwa mine dump between the illegal miners and the "legitimate" mine owners' hints at a possible alternative understanding of power. In the classic Foucauldian analysis of relations of power, power is about strategy and tactics aimed at consolidating and normalising influence, often assumed to be concentrated spatially along certain nodes of control. The possibilities for decentring these nodes of power tend to be quite limited due the historical accumulation and consolidation of an archaeology of discursive mechanisms and disciplinary violence. Pierre Bourdieu integrates these power-building mechanisms into the body as a cumulative of social and cultural capital that is given as a priori, and enacted as a dispositional attitude outwards into the world. In both these views of power, which are often referred to, little account is taken of the confluence of events that gives rise to the possibilities of the emergence of novel forms or conglomerations of power.

While it is easy to acknowledge that there are interactions of factional interests of power that disadvantage several individuals, these relations are not structured in dialectical opposition. The world in which mining trespassers and legitimate mine owners operate is one and the same, and legitimate mine owners, just like the less privileged, have continuously to negotiate for an advantageous position. This requires they improvise, or compromise with the emerging factional interests of illegal miners. Placing this discussion within the broader discussion of contestations of power, I draw from Susan Oyama's (2000) work on developmental systems theory, which departs from a cumulative, archaeological, and thus teleologically inclined perspective of factional interest to focus on improvisational, emergent growth. Informal miners on the Copperbelt are immersed in processes for livelihood where contestations for power emerge not as a separate discourse or solely discursive effect but as a consequence of the material and social conditions they encounter as they go about their business and lives.

The discussion in this chapter points to the nuances of local views about what constitutes legitimate action and about the relevance of westernised notions of legality and illegality. Actors draw on multiple ontologies and moralities. These include moral obligations that are not only social but material and phenomenological in the way experience is seen as integral to bodily corporeality. Harri Englund (2008), for example, quoting Max Gluckman's work on jurisprudence amongst the Lozi of Barotseland, writes that morality, as expressed in moral obligations, cannot be looked at in isolation from the constitution of personhood, itself an unfolding of both material and affective practices (2008, 34). These practices in turn are embroiled in the enfolding of time in contestations of how and in what personhood is constituted, and give rise to the emergence of other types of relationships.

From the perspective of formal law, what is seen as a breakdown in law and order—enacted in the policing and prosecution of illegal miners—could also be seen as an opportunity. Zigon, writing on morality and ethics in post-Soviet states, argues that it is important that scholars "see the ways in which moral dispositions themselves are shaped and reshaped" (Zigon 2007, 148). Unlike his approach, which calls for the observation of the moment or event of moral breakdown and ethical demand (as presented in the moral dilemma, for example, which presents for the individual faced with it a moment calling for tactical or strategic action), I argue that it is important to observe both the performance and the movement across that moment and others.

In the next chapter I demonstrate this by examining women's negotiations of gender roles and identities across various ideals of domesticity present in Copperbelt interactions. In the social history of the Copperbelt these have generally been presented as broken or fractious. In the chapter, I show that women navigate multiple roles, sometimes easily, sometimes less so, in their quest to produce harmonious relations.

NOTES

1. See Jane L. Parpart (2001), who indicates that the moral political voice women lend to economic struggle extends to the articulation of the constraints against patriarchal power and the perception and construction of the good woman.

2. The Zambia Consolidated Copper Mines and the Zambia Privatization Agency faced a lawsuit in 1997 over the decision to sell the Luanshya mines to the Binani Group of Companies. "Zambia's ZCCM Sued by South African Mining Company," Deutsche Presse-Agentur, 8 October 1997. For a discussion of the justification to sell the mines to Binani rather than First Quantum see Kaunda 2002.

3. "Zambian Copper Mine Faces Closure Due to Debt," Panafrican News Agency, 2 November 2000. The article described RAMCOZ's failure to settle workers' salaries, service bills to the mine-drilling company Mpelembe Drilling, and settle a significant debt—of more than US$20 million to the energy company Copperbelt Energy Company.

4. A black market in foreign currency thrives in the urban areas of Zambia. David Chibesa, writing for the *Times of Zambia*, describes its working in an article titled "Forex Seekers Revisit Katondo Street," 24 December 1998.

5. Street-side and front-yard stores have become ever more visible in Zambia's cities.

6. During the period of my fieldwork in Luanshya, a former mine employee staying in Roan Township had used explosives suspected to have been stolen from the mines to commit suicide by blowing himself up in his house. "Luanshya Miner Blows Self Up," *Times of Zambia*, 31 December 2007.

7. As of 2009, about 86% of Zambians were living below the poverty line.

8. On average, a dump site worker manages to sell about four tonnes of flux stone per month. Market price at the time of this part of the study in July 2008 was ZMK 70,000 per tonne. This would mean an income of ZMK 280,000 per month. Most underground miners in the bottom rank would make anything between ZMK 300,000 and 1.5 million per month. The majority of them are not permanently employed.

9. In a study carried out just after the privatisation of the mines in the mid-1990s, Hansangule, Feeney, and Palmer anticipated these contests for land on the Copperbelt. The pressure for usable land is so great that most residents now use their backyards for agricultural activities and small-scale trade.

10. This statement expresses a criticism of the perceived continued engagement of the elderly in economic life well past the period they would have been expected to retire. Ann Schlyter's 2004 study on ageing in Zambia cities corroborates these views.

11. My own survey data show that, for example in a Luanshya street comprising twenty households, eight women had lost their husbands in the period between 1998 and 2008.

12. Comment made in a group discussion with copper dump site workers on 19 July 2008 in Luanshya.

13. According to the Central Statistical Office numbers from 2007, 14.3% of the Zambian population is HIV-positive.

14. The owner of the mine is a Zambian of foreign descent. In the Zambian context, he is seen as a "foreign" investor despite his Zambian citizenship.

15. "Help Us to Solve Illegal Mining Problem KCM Asks Partners," *Times of Zambia*, 18 April 2009.

16. See, for example, "Anti-copper Theft Squad to Be Boosted," *Times of Zambia*, 12 June 2009. The headline "Illegal Mining Must Be Stopped," *The Post*, 11 June 2009, suggests measures like fencing of mine dump sites to prevent the "unlawful" activity of illegal mining.

17. Reports of deaths are common in the newspapers. For example, in June 2009 eight illegal miners at the Chambishi Metals mine in the Copperbelt town of Kitwe died after a tunnel they were working in collapsed, "Eight Illegal Miners Perish," *Times of Zambia*, 11 June 2009.

18. Ingold (1993) describes taskscapes as a temporality of movements and activities that are similar or related.

CHAPTER 5

Performing Gender on the Copperbelt

Much has been written about the fractiousness of familial relationships on the Copperbelt. Often posited in terms of a tension between modern and traditional concepts of family, studies have offered little in terms of illuminating women's own views of domestic harmony and expectations, and their places and experiences of pleasure. This is not to deny that the problems in marital and familial relationships identified by prior anthropologists studying the Copperbelt exist (see summary in Ferguson 1999, 189–204). Indeed, on the whole, one does not have to look far to find disheartening family relations. One of the most recent anthropological studies on the region, by James Ferguson (1999), has argued that framing the problems affecting Copperbelt families as a structural dissonance between modern and traditional concepts of family (a perspective often held by Copperbelt residents themselves) has led to a failure to ask "how progressive it is to project what is fundamentally a bourgeois image of a normative European family onto the diverse domestic arrangements of the Copperbelt" (1999, 205). It is this normative view, which has been responsible for perpetuating a sense of the brokenness of Copperbelt families—one that has done little to allow for the exploration of the ways in which women, old people, and children get by within an economy that has long been dominated by the formal employment of men—that Ferguson critiques.

More recently in anthropology, there has been increasing interest in understanding concepts and the place of romantic love in Africa (see, for example, Cole and Thomas 2009; Johnson-Hanks 2007) and the places of conviviality and aspects of life that foster imagination and hope in otherwise difficult social contexts (see Ross 2010). By drawing attention to these areas, Cole and Thomas (2009) and Ross (2010) motivate an empathetic engagement with the people they represent and their lives. It is from a perspective informed by these works that I explore how Copperbelt residents, women in particular, reconcile customary and Western ideals of marriage and relationships; what they desire and their views of the issues that beset these relationships; and how they try to carve out space for economic independence and pleasure.

In the context of gender studies in Zambia, my aim in this chapter is to follow on from Karen Tranberg Hansen's (1997) study *Keeping House in Lusaka*, which did much to shed light on the "home front" and the issues that occupied women. The prior, more formal and visible presence of men on the mine towns has meant that representations of women have tended to posit a largely chauvinist worldview (mainly as a result of interviewing mainly male informants, as Ferguson rightly pointed out) that character-ises the male-dominated workforce of mine towns (1999, 188). However, in studies of the Copperbelt, Hortense Powdermaker's (1962) *Copper Town* pro-vided vivid insights drawn from the diaries of her research assistants, who kept account of the goings-on on the domestic front in Luanshya. George Chauncey's (1984) and Jane Parpart's (1986, 1994) studies on the nexus of women's labour, marriage, class, and the economy of the household on the Copperbelt provide a historical and structural analysis of the macro- and micro-political and economic issues that extended labour and gender strug-gles beyond the household. Henrietta Moore and Megan Vaughan's (1994) study of gender, nutrition, and agricultural livelihood in Northern Zambia, while not on the Copperbelt, nevertheless provides an excellent account of how changing dynamics of urbanisation and welfare from the early establish-ment of the Copperbelt influenced rural life, including how male migration to the Copperbelt impacted the processes of matrilineal marriage amongst the Bemba, the largest migratory group to the Copperbelt. Audrey Richards's (1956) account of female initiation rites in rural Northern Zambia provides an ethnographic account of rites that Thera Rasing's (2001) study shows per-sisted to the contemporary period on the Copperbelt and continue to be an important part of how women's gender is conceptualised.

In these studies, including the more classic Manchester school texts of Wilson (1968) and Mitchell (1957, 1961), a picture emerges of Copperbelt women as ill-used by their husbands and boyfriends, but also out to assert their social, economic, and sexual independence; and as women who have broken from traditional norms and etiquettes—brash, cheeky, money-grabbing, and fashion-conscious. This characterisation is not out of place with how Copperbelt women are characterised even today. However, absent from this picture is insight into Copperbelt women's attempts to reconcile and find harmony within a contradictory, changing environment.

COPPERBELT VIEWS ON THE ROOT OF FAMILY AND
MARITAL PROBLEMS

In late 2008, over the course of a supper I hosted in Luanshya for some colleagues, all long-term Copperbelt residents, a debate began about the reasons for disharmony in Zambian marriages. None of the five guests were married at the time, though two of the guests, in their late forties, were widowed.

Initially my guests had argued that the problems in Zambian marriages arose from the expectations and obligations of having to support extended family members.[1] It emerged, though, by general consensus, that the problems that beset urban Zambian marriages—from relationships with relatives, marital infidelity, and money—were not simply as a result of the tensions emerging from the differences between a nuclear model of family and a wider, extended notion of family. Rather, as one guest suggested, urban dwellers were confused in interpreting a customary notion of marriage, what they called "traditional marriage," and a "modern one," represented in the Western ideal of a contractual and monogamous relationship. The argument was that this confusion affected all aspects of life—including relationship aspirations, social expectations and proprieties, interactions, and modes of communication. Giving an example of the problems that may arise from the style adopted to communicate within a marriage, one guest spelt out that within the ideal "traditional marriage," a couple was able to address issues by a deployment of symbols and actions that stemmed from a "cultural education," such as was bestowed through female initiation rites, and consultation with traditional marriage counsellors, otherwise known as *banachimbusa*. In a "modern marriage," by contrast, the proper means of communication involved "explaining yourself" in as direct a manner as possible. The gist of the argument was that in a "proper" traditional marriage, there was a greater reliance on symbols and other non-verbal modes of communication that sought to transmit affect through a bodily material engagement in the environment. This was in contrast to a more direct modern, or "Western," communication style that was more loquacious and direct and tended to abstract from the environment by "overanalysing" what was said. My guests were in general agreement that the root of "the confusion in Zambian marriages" was that both systems were in play, resulting in misinterpretations of what was conveyed.

However, when my guests also said that Zambians "had no culture," that Zambian men did not know whether they wanted a traditional or modern wife, and that "modern-looking women" trapped married men by playing out the role of a "well taught" traditional wife, they indicated the ambiguity, fluidity, and improvisory nature of Copperbelt residents' gendered domestic expectations, actions, and representations. During the course of my research, I found that, in contrast to men, many Copperbelt women did not engage with these two systems as separate, but rather, as Thera Rasing (2001) noted in her research on the Copperbelt in the mid-1990s, saw Western norms as part of a range of repertoires that included social mores associated with tradition (2001, 188). Women experienced social misunderstandings as a dissonance that underlay the tension in straddling what Ferguson (1999) referred to as "streamlined" expectations of domesticity and those conventions that revered compliance to a muted way of being in the environment, particularly in the presence of men or senior women. On the Copperbelt, this meant that women were expected to project "progress" in how they kept their homes and raised their children, and yet at the same time were expected to go out and find a means to get by, but in ways that maintained their respectability as proper traditional wives rather than as "brash modern women."

EXPLORING THE PROBLEMS FROM A THEORETICAL ANGLE

To explore the notion of dissonance in the gendered expectations of domesticity, I draw loosely from Gregory Bateson's conceptual framework for the analysis of human communication. Bateson (1972) noted that human communication involves the use of multiple logical types, both verbal and nonverbal. He lists a selection of the former as play, non-play, fantasy, sacrament, and metaphor; and the latter includes posture, gesture, facial expression, and intonation (1972, 206–207). By logical type, Bateson refers to that which can be abstracted from interaction that is drawn on here as a useful tool for formal analysis. Although Bateson differentiates between the verbal and non-verbal, in practice they are entangled and inseparable, in that fantasy, play, and metaphor can be evoked in bodily gesture, intonation, and posture. In addition, these logical types invoke movement; they are temporal, shifting, and as such, in the analysis of social interaction and in reading or communicating ways of being, what they leave are not fixed readings of a situation but impressions from that interaction or observation. As in musical impressionism, the focus in the analysis of the cases I present in this chapter is not so much on the "clarity in structure" as on the "harmonic effects" or the "tone." This approach lends itself well to the less visible aspects of life. It also allows for a discussion of power as a dissonance in the tone of habitual expectations. This is not to deny the more outwardly visible manifestations of gendered contestations of power, as I have demonstrated in Chapter 4, but I argue that it is not enough to focus on these without also assessing the more hidden aspects of gendered power relations and how they are inscribed and generated within a wider body polity.

An early proponent of identifying and examining the hidden aspects of power in gender relations was Henrietta Moore. In her brilliant study of gendered, spatial, everyday practices amongst the Marakwet in Kenya, Moore draws on the idea of cultural text as a way not simply of looking for meanings in the visible symbols of place and action, but of looking beyond, into people's strategic interpretations or translations of their actions as they go about their everyday lives (1986, 75). As not all that the Marakwet did was easily explainable in words, Moore (1986, 76) drew on Lakoff and Johnson's concept of metaphor as a work of poetic imagination to read into not only what was said but also what was done, for example, how recurring everyday domestic activities come to be inscribed within place and rendered as natural, and thus serving as a way of legitimating gendered and power relations. A metaphor is a logical type that is not literally translatable as such; it is open to multiple meanings and readings. Thus, in Moore's analysis of relations amongst the Marakwet, gender and power were not one thing but were subject to multiple contestations and transformations, not all of which were readily visible.

On the Copperbelt, this invisible realm was also shrouded in the symbolism of female initiation rites that, as the anthropologist Thera Rasing (2001) noted, play an important role for Copperbelt women in the making of respectable womanhood. There is widespread social discourse about the rites and their place in the making of gender relations. That these rites were shrouded in secrecy also allowed Copperbelt residents to make their own interpretations of what was ideal or not in this customary view of womanhood. As a practice stemming from rural life and enacted in what Rasing argues is almost unchanged format, they provide for Copperbelt women a ritualised link to the rural area that allows women better than men to embody the village in the town—and hence customary notions of tradition—while at the same time negotiating their place within the urban as modern women.

Female Initiation Rites and the Making of Womanhood on the Copperbelt

Female initiation rites are a common practice across almost all ethnic groupings in Zambia. They foster the transition to womanhood when a girl reaches puberty, after the start of her first menses. The most well-known study is Audrey Richards's (1956) study of the *chisungu* female initiation rite among the Bemba, a matrilineal group in Northern Zambia who comprised the largest section of mining migrant labour to the Copperbelt at the turn of the twentieth century.[2] Richards's study of the ritual highlight the performative aspects of the making of gender, and the engagement of the body as a discursive site. This drew my attention to bodily gesture and its communication of moral values. Wim van Binsbergen (2003), writing of female initiation rites amongst the Nkoya in central western Zambia, looks to the affective and interactional aspects of the rite, showing that ritual goes beyond the time and space of its enactment. More recently, Thera Rasing's (2001) work[3] on the *chisungu* rites in Mufulira, conducted with mostly Catholic women, shows that these rites, similar in form to those Richards studied almost half a century before, had not died, even in the face of the attempts of early mission Christianity to suppress them, but had endured. Both Richards's (1956) account of the rites in rural Northern Zambia and Rasing's (2001) urban Copperbelt study give excellent descriptive accounts of the *chisungu*, providing their form and function, the way that values and virtues of womanhood are performed and learned through songs, dance, and the symbolisms of the *mbusa*[4] clay models. Through these means, moral insights are passed on. The *chisungu* trainers, known as *banachimbusa*, who, in Rasing's study also identified as Christian, are the female diviners who link the transition to womanhood to a broad African cosmology whose underlying ethos is a generative communitas mediated by powerful women.

Though I did not conduct a survey on how many of my female informants had undergone female initiation rites, discourse on the importance of these rites was common, not just amongst women, but also among men. It is usually couched as a narrative of the "ideal traditional woman." Rasing found that only 4 of her sample of 120 women who had grown up on the Copperbelt in the 1970s had not been initiated (2001, 12). This indicates that female initiation rites may not have been uncommon at the time of my research. In discussions with some of my female informants I found out, as in Rasing's study, that these rites were often carried out during school breaks over a period ranging from a week to a month. Unlike the periods before the worst effects of the economic depression on the Copperbelt, where some young women had been sent to their "villages of origin" to be initiated, more often than not the rites were conducted within the towns and nearby "bush" of the Copperbelt. Women who did not undergo these rites at puberty usually underwent similar training prior to marriage, often tagged to the kitchen party, a kind of bridal shower that I describe later in this chapter.

Chisungu rites are individual, not age-group, coming-of-age ceremonies. At the core of these rites, as evidenced in the narratives of Copperbelt residents, are concerns on the management of sexuality, fertility, and production of food for the household.

The *chisungu* training covered a woman's relations with her in-laws and handling marital problems (for example, being cautioned not to reveal household secrets, which really related to keeping domestic matters private).[5] It covered learning about sexuality, for example, how to please a husband, but also the cosmological danger of sex, for which purifying rites were passed on to the novice. The training also involves significant harshness, in some reported occasions spilling into outright cruelty and abuse.[6] This hardship is intended to serve as a lesson and experience for enduring hardship in life and in marital relationships and is used as "a gauge to check if [a girl is] ready for marriage" (Richards 1956, 123). Indeed, many Copperbelt women refer to marriage as the *shipikisha club*, or "endurance club." Despite the instability of marriage, noted by many anthropological observers of the Copperbelt, there is a Bemba cosmological view of marriage, still relevant today, that mystically linked man and wife by a mutual need to ritually purify each other when either engaged in cosmologically dangerous affairs outside marriage (Richards 1956, 34).[7]

The *chisungu* rite does not serve as a ritual through which to learn womanhood per se. The process of knowing gendered ways of being starts, as Richards observed, from the time that a girl is very young, for example, helping out in childcare, in the kitchen, and in the garden. Richards (1956) noted that the training in the *chisungu* ritual involved learning a secret language that drew on song, dance, and *mbusa* clay models. This training was not, she argued, discursive (1956, 127). Both Richards (1956) and Rasing (2001) observed that novices spend much of the time sitting and looking downwards, dancing, and singing. Both scholars concluded that the learning was not instructive or directive but drew more from metaphorical evocation. René Devisch writes that "metaphoric production in ritual breaks away from linguistic ones which impose a hierarchy between body, senses, and cognition and thereby limit the capacity to generate meaning and empowerment in ritual practice to coding and communication" (1993, 43). In this way the rite, as a process of metaphoric evocation, works not as a "text, a predication, or an expose, but, primarily as showing, spelling out something by displaying its ingredients or motto" (1993, 43). I suggest that this is precisely how the *chisungu* ceremony plays a role in the making of womanhood.

In bodily comportment, such as being still or undertaking activities that require the novice to jump and use parts of the body such as the mouth to carry out various tasks (like digging and planting seeds, moving on one's back, hanging from a house post, dancing and singing and being shown *mbusa* models), the *chisungu* rites urge a tuning into the multisensory realm of the body. Henrietta Moore, in her re-analysis of Richards's account, draws attention to the way in which the "bodily praxis of the initiation rite literally incorporates its moral teachings" (1999, 12).[8] In these performances I would argue (as does Devisch for the gynaecological healing cults amongst the Yaka in Congo), "Ritual encourages the senses, emotions, and *habitus* to be very active . . . informing the participants [as] to what is going on in an endeavour in which physical, social, ethical, and spiritual [dimensions] are interactive and weakly demarcated" (1993, 43).

This indicates that the meaning of the rites resonates beyond the bounds of praxis. For example, an important ethos of the *chisungu* rite is respect, or *umuchinshi*, as a basis for fostering both kin and wider community relations. In Devisch's view of ritual, the communication of respect not only would be a dramaturgical expression of the social order and norms, in which actors behave as mere vehicles for their transmission, but also would be generative of other forms of meaning-making and life transmission. Devisch notes that Turner's seminal account of ritual excludes "bodiliness, senses, and emotions" and cosmology (1993, 252).

UMUCHINSHI ("RESPECT"): THE ETHOS OF GENDERED PROPRIETIES ON THE COPPERBELT

A woman was expected to conduct and carry herself with *umuchinshi*. A woman who carried herself with respect was one who gave respect to her elders, both women and men. *Umuchinshi* was shown in various ways: in the way you greeted your elders, for example, kneeling to the floor or a slight curtsy if standing; not interrupting or intruding when older people were speaking, and only speaking when invited to do so; bearing gifts to share when visiting extended kin as acknowledgment of reciprocal relationships; sharing food; and observing the rules of avoidance with regards to in-laws. Showing deference in the company of elders or social betters was extremely important, often communicated in bodily gesture by looking downwards, with slightly hunched shoulders and speaking in a tone that was loud enough to be heard, but not too loud as to sound authoritative.

Even though this was considered the appropriate way for a woman to conduct herself, as I write in the next section, I was aware that I too embodied multiple ways of being, both consciously and unconsciously. These were entangled in both the visible and the invisible aspects of social and material interactions, an awareness I needed in order to be competent and not misinterpret social situations in which I found myself.

Umuchinshi in a Social Situation

In November 2008 Jane, a close female work colleague from the Copperbelt University, and I were invited by one of our workmates, Peter, to join him on a visit to Ndola see a female friend of his, Margaret, whom he held in high esteem. He explained to us that Margaret was a high-ranking civil servant and a widow about a decade older than Jane and I. Peter and Margaret had been friends from their university days in the late 1980s. Peter had invited Jane and me because he thought Margaret, who was a bit socially isolated because of her job, would benefit from having new friends, and he thought we would gain in having a female mentor to offer us, in his words, "broader perspectives on life." So off we went to Ndola to see Margaret. This visit was illuminating to Jane and me as it highlighted the gendered nuances of social interaction and communication in urban Zambia.

When we arrived at Margaret's home in a plush suburb of Ndola close to lunchtime, we found Margaret having her hair braided in the company of a group from her church that she met with occasionally for prayers. This was a little perplexing because from the many effusive things Peter had said about Margaret, I did not get the impression that she was an overly religious person.[9] After Peter greeted Margaret with a friendly embrace and proceeded to introduce us, Jane and I were a little unsure of how to greet her. If we had to draw on the cues provided by Peter, an informal handshake would have been fine. However, the fact that she proceeded to sit down after she had hugged Peter meant that this would not be possible, and in fact signalled that she expected a "traditional" greeting that required our getting on our knees to shake her hand. This we did, and thus it communicated that we acknowledged her social standing, both as an older woman and a high-ranking civil servant.[10] She appeared pleased with this, because she went on to jokingly ask Peter where he had acquired two beautiful girlfriends, and whether she should be jealous. At this, Peter had laughed, and said he brought her two younger sisters. During this interplay, Jane and I did not laugh, as this would have showed too much familiarity,[11] but nonetheless, despite feeling slightly discomforted, we sat down after greeting the members of her church prayer group. After making small conversation in which Margaret asked us about our work at the university and our social lives, we left after it became apparent to Peter that we would not be invited for lunch, as he had expected. Margaret, though, did invite us to her place again for dinner, as long as we prepared it. By asking us to prepare the meal for which we were invited as guests, Margaret was indicating her acceptance of us within a "traditional" family-like setting, of which we would be incorporated as "younger sisters," and, in a show of respect to her age and seniority, we would be expected to serve her.

A week later, we were at her place, preparing a meal for a dinner party that comprised Margaret, Peter, Jane, me, and three other guests. As is often the custom in Zambia when formally entertaining guests, there were numerous dishes to prepare; three meat dishes of beef, chicken, and fish; a variety of vegetables; and nshima, rice, and potatoes. We also made a dessert—not usually requisite for meals in Zambia. The preparation overall is lengthy and labour-intensive because even in upper-middle-class homes such as Margaret's people tend not to buy pre-cut, ready-to-cook ingredients. Thus, Jane and I spent the evening cooking, serving drinks, and cleaning up afterwards, as well as being guests.

The experience was not unusual to either Jane or me, who then, as single, childless women, often found ourselves taking up this role at large family gatherings. While in the post-mortem of the dinner we were critical of having to play a similar role, commenting ironically that we had been "badly" taught—though some would say "well taught"—on how to behave, we were also aware that by tasking us with preparing the meal Margaret was signalling her acceptance of us into her home. By serving Margaret, Jane and I had acknowledged Margaret's social status and thus shown her respect.[12] As Richards noted, Jane and I as younger women were expected to accept the dominance of older women (1956, 48). However, our subsequent interactions with Margaret were varied, and there were more social occasions when we did not need to work serving her and we were treated more or less as equals.

Despite having a general sense of "knowing" that was attuned to gender, age, and status, was subtle, and called for careful attention to almost invisible cues of what to do or what was expected, I found myself on several occasions out of step, reading some social interactions wrongly or being misunderstood. As in Bateson's schizophrenic bind, it was not always clear how one was meant to behave, and I was sometimes blind to the social cues or failed to interpret them correctly. While at times this being out of step was a result of a deliberate attempt to assert some kind of autonomy in refusing to behave as expected in terms of idealised traditional mores, at other times it was as a result of another type of habituation that stemmed from the other rules of social interaction and comportment I had learnt from the ZCCM-run primary school I had attended, which had, in the 1980s, been staffed by a large expatriate British staff. At school, looking down when being addressed by someone in authority was considered rude, as was not explaining oneself when asked to explain. In contrast, in interactions with family and family friends, one looked downwards when being addressed by an elder, and questions as to why one had done a particular thing were often rhetorical: one was not expected to respond. Socialisation and learning about the world outside a formal educational setting was much as Devisch described amongst the Yaka: listening as a form of attentiveness, a way to tune in to the broader meanings of what was said.

In general, women more than men were expected to embody a more "traditional" habituation; at the same time some men expected their friends, lovers, wives, and/or mistresses to project what was perceived as a more progressive modern outlook, either in appearance or in manners. In the playing out of such expectations, misunderstandings were easy. For example, an interaction where a woman looked straight into the face of a man she was talking to could be misread as bold, and she could be subject to unwanted attentions; on the other hand, a downward glance could be perceived as coquettish.

It was in the analysis of situations such as these that the Manchester school adopted situational analysis to explore Copperbelt identities in a social setting that was considered to be rapidly changing from rural to urban. Members of the school came to the conclusion that Copperbelt residents enacted both rural and urban identities,[13] dependant on social context. It was and still is a useful framework for looking at identities, in this case gendered ones. However, a Batesonian perspective on communication may also illuminate the misinterpretations that may arise out of multiple modes of communication, such as that set out in the example above in how a woman's comportment may be misunderstood. Second, if we draw from René Devisch's notion of borderlinking,[14] the emotions of protagonists may not be readily visible in the gendered performances of daily interaction and tasks. For example, despite Jane's and my genuine desire to make a new friend, we were also

mildly resentful of having to adopt a subservient role. However, our habituation to this role meant that we took it up without breaking step, thus not
disrespecting Margaret, who expected to be served as an older woman. In
this way, all of us were connected to a body politic that was not only based
on an ideal of appropriate behaviour but one that resonated with feelings of
resentment, pleasure, shame, and other emotions arising out of various interactions. This is reflected in the subtle cues of bodily comportment, where
even the person performing an approximation of a bodily gesture of respect,
for example, kneeling, can still offer clues to having feelings of resentment,
either by exaggeration, feigning the movement slightly, or a number of other
subtle cues that too may be open to misreading.

Thus, a woman who did not "carry herself" with respect would be referred
to as having no shame.[15] For example, in disciplining young persons, an adult
might ask, *taunfwile insoni?* ("Haven't you felt shame?"). Just as when Copperbelt residents say *sebanya wikute* ("Get embarrassed but get full"—see
Chapter 4), the shame of subverting moralities in order to get by and survive,
shame as a painful feeling of humiliation and distress and as a loss of respect
and honour, becomes not only emotive but also bodily. Similarly, behaviours
like extramarital affairs, excessive drinking, not observing respectful in-law
avoidance, and symbolic seclusion for menstruating women[16] are not only
seen as shameful and disrespectful but, as I mentioned earlier, but are also
seen as polluting and dangerous in that they can cause illness and even death
to innocent parties who are part of this cosmological view of communitas.

Thus, the desire or aspiration for the respectable traditional wife in popular Zambian discourse should be seen not only as a somewhat chauvinist discourse critical of modernity, but as one that also goes beyond this surface to
indicate the experiential and existentialist struggle to reconcile ways of being
and behaving that are locally understood as modern or traditional.

REFLECTIONS OF MODERNITY AND TRADITION IN IDEAS OF
MARRIAGE IN ZAMBIAN MEDIA

To reflect on the gendered narratives of modern and traditional ideas of marriage in the popular realm, I present extracts from articles from the Zambian media. These stories provide some insight into how the narrators use
examples and metaphors from the material and embodied expectations of

womanhood to criticise what they see as modernity's erosion of traditional values. While largely based on a nostalgic view of the "village" or "tradition," they nonetheless reflect, as shall be seen in the cases presented later on, contemporary practices and preoccupations such as class and global inequities.

One story, titled "Trouble in the Womb," by The Journey Man, a popular columnist for the *Zambian Post* newspapers, published 1 March 2012, reflects on the abuse and rape of the maternal figure, a powerful symbol in the cosmologies of many Zambian groups. As a generative figure, the maternal figure embodies and encompasses both male and female genders. In the story, the author writes of how a midwife, traditionally a role undertaken by *banachimbusa*, urges a mother-to-be (presented as mother nature Zambia and with the desired characteristics of a generative, sharing, and interlinking being) in the throes of a long and painful labour to reveal the truth of who is responsible for her pregnancy. In the story, the mother, who has escaped from her local but abusive husband with whom she had numerous pregnancies all of which had resulted in stillbirths (indicating that he or she had been unfaithful and had thus brought misfortune on the innocent lives of the babies), seeks liberation by courting foreign outsiders, who then betray her trust by raping her. The rape results in a pregnancy and difficult labour. The pregnancy's genesis raises for the mother and midwife the anxiety that she may give birth to a monster.

This story is a betrayal of the maternal figure by the state that dishonours it by denying the reciprocal and convivial values it embodies, and allows an indolent and abusive masculinist view to pervade. The maternal figure turns to the outsider and instead encounters the rapacious entry of capital that pillages its fruits and from this interaction potentially spawns a monster. As a reflection of power relations, the story hints at the erosion of feminine "power" embodied in the powerful figure of the maternal within a modern context. It also reflects the importance of fertility and children, for many Zambians a hallmark of adulthood and the gaining of societal respect. Thus, even though there is a preoccupation with sexual mores in discourses of respectability, fertility and children may afford respect even to those considered to have behaved immorally.

Another story by the same author, titled "Modernity" and published 4 October 2012, reflects on the "demon" that possesses the village girl he married and loved. It changes not only her outward appearance and behaviour, but also, he fears, his own moral outlook on the world.

She was from the village. Many had told me not to marry this woman but you see, when you are in love, the ears fail. I followed my heart and married her anyway.

The early days of our marriage were blissful. Now things are different. I don't know what demon now possesses my wife. . . .

. . . She used to cook me *munkwani*, *bonongwe* and *gwada* but now she says these dishes are for the poor, beneath her. She had nothing when I first met her. She was only a village woman with little education and no material possessions. Now she laughs at the poor. I am surprised.

She had this captivating dark skin, without a blemish. Her skin was the colour of the finest clay. Her hair was shiny black. Sometimes she would tie it in fascinating and alluring knots of the *mukule* kind. . . .

. . . She bleaches her skin now. She has an orange face, like a ghostly character in an Alfred Hitchcock movie. Now she also has long and artificial eyelashes. Her face now scares me. She calls this look modern. I call it lost. . . .

. . . When I first found our maid in our bedroom making the bed I chased her. This action on my part led to my being severely chastised by my wife.

She defended the maid. She said that she couldn't keep the house by herself, that she needed the help of the maid. I wonder whether she was really listening to herself when she said those words.

Does she know just how ambiguous she sounded when she said that she needed the maid to help her? So now, for fear of annoying my wife, the maid enters and leaves our bedroom as if she was a licensed occupant of that room.

When male visitors come to our home these days, my wife no longer genuflects as she greets them. She even shakes their hands instead of merely cupping them from a distance.

Sometimes, she comes to the sitting room to chat with them, wearing only a pair of shorts or a mini-skirt. When I tell her to cover her bare legs with a *chitenje*, she accuses me of morbid jealousy. One day I even caught one of my friends looking up her legs leeringly.

I couldn't blame him but my heart badly hurt. It reflected very poorly on me, I achingly thought.

These days I catch myself looking at the maid in a strange way. When doing this, I have dirty thoughts on my mind. I worry about this. Now I see that my maid has buttocks. I had never seen them before. My wife has changed. I fear that now she is changing me.

Instead of dressing for me, she now dresses for work.

Maybe I am really old-fashioned, a cultural dinosaur. But then, when a way of life is beneficial, should one abandon it, pilgrim? I refuse to adopt ways that are alien to me, ways that could endanger my very survival and prosperity. Or should I?"

Discussions of whether to adopt ways of being that are associated with the modern or the traditional pole are like the debate with my dinner guests taken to public forums. For example, the popular radio station Radio Phoenix spurred an online debate on the similar topic by posting an image by the Kenyan cartoonist Stanislaus Olonde aka Stano on its Facebook page on 11 March 2013 (see Figure 6) and asking followers whether the picture presented a "true reflection of *Mayadi* wife vs. *Komboni* wife" (wife from the yards, or low-density suburb, and wife from the compound, or high-density suburb), or, as Ferguson categorises it, the cosmopolitan or localist. These categories on the Copperbelt reflected virtuality in imaginings of place, where the *Mayadi* pointed to the modern and urban and the *Komboni* to the traditional and rural.

The image and the question elicited various responses, but several writers pointed out that the representations in the image did not reflect domicile or area of origin, but indicated whether or not the woman embodied customary traditional values.

Female commenting: "First picture shows a couple that got together with total disregard for traditional pre-marital counselling and guidance. The second picture shows you a very lucky guy who married well. Have seen real life examples of both cases and problem was not domicile but content of heart and mind, especially of the woman since she is by tradition and by biological design the homemaker."

Male commenting: "Its neither *mayadi* nor *komboni*, think it's about being cultured and showing respect to a husband."

Other comments reflected the social expectations that women should be hard-working.

Female commenting: "Nope . . . These days so called '*mayadi*' or 'polished wife' is very busy working and has no time to lay around in the sofa reading a mag just waiting for the man to come home with the bucks and waiting to 'take off his shoes!'"

Figure 6. *Mayadi* wife versus *Komboni* wife. Illustration by Stanislaus Olonde "Stano," October 2020. An earlier version was sourced from Radio Phoenix.

Male commenting: "It all depends on the status of the *mayadi* wife, if she also works then its normal but if she stays home the whole day watching movies and magazines then she is a problem. The *komboni* wife is doing the right thing coz she was home the whole day."

Yet others commenting on the post debated on which representation reflected the caring spouse.

Male commenting: "This is a serious misrepresentation. . . . Are we trying to say the those in '*Mayadi*' are more caring than those in '*Kombonis*' or the opposite; this is pure NEGATIVE in all senses."

Female commenting: "If the opposite were true for the *mayadi* arrangement, would anyone care? I think the tendency for men is to demand to be taken care of when they don't make an effort to show even better care for their partners."

A female writer took umbrage over the untidiness of the localist wife, whom she also saw as signifying exploitation, writing that the "second picture shows how a wife is supposed to be, but should keep herself clean not look like a slave."

At the same time that women were expected show *umuchinshi*, which both men and women also associated with a showing of care and also as a comportment to show respect for oneself, they were also expected to project an air of worldliness that was becoming, especially to men who wanted to project themselves as modern or cosmopolitan. This may have meant dressing in a way that was considered stylish and within reason, being able to contribute and give an opinion in conversation. Men also desired that women contribute a livelihood to the home, but as I show in the cases presented, this aspiration was also tempered with a tendency to inhibit women's activities that fostered this economic independence. In my observations of interactions and ways of being on the Copperbelt, and also in my own actions, I realised that people's repertoires of being were variable and nuanced and that they fluctuated. Neither men nor women were fully versed in their perceptions of how they were expected to be. In addition, the expectation of what they wanted a partner to convey in various interactions, or how they expected them to behave, was at times fuzzy, and occasionally went against what they vocalised. All these interactions played out as Copperbelt residents sought places of pleasure and harmony, and while women in particular also tried to maintain social proprieties.

WOMEN'S LEISURE ON THE COPPERBELT

When a young woman who had moved from the capital city, Lusaka, to the Copperbelt asked me, "What do young Copperbelt women do for fun?" I was initially at a loss. What did they do indeed for leisure?

I realised in my everyday encounters with women on the Copperbelt that their predominant realms of amusement were embedded in the tasks they engaged in daily. Play as a pleasure-seeking activity was to be found where women sat in the yards, or by the side of a stall getting their hair braided, or as they walked in the companionship of their friends to buy some tomatoes or visited each other's homes. Through this I realised that play for many women meandered along with the many other activities they engaged in.

The kitchen party, however, is the social event that women young and old

Figure 7. Two women wait for service at a small front-yard store made from off-cut timber and covered in tarpaulin. The store sells tomatoes, bread, and candy and advertises a hair salon. Photo by Mulemwa Mususa, December 2008.

turn up at expressly to have fun. Mainly held on weekends, it is a space where men are, for the most part, excluded, although of late it has become a trend for the prospective groom to arrive with a bouquet for his bride-to-be. The kitchen party was modelled on an abridged version of a traditional marriage ceremony and a Western bridal shower. It is a pre-wedding event, which in many ways is considered more important that the wedding itself, even by the potential groom, as it provides the couple with starter household items. The kitchen party is the highlight of many women's social occasions; it allows them to wear fine clothes and interact unfettered by the presence of men, where in other mixed social situations women are expected to show decorum in their comportment and interactions.

Wedding gifts are often presented to a marrying couple at kitchen parties. These are usually arranged in a pile in full view of all the guests, or, as has become common, they are displayed as in a store, with gifts from the family and friends of the bride on the left, and those from the groom's family and friends on the right. There are several features of the celebratory finale of the Bemba female initiation rites in the kitchen party, such as dancing to traditional drumming and the immobility of the bride-to-be (who sits through the entire party on a mat looking downwards and sometimes covered in a blanket). Gifts, ranging from cooking sticks and pestles to electrical appliances like irons and sometimes refrigerators, are presented to the bride-to-be, as are instructions on when and how to use them. These presentations are often playful, sometimes accompanied by bawdy jokes and dancing. At these parties, women drink alcohol freely, and even at the Christian parties, where alcohol is not served, some guests nevertheless smuggle alcohol in their handbags. Buffet food is also served. Much store is given to the marital counsellor and the drummers, who are usually female and are paid in cash, alcohol, and cloth. The success of a party is often judged by the amount of alcohol and the atmosphere created by the drummers and the "matron," an older woman usually with extensive social networks and some status within her family and community.

For many women, being able to attend a kitchen party requires having means to provide a gift. Being able to attend these parties regularly also means that women need to have some access to an independent income. As the majority of the Copperbelt women I interviewed struggled to make ends meet, many of those who formed part of a regular kitchen party circuit turned up to these events with gifts from their own kitchen parties or those of their daughters or other female relatives. For family members and close friends to the bride-to-be, the pressure on their pockets was even greater because they were also required to contribute a sum to the hosting of the party that would go towards hiring of the marital counsellor and the drummers, and paying for food and drinks. The agreement to contribute to the kitchen party was often elicited as a pledge during the numerous preparation meetings, which also provided women another opportunity to socialise.

Kitchen parties not only offered women a liberating space for fun, but were also valuable as a place to network and expand their business opportunities. As a number of women on the Copperbelt were involved in trade, for example selling clothes and other items bought from China, Dubai, South Africa, and Tanzania, they needed a broad customer base to which they could sell these items. As many of these goods were paid for in monthly instalments, they needed to understand who was connected to whom in chasing up their payments. Women who were unable to attend kitchen parties were also thus denied the potential to grow their businesses. Amongst my informants, one such case was Susan, Mr Mubita's wife.

Mrs Susan Mubita: A Woman Whose Husband Stops Her from Attending Kitchen Parties

Susan and Mr. Mubita married in 2003 in what Susan described as a simple wedding ceremony. *Lobola* (bridewealth) was paid to her family. Before meeting Mr Mubita, who had been divorced for several years, Susan, who was born in the early 1980s, had worked as a dressmaker in Roan Township, a high-density former mine suburb. There she had a reasonable number of clients till she moved briefly to Kitwe in 2003 to stay with an "aunt," really a former neighbour. In that same year, the "aunt" said she knew someone who wanted to marry Susan, and introduced her to Mr. Mubita. There had been no kitchen party for Susan because neither Mr Mubita nor her family then could afford it. Susan seemed disbelieving, implying that Mr Mubita could have helped her fund the kitchen party as they met shortly after he had received his retrenchment benefits. Mr Mubita, however, used his benefits to pay for the college education of the two children from his first marriage and to set up the business enterprises I have described in Chapter 3.

Susan was sceptical of Mr Mubita's self-employment activities. The problem, she said, was that Mr Mubita "wants to do things himself. He survives through hard work." She felt he would have no problems finding a job given the new copper boom, but said that "he refuses to work," adding, "Life is very difficult my sister, especially as a mother of two." Mr Mubita himself was keen to be self-sufficient. In one interview, he vocalised what he saw as Susan's lack of support for his activities and compared Susan to his first wife, who "was very industrious. She was a businesswoman, she baked cakes, scones, etc., which she sold to people. She learnt to bake from the sisters."[17]

During visits to their place, I had observed that Susan appeared to take little interest in Mr Mubita's business activities and seemed to spend a lot of time indoors with their baby, unlike other women in the area I had interacted with, who, even with small children, spent a lot of time outdoors, where they could interact with passing neighbours or go visiting the homes of their friends and neighbours. On the occasions that I saw her alone attending to the little store Mr Mubita run in his front yard, I heard her tell customers to come back later, as she did not know the prices of some of the items. On one occasion, I met her running along the road looking very distressed because the shop had been robbed while she was indoors changing the baby's nappy. Susan's distress and her lack of knowledge of the pricing of items in the store suggested the control Mr Mubita exerted over their household finances.

Mr Mubita's views on the management of household finances were also illuminated in a conversation I had with him on the benefits systems of the mines. According to Mr. Mubita, following the privatisation of the mines, benefits and other amenities "started fading." According to him, the removal of a benefit that caused the biggest protest was that of the child allowance. "Women and children protested that they wanted it to remain fixed. Sometimes children would abuse the parents when they were not given the money, saying it was theirs and so certain parents, especially us men, were happy it was withdrawn." He said that wives did not get any money directly from the mines but were entitled to use mine facilities such as the hospitals and recreation facilities. However, Mr Mubita also described situations where women were entitled to collect their husband's pay cheques, saying, "What would happen is that the wife would approach the welfare section and log in a complaint explaining the problem, and if they were convinced, they would get her details, and during the payday, the wife would go and get the pay cheque and the money. The husband would not be given the money, no matter his protests." According to Mr Mubita, some men had voluntarily asked their wives to collect their monthly pay, but this was uncommon. This tallied with what was frequently recounted by my female informants, who complained that their husbands allowed them little access to their earnings.

Susan did not make her own money. She claimed that clients for her dressmaking business had dried up when she had moved to the low-density former mine suburb to live with Mr Mubita. She put this down to a class difference: "The people here are different; they like expensive wear, so they go into town." This could not have been the only reason, though, because there were other reasonably successful dressmakers in the area, mainly doing alterations on second-hand clothes bought from the town's markets, which were also patronised by those who lived in Roan Township. Second-hand clothes were generally cheaper than buying fabric and making a new item (see Hansen 2000). The main reason seemed to be her social isolation.

Susan's contact with her former friends, most of whom lived near her parents in Roan Township had dwindled over the years. She attributed this to her having cut back visits to her parents because one can't go with "bare hands"[18] and "Mr. Mubita wants me to stay home." Once I found her despondent at her home because Mr. Mubita had refused to give her money to attend a kitchen party. She needed ZMK 120,000 (about US$24) to attend. On this occasion, she mused about her options for an independent income from something like trade, but discarded the idea, noting that the women she knew who were running their own businesses, such as stores selling second-hand clothes, or doing *makwebo* (cross-border trade) with places as far away as Dubai and China all had start-up capital, and she did not have any. Susan observed that such business was risky because people would buy goods on credit but then fail to pay.

Attending kitchen parties could have extended Susan's opportunities. In some cross-trading business activity, groups of women would pool resources to have one of their friends travel to buy goods and thus save on travel expenses. It also allowed a lower threshold of entry into a business. In addition, as one woman cynically pointed out to me, having a younger woman such as Susan in a *makwebo* group was also helpful because in freight and customs negotiations the men who normally facilitated these processes tended to be more amenable to helping a young, attractive woman than an older one. It was notions and ideas about such interactions, where young women might be egged on by others, that made men uneasy about not only *makwebo* but also kitchen parties. Both activities were unpopular with men because of the perception that they encouraged women to "behave badly."

Though many women, both married and single, socialised as well as engaged in business activities largely separately from men's sphere, men as well as women were concerned with the proprieties of these activities and how they appeared to others. In these spheres, marriage offered respectability, whereas single women were often the subjects of rumours concerning their sexual and moral conduct. Situations such as Susan's were what influenced older women to keep some of their earnings hidden from their husbands.

WOMEN KEEPING ECONOMIC SECRETS

On 5 July 2005, the BBC 2 series *Africa Lives* broadcast a documentary called *The Real No.1 Ladies Detective Agency*, based on a private detective agency in Lusaka that employed mainly female investigators. One of the cases pursued by the investigators was that of a female teacher who was suspected by her husband of having an affair. It turned out that the woman was instead setting up a small business without her husband's knowledge. According to "our culture," the male head of the agency said, this was tantamount to adultery.

While conducting fieldwork in Luanshya, I learned that most of my female informants were keeping economic secrets from their husbands. Those who weren't were perceived by their female counterparts to be foolish. It was thought that their openness would only result in disappointment or, more pointedly, disenchantment with their husband's ability to look after their children. Women, especially older ones, urged those women inclined to share everything with their husband to keep something away for a rainy day. Women's economic affairs, especially when they were running an independent business, were a source of great domestic strife on the Copperbelt. I was told that if men were aware that their wives had money, they would pressure them to part with it. The Domestic Health Survey of 2007 indicated, for instance, that women who were working and paid in cash were more likely to experience physical abuse (2007, 276). Some NGO projects, such as the Lusaka Peri-Urban Slum Upgrading project, supported by CARE International, had, in recognition of these problems, even designed mechanisms to ensure that women involved in slum-upgrading activities would not be paid in cash but in food parcels to prevent men from diverting from the household what women earned.

Women were anxious, too, to hide their earnings from their husband's relatives. In the largely matrilineal groups in Zambia, the husband's matrilineal relatives' children, in particular a man's eldest sister's,[19] customarily had claim on their uncle's property. As a result, as Hansen noted in her research on urban households in informal settlements in Lusaka, when a woman's husband died, it was not uncommon to have his relatives descend upon the household and grab everything (1997, 97). The Zambian Intestate Act of 1989, which was put in place to ensure that a widow and her children were not left destitute and which allowed them to sue property-grabbing relatives, did not prevent the continuation of this practice (Hansen 1997, 97). The act, implemented in the absence of a will, apportioned the deceased person's property roughly as follows: 20% for a surviving spouse or, in the case of polygyny, shared between spouses; 50% to children (both legitimate and illegitimate) apportioned according to their educational needs; 20% to the deceased's parents; and 10% to other dependants. As I found in my fieldwork in Luanshya, deceased husband's relatives found creative ways in which to use the Intestate Act to assert what they viewed as rightful inheritance within the matrilineal system, and even people charged with helping widows understand the act, such as legal aid counsellors, used it for personal gain. As I sat in the office of one of these legal aid counsellors, a Mr Bwalya, I heard him persuade a widow whose husband had left nothing but the house that had been part of his retrenchment package to sell it in order to give a share of the proceeds to the deceased man's relatives, even though the sale would have left the woman and her children homeless. Mr Bwalya allayed her fears of homelessness by telling her that he had on his books a property in a high-density neighbourhood that she could buy from the proceeds of the sale of the family house. Mr Bwalya ran from his legal aid office a brisk real estate business. When I interviewed Mr Bwalya later, he argued that the Intestate Act was unfair because it disrespected the "culture of the people" and the "Zambian extended family." Mr Bwalya also thought it dangerous for the widow and the children not to respect this "culture" because of retribution relatives may mete out. While Mr Bwalya did not mention fear of witchcraft, one woman, the widow of a former mineworker who was renting a one-room servants' quarters in the low-density suburb in which she had once owned a home, told me she had given up the family home for fear of her children being bewitched by her late husband's relatives.

It was not only during the period following the death of a spouse that relatives interfered in matters of household property. Mrs Mwenya, introduced in Chapter 2 as a young woman who with her husband had tried to set up an oil-processing business, informed me that her husband's relatives had been very upset when they found out that he had bought her a car. According to Mrs Mwenya, it was such a serious matter that the relatives convened a family meeting where her husband had been advised that buying such big gifts for his wife would make her proud and unmanageable. Mrs Mwenya was of the opinion that her husband's relatives were concerned that "he loved her too much," that "he would do anything for her," and that because of this, they could not control him.

Mrs Mwenya husband's relatives' worry that she would become proud indicated a concern with the decline of the extended family, the subject of an ongoing debate among Copperbelt residents. Though many people had long supported their relatives even under great financial stress, the loss of men's formal jobs meant that few could divert incomes to their relatives as they did before. The fact that following the massive layoffs in the mine many women had unofficially become the breadwinners in their households meant that they could have a greater say whether they supported extended family members. As one woman who ran a successful backyard poultry business put it, "For many years I looked after my husband's family. They would come here and even say bad things about me. I kept quiet. My husband would give them money then fail to buy clothes for the children. Now he has no money, so I tell him that if they want to come and stay here, they must work." With increasing economic independence, some women were able to have a greater say in matters of the household—though at some social cost, with the risk of being called fast or having their husband "under petticoat government," as one informant told me, using a Victorian phrase that speaks to colonial influences on the Copperbelt.

Mrs Phiri: A Woman Whose Husband Is under Petticoat Government

Mrs Phiri, introduced in Chapter 4, was accused of Satanism by neighbours in Luanshya due to the relative success she and her husband enjoyed. She, much more than her husband, was the visible head of their household. A successful business person, as her husband was ready to admit, she had been key to helping her family weather the worst of the town's economic crisis. She managed—with the help of her husband, their children, and the occasional extended family members—a diverse portfolio of small investments, including a landscaping business, trade in hardware and household goods, transport and grain marketing, and foreign currency trading. In my interactions with the Phiris they appeared to me to have a solid and happy marriage. However, several neighbours spread gossip that Mrs Phiri was "fast" and that her husband, a mild-mannered man, feared confronting her over her supposed infidelities because he was "under a petticoat government," implying that he had failed to control his wife.

That Mrs Phiri had significant say in the household affairs was clear, and Mr Phiri was unstinting in his admiration of how his wife ran their business and household. Mrs Phiri appeared to hold, at least within the spheres of her home, a comfortable reconciliation of the traditional values of *umuchinshi* and the values of a Christian marriage, in speaking of love and the need to respect the head of the household. She was active in a Catholic women's church group and emphasised the values of a Christian marriage and family life, ensuring that her daughters participated in the lay activities of the church. Mrs Phiri also frequently attended kitchen parties and was a popular matron to host these parties.

Despite the good relationship Mrs Phiri appeared to share with her husband, she was adamant that men should not have full knowledge of how a woman kept her books. If men knew how much women were earning, they would not take their responsibilities seriously and would be tempted to "squander" the income. Mrs Phiri conspiratorially told me that even though Mr Phiri was a good man, she did not tell him all her earnings, pointing out that it was easy to hide what she was making, especially her foreign exchange earnings, because "the dollar is always changing."

Mrs Phiri considered Mr Phiri a soft touch with regard to his relatives. One afternoon I noticed that Frances, the Phiris' eleven-year-old nephew, was not around. He had been a visible feature of their home, washing dishes, feeding the chickens, and running small errands. The orphaned son of Mr Phiri's late sister, he was brought to live with the Phiris to provide him with a better education in the town, after having stayed with another relative in a rural area in Eastern Province. When I asked after Frances, Mrs Phiri told me that she sent him to the "village" to live with another of Mr Phiri's sisters because he had been "lazy," wanting to play after school rather than do household chores. There, she said, "He would learn real work." When I responded that it was unsurprising that he wanted to play, as he was young, she justified her actions by saying that times had changed and no one could expect to "stay for free," as there were no free services being offered any longer. Mrs Phiri's actions reflected a general mood, giving rise to what was perceived as the breakdown of convivial extended family relations. The increasing domestication of business enterprise added to the exploitation of unpaid kin, increasingly without recourse to other areas of reciprocity, such as clothes and occasional gifts of money. This, as I point out in Chapter 6, contributed to young persons' taking up risky modes of livelihood.

While envy may have played a part in gossip that circulated about Mrs Phiri, part of her notoriety stemmed from her business activities, which required her to network beyond the kitchen parties she attended and hosted and her church's women's group. Mrs Phiri herself was aware of how these interactions appeared to others. For example, I met her once in the town's small centre talking to a young man who helped her sell and buy foreign currency to workers in a mining camp in the Democratic Republic of Congo, just over the border from the Copperbelt town Mufulira. Mrs Phiri introduced him to me as her business colleague, her manner warm and affectionate towards him, noting that he helped her get the best foreign currency rates. Later Mrs Phiri used the example of the young man to highlight how people in the town were very concerned about appearances and tended to misread social situations. She said, "People here like to see what they like to see, so the way you saw me greeting that boy, someone else would have said, that is Mrs Phiri's boyfriend. People like to think bad things of others. You see the way Mr Phiri drops Ida off by her place and gives her a hug. She is my best friend, and we have known each other for a long time. I trust her. But people would say, 'Mr Phiri is always at Ida's place,' even if I am the one who tells him to take her there."

Mrs Phiri was also highlighting the general suspicions that were rife in relationships between men and women, which she blamed squarely on men's poor behaviour and the failure of women to mould the men into what they wanted. She commented,

> When I started seeing Mr Phiri, the first time I went to visit him he did not pick me up from the station. When I saw him, I cried. I said to him, "How can I know you love me if you are not even there to meet me the first time I come to see you?" I want to be loved. I told him that if I am not loved, I could die.

Mrs Phiri explained that women failed to have happy relationships because they had not learnt from their parents good ways to live together as a man and wife. She also laid blame at the feet of traditional educators, *banachimbusa*, who prepared women for marriage. They urged women not to voice their displeasure at their husbands' misdemeanours, encouraging a stoicism that had no place in a society where women's rights were respected.[20]

Despite Mrs Phiri's criticism of the *banachimbusa*'s training, her own daughters, who were also staunch Catholics, had undergone the traditional initiation rites. I heard her tell one of her friends, who was unsure whether to have her daughter initiated, that it would be wise for her to do so. Otherwise her daughter might fail to marry or "hold" a marriage. What Mrs Phiri was pointing out was that in a social context as dynamic and fluid as the Copperbelt, a woman could not rely on meeting a man who did not uphold customary notions of domesticity. It was not only the expectations of men that Mrs Phiri was concerned about with regard to the marital options of her daughters, but what kind of reception they would receive from their in-laws. She was worried that an uninitiated daughter-in-law would attract ridicule from her new relatives, and possible mistreatment at their hands. Similar concerns, as well as the unclear expectations of men, are illuminated in the case of David, a widower who was seen as highly eligible for remarriage.

David: A Widower Eligible for Remarriage

David, a widower in his early forties, was dating two women. He had two children with his late wife who had passed on a decade before, and was being helped with their care by his late wife's younger sister, who had moved in shortly after the funeral. The presence of his sister-in-law had led for some time to rumours that his late wife's relatives had foisted a "replacement" wife on him, now a rarely implemented custom of some of the matrilineal groups in Zambia like the Bemba.

A successful corporate executive, working in private practice, David lived a comfortable life, epitomizing James Ferguson's category of "the cosmopolitan." When we first met, he introduced himself by his first name. Highly sociable and well travelled, he often hosted meals at his well-presented home, with its landscaped gardens and an interior with a collection of African art. David was considered highly eligible for remarriage but eluded it, stating he that he did not want his children to have a stepmother, and that he did fine as both a father and a mother figure for them.

David's girlfriends Carol and Brenda could be seen as having a "modern" outlook. Carol was working within the NGO sector, and Brenda was a banker. Both were widows, each with a single child, and they lived what appeared to be independent, comfortable lives. Unlike the majority of my informants on the Copperbelt, they were able to afford a leisurely lifestyle that included the occasional holiday "abroad" within the sub-Saharan African region. David's, Carol's, and Brenda's lifestyles were quite unusual on the Copperbelt, as they represented the small section of country's working professionals with earnings around 2009 estimated to average about ZMK 5 million after taxes (approx. US$1,000).

Unlike other informants on the Copperbelt who expected their girlfriends to take on a domestic role, which tended to blur the line between girlfriend and wife, David went out of his way to ensure that his girlfriends did not behave like wives. This was because a person who in the Western sense could be said to be dating could be sued either for a conjugal relationship or for "wasting one's time."

David, however, was taking a temporary break from Carol. While it was nice to be with a "well-taught" (i.e., initiated) woman, it was better that she behaved as such in private and not in front of his friends. Carol had allegedly informed him that dinner was ready by kneeling at the threshold of the living room, where he was entertaining his friends. This act indicated a propriety that was out of place in relation to how he saw their relationship. I had observed his sister-in-law, domestic worker, and gardener kneel at a little distance before him to make some request, so it was not the act itself that was a problem, but what Carol's behaviour signified to others. It turned out that Carol's kneeling was not the act that most upset him, but the rumours that circulated about her that David heard courtesy of a concerned friend. The rumour was that Carol regularly consulted traditional healers and *banachim-*

busa. In conversation amongst a mixed group, David queried the womenfolk why they needed recourse to "primitive methods" to catch a man. Yet, as I had observed, he also appreciated her modesty and education in these matters. His concern, as well as that of the other men in the room, was "sneaky methods" to elicit affection, and he was worried about what women had fed him. Here he was referring to love portions that in the popular realm were perceived to "tame" men and focus their affections on the person who set about to entrap them.[21] In addition, Carol's innate reserve, precisely that which gave her a respectful demeanour, that which characterised her as someone with *umuchinshi*, did not endear her to David's friends, who considered her unfriendly and *uwai finya*, "someone who carries herself heavily."

Around the time that rumours circulated about Carol's visits to traditional healers, David's relationship to Brenda appeared to get closer, with David telling colleagues that he was considering remarrying. Brenda, unlike Carol, was loud and engaging; on social occasions, she circulated widely and appeared to have no worries in expressing contrary social opinions. However, David was concerned about how Brenda would be received by his relatives, who expected traditional conventions to be observed. In addition, he was worried that the fact that she was from a different tribe (he was Bemba and she was Lozi) would be used by his relatives to alienate her—this despite widespread intertribal marriage. David said he was worried that the expectations of his family would change her and turn her into someone who was "no longer fun" and that he would rather continue their relationship as it was.

As David learnt, it was difficult, however, to remain friends with women once they got married, even if the relationship was platonic. For many of the older Zambian generations and some of the young, there was no such thing as a platonic friendship, with the Bemba saying *koswe tayikala apepi ne mbalala*, "A rat cannot be left near groundnuts," a caution on such a relationship. When Charity, a female executive and David's best friend, whom he had known since childhood and with whom he had a platonic relationship—despite the scepticism of many—got married, he found it increasingly difficult to socialise with her openly. According to David, Charity's new husband was a traditionalist and would not condone her meeting him. This was not because Charity's husband viewed David with any suspicion, but, as David explained, because Charity's husband, a considerably older and respectable businessman, did not want to attract ridicule from his peers by his wife's "consorting with a younger man."

There was a perception of social danger in befriending unattached young men. Young men were seen as only interested in playing around, and a woman seen to hang around them was likely to risk being labelled "loose" or as "moving around." Hansen made a similar observation about an informal settlement in Lusaka, where being single and conducting a single lifestyle as a woman also implied being loose (1997, 135–136). These aspersions on the sexual conduct of single women interacting with men indicated, for Hansen, a society that was overly concerned with sexual misconduct (1997, 135). For example, sexual relations conducted without cleansing rites were a danger to innocent persons. However, aspersions of sexual misconduct applied not just to women's interactions with young men. Young men were also considered less eligible than older men, as they were unlikely to have proven themselves in looking after a household. This ability to "take care" of a woman and those related to her is what made married men, divorcees, and widowers more eligible than single, unattached, young men. This outlook was illuminated in the case of Idess, a young woman who was on the lookout for a husband.

Idess: "Looking for Someone to Look after Me"

When I met Idess, she narrated her difficulties, saying, "My dear, it is not easy." Idess was not born on the Copperbelt but in Luapula Province in 1980. At the age of seven, she was sent to live with her mother's brother in Luanshya to get an education in the better schools of the Copperbelt. In 2000, the year that she completed her secondary school education, her uncle was retrenched from his job in the mines. Life in her uncle's household was busy, as she carried out many domestic chores requested by her uncle's wife, but she was not treated much differently than her uncle's children and the orphaned child of her aunt's late sister.

However, life became hard when, with his retrenchment package, her uncle decided to move in with a Lamba woman on the rural outskirts of the Copperbelt town. The rest of the family remained in the former mine house that formed part of his retrenchment package.

Following her uncle's departure, Idess's aunt expected her to do more work, helping out with growing food on the perimeter of the town. Her aunt also started to ask her, when she saw her talking to a certain man, if he had given her something. This could be seen as a direct way to ask Idess to transact herself. It could also be seen, as Liv Haram (2005) notes in her research on love and relationships in Tanzania, as an attempt to normalise Idess's relationship with her male friend by enfolding him into a sharing of food and resources, seen as a respectable form of reciprocity.[22]

When Idess's aunt got ill and passed away, Idess was left looking after her cousins. Two were under the age of five, while three were teenagers still at school. In time her uncle moved back to the house with his new wife, a choice that pitted him against his older children, who accused him of killing their mother.[23] Idess told me that she could not live with her uncle's new wife, whom she suspected of having entrapped him with "roots."[24] She expressed her desire to have her own house and get married.

I bumped into Idess a number of times in town in the company of various men, who ranged in age from thirties to sixties. Her demeanour was strikingly different from her manner at home or amongst her female friends, when she was vocal and often boisterous. In her interactions with these men she looked much more subdued, and on all these occasions the men seemed to be asking her when they would see her again. Idess would say she would call them, only she did not have money for cell phone airtime. On two occasions, I witnessed her being given money. It was clear that Idess was engaged in some form of courtship. When I asked whether she was seeing anyone, she told me that a young "working-class man"[25] had offered to marry her, but that "lies" told about her had resulted in marital negotiations not going beyond *kambale*.[26] Her friends told her that she was lucky she had not fallen pregnant with him because a young man *teti akusunge*, "couldn't look after her," and that it was better to have a child with an older, married man as they were more used to the responsibility.

Despite the increasing idealisations of love for love's sake, love detached from material goods, as vocalised in Zambian contemporary music,[27] material exchanges, often referred to in development aid circles by the value-laden term "transactional sex," still forms the basis of most courtship on the Copperbelt. This exchange, as in Idess's case, took the form of cell phone airtime, money, clothes, and food. A gift of money was not seen as belonging to a separate realm from other gifts such as food, the way it would be seen in the West. Money was as easily given away as food, and not to give it when one had it was stingy. When Idess's friends saw older, married men as more responsible, they were in part referring to the fact that in Zambian marriages, especially those involving matrilineal groups such as the Bemba, sons-in-law would share gifts with their in-laws as a way of showing respect, or *umuchinshi*. However, as many young people did not have the resources to do so, due to high youth unemployment, these views of Idess and her friends made many young men anxious about their relationships with women. They were suspected of seeing older men on the side, whom young men saw as killing young women like "flies." This was also a reference to the fear of HIV/AIDS, whose effect I discuss in Chapter 6.

This anxiety was also reflected in young men's views of women who were dating "white men" or "foreign men," whether they were Zambian nationals or not. Such women, as in the case below of Beauty, were likely to be characterised as loose and only interested in money, possibly reflecting the paternalistic nature of foreign capital on the Copperbelt and the long-running disparities in wages between local and expatriate staff. When Idess jokingly requested I help her find a "white husband" because they did not behave badly, "like us Africans," she was also communicating a need to be looked after.

Beauty: A Woman Interested Only in Money

When I first met Beauty, she was walking down one of the Copperbelt town's potholed roads. She was an incongruous sight on the town's street. A tall, graceful, slender woman with short-cropped hair dressed in a dark, pinstripe skirt-suit and stilettos, with an air of polish, she would not have looked out of place in a fashion magazine. Curious, I said hello, and thereby began a conversation that provided insight into the life of women on the Copperbelt characterised as "loose" and "interested only in money."

Beauty was not working in a bank, as I had initially presumed, as banking was the only sector I could think of in the economically sleepy town. Rather she was a businesswoman who ran an unsuccessful restaurant, as well as occasionally trading in clothes imported from South Africa that she sold on credit to a network of female clients. She was also pursuing a marketing course, taking evening classes in a nearby Copperbelt town. After hearing about my research interests and my growing up on the Copperbelt, Beauty, unlike some of my female informants, was happy to talk about what was going on in her life in relation to the region's mine economy.

She had moved from Western Province as a young girl, where she had lived with her mother, a widow, and other siblings, to stay with her aunt,[28] her mother's sister. Her aunt was married on the Copperbelt and worked as a nurse in the mine hospital. Her aunt, who had three female children, also became widowed when her husband, according to Beauty, died from depression following his retrenchment from the mines. Life became very difficult, with her aunt struggling to support her children and Beauty, at that time all teenagers. Her aunt decided to emigrate abroad to work as a nurse, with two of the younger children joining her later. Beauty and one of her cousins were left in the house that the family had gained as part of the retrenchment package from the mines, receiving subsistence money from the aunt. This money allowed Beauty and her cousin to complete their secondary school education. For reasons that Beauty could not elaborate on, the remittances from abroad dwindled, and Beauty and her cousin were forced to take up paid work rather than go to college. Beauty found a low-paid job as a bartender, but her cousin did not, forcing them to put the house up for rent and move into "servants' quarters." Both started dating, but Beauty described these relationships as just *ukwangala*, "playing," connoting a courtship not necessarily leading to marriage. It was during this phase that she got pregnant and had a child with a boyfriend who was unable to support her. Beauty's son had just started attending primary school when I met her in 2007. She said the boy's father did odd jobs and was still living with his parents.

At the time I met Beauty, she was staying in a rented three-bedroom house in a former low-density mine suburb. Her rent, she told me, was being paid by her current boyfriend Craig, an expatriate mine manager, one of a wave of foreign mineworkers[29] hailing from South Africa, Australia, the United Kingdom, Peru, India, and China who began to move into the Copperbelt with rising copper prices. Craig was already married and had a family but, like other expatriate workers, had moved without his family because there were few good schools and housing was poor.[30] I found out by chance that he was also "keeping house" with another woman, Bwalya, who like Beauty was running a restaurant, but a much more successful enterprise. While Beauty knew of Bwalya, as the two moved generally in similar circles, neither, as far as I knew, had ever confronted the other over this arrangement.

While Beauty's critics and sympathisers both described her relationship with Craig as commercial, in practice it resembled a settled, familial, domestic arrangement. According to Beauty, Craig settled the rentals, paid for her son's school fees and her college tuition, and provided a monthly household income, for which she had to account. She in turn provided meals, got his laundry done, arranged for the servicing of his car, booked their holidays as well as his trips abroad to visit his legitimate family, and was his companion for social gatherings. Their relationship was conducted openly among his peers, some of whom had similar arrangements. They often had arguments about money, as Beauty claimed he refused to give her money outside running their household and her personal care. Beauty needed the extra money to help her mother and her siblings, whose expectations for help had risen when she started seeing her "white man."[31]

I once saw Beauty adopt the demeanour of the traditional wife in her home, semi-curtseying when serving Craig his drink and calling him "ba-Craig," adding the prefix that connoted respect. Later she laughed and said, *kaili fye ashile umukashi kubusungu, pantu ta mutasha*, "That is why he has left his wife in the West, because she doesn't thank him." She was referring to local, customary notions of *umuchinshi*. However, whenever I bumped into Beauty at a popular beer garden in the company of Craig and his friends and their partners, Beauty's behaviour was often openly flirtatious, not unlike that characterised by Ferguson and other anthropologists who observed women in these social settings. What was surprising about Beauty's behaviour at the beer garden was its sharp contrast with how she presented herself at home and at the restaurant she ran. There she appeared relaxed and demure, chatting with her staff while cleaning fish or vegetables, or talking to her customers and passers-by. She was often generous, offering meals and cash to people who loitered in the shops, hoping for "piecework." She did not demand that clients settle their bills there and then, and she would often insist that the meal I ordered was on the house. Beauty's behaviour drew on a varied repertoire of ways of being, to project not only a certain style, that is, the modern woman in a bar or the traditional woman respecting the customary ideal of generosity, but also her conscious or unconscious adeptness at weaving relationships and modes of comportment across various settings.

It was not uncommon for both expatriates and local Zambians to set up women "on the side." These extramarital affairs, which resembled polygamous arrangements without the consent of the wife, were a source of worry to the women of the older Copperbelt. Like the stories of the Lamba women that characterised the establishment of the Copperbelt, stories about enticing Kaonde and Lunda[32] women were circulated, eliciting fear among women whose husbands had found work in the new Copperbelt of North West Zambia. It was not only women who worried about the husband's fidelity; as Ferguson points out, men too had suspicions about their wives (1999, 185–186).

In 2009, after not having seen Beauty for almost a year, I bumped into her walking her son to school, looking very different from her usual immaculate self. She told me she was doing badly. She was looking for a job but had little prospect of finding a reasonably paid one, as she had not completed her marketing course. She had been evicted from the house she was renting and was struggling to meet her expenses. I enquired after her some weeks later and found that she had left town.

I heard varied explanations for her departure and the decline in her fortunes. She was said to have fallen in love with a good-looking and notorious young man. He was only interested in getting money from Beauty, running her businesses into the ground and coercing her to get money from Craig to finance a trade in spare car parts. The story went that when Craig found out about this relationship he "chased her" from the house. In another account, Craig's wife had found out about Beauty and Bwalya and forced her husband to terminate both relationships. In a third story, after Craig ended their relationship she dated a married man who had taken her on as a second wife. When Beauty reappeared in town some months later, once again dating Craig, the gossip was that Craig had forgiven her for her indiscretion with the young man. I later learned from Beauty herself that she had accompanied Craig to an outlying rural mine post in the North West Province, where mining explorations were being carried out.

One of the assumptions that underlay the rumours of Beauty's departure was that she could not feel genuine affection for Craig and that she could only turn to a Zambian man for love and marriage. The Zambian popular song by the late renowned electric guitarist Paul Ngozi, "Half Muntu, Half Mwenye," and more recently the artist Petersen's "Maoffals" (2012), are about Zambian women's relationships with Asian men, and the unlikelihood of marriage. They reflect a discourse of the racialised other that was antithetical to Kaunda's nation-building under the motto "One Zambia, One Nation." While not colouring the entire landscape of Copperbelt domestic arrangements, relationships such as Beauty and Craig's were more visible with increased mining activity, especially in the rural outposts of North Western Zambia. However, despite the "othering" that formed part of the narrative that criticised women who had relationships with "foreigners," "outsiders" were brought into the fold of the Copperbelt's customary ideas of domesticity.

PERFORMING GENDER

As Ferguson noted in his research on the Copperbelt, it was hard to find domestic arrangements that resembled the Western ideal of a nuclear family, even though that ideal was used to critique marriage and relationships on the Copperbelt. In what appears to be a contradiction, Copperbelt residents also looked to the customary, non-Western ideal of marriage, referred to as a traditional marriage. Just as it was hard to find the ideal Western domestic arrangement, it was also hard to find one that looked like the traditional marriage, which upheld values of respect towards elders and men, as well as reciprocal relations amongst kin. What one found was a variety of domestic arrangements, of which I have presented a small cross-section. Many of the issues illuminated in these disparate domestic settings were of concern to the general population of the Copperbelt.

There was a concern over the management of household finances. As Hansen (1987) noted in her study on the dynamics of gender and the management of the domestic sphere in Lusaka, younger married women on the Copperbelt found it harder than older women to have a say in how household finances were spent. There was a perception amongst many Copperbelt women that men were not very responsible in the handling of money. As a result, women urged each other to keep what they earned (largely from informal sector activities) secret from their husband, and in acknowledgement of the claims that a husband's relatives might have on a household's assets, women also kept their earnings and assets secret from their husband's relatives.

This attempt by women to keep their earnings invisible is also reflected in the invisibility of female initiation rites that a number of Copperbelt women undergo, as well as in the popular female-only kitchen parties. The "secret language" of the female initiation rite, a coalescence of a lifelong education in the embodiment of moral values—like the expectation of industriousness, the sharing of food, and respect manifested in the bodily comportment of deference—hides from view women's affective engagement with these norms. In their engagement with a customary ideal of womanhood that may appear subservient, Copperbelt women do not necessarily contest this ideal by discarding it in favour of a Western notion of female liberation, as represented, for example, in outright assertion of their desires; rather, they tend to undermine these values in ways that allow them to go about their business without being cast loose from social networks they may come to rely on. This means that while rumours and gossip may act as a sanctioning mechanism, women labelled as fast or loose are unlikely to be cut off from interactions with other people as long as they draw upon a repertoire of relationship-making interactions, such as respect for elders and men, and reciprocity.

The key lesson of the initiation rite that women were expected to take away from it was cleverness (Richards 1956; Moore 1999). Women were expected to be clever in how they negotiated a space for economic independence, a place for leisure, and harmony or love. This, as in their livelihood activities, necessitated an improvisational approach to the performance of gender. Gender identity not as a static given, but as Moore (1986) and Judith Butler (1993) argue, is the enacting of recurring practices that are largely unconscious, are bodily, and in their everydayness tend to be inscribed as natural. This process of inscription, as a reiterative performance of what Butler calls the "doing" of gender, constitutes a temporal condition of the subject. As such, she argues, the gendered subject is not a stable identity, but rather is unstable (1993, 95). It is this instability of the gendered subject that provides the opening for "cleverness" to subvert the gendered expectations of domesticity represented in both the traditional and Western ideal of family and relationships.

Copperbelt residents' engagements with these ideals were not a movement from one ideal to another, but rather comprised the creation of homologies "between different levels of experience and different domains of life." As such, they were not "over-determining" (Moore 1999, 15). This means that "oppositions and symbolic principles are invoked, brought into play, but never resolved, never finalised" and that "there is only processual movement through them" (Moore 1999, 15). The idealisations of the "traditional" or "modern" woman, as presented in the popular sphere, operate in the lived world for Copperbelt residents and urban Zambians like a symbolic template from which from multiple meaning are drawn, and in this way, they work like "technological systems" with which people engage (Moore 1999, 22–23). Thus, the idealisation of a gendered identity is not fixed, but may be open to contestation whereby "actors seek to freeze process and impose particular interpretations" (Moore 1999, 15).

These processes, as reflected in women's involvement in the informal copper business, and in their determination for economic independence, show that Copperbelt women's elaborations of gendered identities were not detached from the materiality of their environments. Their growing importance in the support of their families and their presence in wider spheres of economic activity, albeit still largely informal, was firmly "implacing" (Casey 1987) them in the landscape, making the performance of gender on the Copperbelt not only discursive, but also material in its inscription and thus in the environment.

However, this process goes beyond inscription, as it includes an emotive dimension partaking of the material and the discursive in the making and doing of gender. This affective realm was influenced by the variability, fluidity, and contrariness of domestic expectations and social relations. Women's aspirations were expressed in Idess's desire to have someone to look after her; Susan's wish to attend kitchen parties as a space for pleasure; the clever plays of Mrs Phiri to maintain harmony and financial security in her household; and the critique of Beauty's relationship with Craig as mercenary and devoid of love. Amidst the emotions expressed explicitly and implicitly was the awareness of the need to maintain social proprieties. This is elucidated in David's case, played out as a tension between his desire to enjoy female companionship without the inhibiting stricture of the customary or traditional marriage.

The concern with proprieties was not predicated on a static structure of embodied social norms, but rather was relational to the wider environment in a way that becomes clearer in Chapter 6, where I explore how people coped with the hardship and precariousness of life on the Copperbelt. In the next chapter, by drawing on popular music, I show how the body, emotion, and environment are "interwoven" through the rhythms that make the reiterative process of life. The contestations of the interpretations of gender identities and practice, in my view, do not lie within a body as a structure of learned norms, nor "out there" as abstract values, but rather are enacted across all the spheres of phenomenological engagement, the body, emotion, and environment, and within the rhythms of everyday lived experience. In this way, the problems in marriage and relationships that Copperbelt residents identify as a failure to adequately interpret the customary and Western ideal of marriage reflect dissonances in the rhythms of the reiterative doing of gender.

NOTES

1. All but one of my guests was supporting relatives.

2. A more detailed discussion of the effects of this migrant labour on rural communities in Northern Zambia is provided by Henrietta Moore and Megan Vaughan (1994).

3. Conducted in the mid-1990s mostly amongst a Catholic women's group who lived in a low-density suburb on the Copperbelt town of Mufulira (Rasing 2001, 17).

4. *Mbusa* means "things handed down."

5. Though domestic privacy was valued, as Hansen (1997) demonstrates in her study of women's lives in an urban, informal settlement in Lusaka, women tended to take intimate domestic problems to the public local courts. I made similar findings in Luanshya.

6. "Alangizi: Victim Relives Counselling Nightmare," *Times of Zambia*, 8 February 2003,

7. In a nutshell, if extramarital affairs were not admitted to and ritual cleansing did not take place, the ensuing pollution could cause the death of innocents, with babies being particularly vulnerable. See Richards 1956 for a more detailed discussion of this and the Bemba cosmological world view.

8. Moore (1999) draws attention to the amount of time invested in the "preparation, presentation and handling of the mbusa" clay models. Audrey Richards also describes this. Writing of the making of a clay snake, Richards notes that it took almost an entire day. The women worked on it until it was neat and well presented (*ubusaka*). Once presented to the young initiates, it was dismantled. Moore also notes that "in the many of the individual rites of the chisungu, instructors and initiates use the mouth as much as possible to handle the mbusa and complete various tasks—embodied transfer of knowledge by mouth from one woman to another" (1999, 12).

9. The majority of Zambians identify themselves as Christian. Outward appearances of practicing the Christian faith were especially important for women in identifying themselves as morally upstanding.

10. The custom of showing what Audrey Richards (1956, 48) described as "extreme deference" to age is not uncommon on the Copperbelt. This custom, as well as the prevalence of female initiation rites modelled on the Bemba rites, indicates the influence of Bemba practices on the Copperbelt, largely as a result of the large in-migration of the people from Northern Zambia in the early mining days. However, as Debra Spitulnik (1999) notes of the lingua franca of the Copperbelt, Bemba, the fluidity, hybridity, and inventiveness of the language could also be applied to spheres other than language.

11. As Thera Rasing observes, young women in the company of older women usually did not speak unless invited to (2001, 112).

12. Audrey Richards noted that social relations predominantly consisted "of the giving and receiving of services" and that "status derived from the ability to demand service," with "giving service as an expression of respect" (1956, 46–47).

13. It is worth noting that in the contemporary context, these identities are idealised in practice, not necessarily in one or the other locality.

14. A cosmological view of the world that does not see human interaction and communication as happening in discrete territories, but as woven through the body (bodies) by rhythm and, in turn resonances that lie beneath and beyond the surface and frame of what is visible to analysis.

15. The idea of *carrying* oneself with respect, in contrast to *conducting* oneself with respect, implies a habituation that seeks not merely to display respect, but to embody respectful mores. For example, sometimes people are said to *ukwi finya* (carry themselves with "heaviness"), implying an excessive embodiment of values that literally weigh them down, in contrast to someone who is described as conservatively rigid.

16. This can range from full avoidance of preparing meals to preparing them but not adding salt.

17. Church mission sisters who run homemaking classes.

18. Susan recounted that her parents, who were farming in the "bush," were struggling, and remembered that when she stayed over, they went to bed without eating.

19. In matrilineal societies such as the Bemba, the majority population on the Copperbelt, a man's older sister is considered a classificatory male and has significant say in his household affairs.

20. Here Mrs Phiri was referring to the generally widespread discourse on women's rights supported by various NGOs and other multilateral and bilateral organisations, which also fed into government policy.

21. This fear of love potions reflected a fear of a loss of agency or autonomy, similarly noted in studies by Wilson (2012) on Malawi and Goebel (2002) on Zimbabwe.

22. It was not uncommon for men on the Copperbelt, whether stopping by to see kin, lovers, or platonic friends, to bear gifts of food. Peter, a friend and colleague from the university, would, after a trip to an outlying rural area, present gifts to Jane and me of fish, mushrooms, or vegetables. This formed part of a mutually reciprocal relationship, because on the occasions that Peter visited our homes, he was also often welcomed to a meal or likewise received gifts of food.

23. A reference to the possibility that she had died from AIDS.

24. "Roots" used in this context meant love potions.

25. A reference to a formal sector employee, regardless of rank.

26. A contribution of money to the potential bride's family to open bride price negotiations.

27. For example, the Zambian artist Nalu, in her song "House, Money, Car" (2005) asks what remains in a relationship when a couple falls upon hard times if material goods are the basis of it.

28. Beauty had moved to stay with her mother's sister not simply for economic reasons, but through a kinship system that allowed the "adoption" of children by members of the extended family. In this case, Beauty's aunt liked her disposition and requested that Beauty live with her and be treated as one of her daughters.

29. There are several studies that document international migrant workers' experiences on the Copperbelt. There are historical studies of European (or European heritage) migrant workers and settlers (Phimister 2011; Milner-Thornton 2011; Money 2015), but less work on the contemporary period and on new players such as India and Brazil. Given the visibility of China's investment in Zambia and its global economic clout, more recent studies (Lee 2018; Sautman and Hairong 2016) have tended to focus on Chinese migrant workers and investment, providing nuance and balance to the sometimes xenophobic discourse about foreigners.

30. An estate agent and the few expatriate workers interviewed during a survey confirmed the lack of decent accommodation, citing the dilapidation of much of what was available on the market.

31. "'Whiteness" in Zambia, much as in the rest of southern Africa, is seen as a social currency both by those who identify with it and by those who interact with those who identify as "white." It reflected not only in wage disparities, but also in access to capital and social networks. The materialisation of this perception is exemplified by a relatively successful Copperbelt farmer who told me he failed to get a bank loan to expand his farming business until acquiring a "white" business manager, whom he sent in to negotiate it on his behalf.

32. Ethnic groups found in North Western Province.

CHAPTER 6

"Topping Up"

Life amidst Hardship and Death

In the previous chapter I gave insight into the variations of the Copperbelt "home front," and how women in particular are managing expectations of domesticity in an economy long dominated by male work in the mines.[1] In this chapter, I cast a lens on the experience of young people, and particularly on how they try to maintain a hopeful stance on a future that implies hardship and death. I argue, just as I have in Chapter 5, that it is important to examine the intersubjective experiences that are both readily visible and invisible in exploring how life in such contexts is conceptualised.

INTRODUCTION

The benevolence of family patrons who supported extended family members with the benefits provided by the mines and the state has contracted. Fear of falling into extreme poverty, combined with the desire "to arrive"—*ukufika*—in the consumerist world, has led many young people to move beyond the extended kin system[2] to seek opportunities for themselves. Many young people and women have entered the informal economy. For women, this shift has largely been motivated by the need to provide "food for the pot" (Hansen 1996, 80). For young men, many of whom live with relatives, it has been driven not only by a need to contribute, but also by a strong desire for personal autonomy—*ukwi monela*, "to see for yourself" or "to fend for yourself"—outside the control of "aunties and uncles." This loosening of ties has gone hand in hand with a reworking of moralities, *sebanya wikute* ("Get embarrassed but get full"). As I described earlier in the book, this phrase covered a range of strategies that included "theft," begging, and other activities, even if they might embarrass one's relations, for example, illegal copper mining[3] and transactional sex.[4] Underlying these strategies was the heavy presence of death, which directly and indirectly correlated to precarious economic activity and changed circumstances.

This chapter is not a descriptive account of death and funerals on the Copperbelt. Rather, like Monisha Bajaj's (2008) description of how schoolgoing youths in Zambia encounter HIV/AIDS as an ongoing process in making sense of death within everyday experiences, I address the notion of life when death abounds. Most of my fieldwork activities involved following people as they went about trying to make a living, a lot of it labour intensive. Through these activities, the body had emerged as a thing over which people had little control, but which they used like a vehicle through skilful practice to find the paths from which the possibilities to extend its journey would emerge. The pitfalls, like potholes along these paths, damaged the body of the vehicle, leaving it up to the skilful improvisation of the drivers to keep on and up to their willingness to "top up" on their lives. I use vehicular metaphors, often used in Zambian popular music and language, as a way of describing the anxieties of Copperbelt residents. This form of expression was not uncommon in the central African region in people's expressions of colonial anxiety (see White 1993).

In this context, life in Zambia is increasingly conceptualised as a precarious journey, one that could come to a halt anytime. Death in Zambia has become an inescapable experience of the everyday and woven into the social fabric of life on the Copperbelt. It was in the sounds of mourning that one heard frequently in the night and the everyday discussions of illness. It was in the *chitenges* (wrap clothes) that many women carried in their bags in readiness to attend a neighbour's or work colleague's funeral, and in the living room suites of chairs set around the dying embers of a fire out in a front yard. It was also in the sheets of paper passed around the passengers on a bus for monetary contributions by a young boy or girl who had been orphaned. No one was untouched by it. At Copperbelt University, where I worked between the years 2005 and 2008, it almost seemed there was a funeral every other week, of either staff members or their families. Statistics confirm this grim picture. The Central Statistical Office 2006 Living Conditions Monitoring Survey (LCMS) recorded that 27% of the households surveyed on the Copperbelt had experienced at least death of someone between thirty and forty-four years of age in the twelve months prior. The leading cause of death, 19.8%

of all deaths recorded, was fever/malaria, a disease that in Luanshya had been well controlled by 1931, following the beginning of commercial copper mining in the late 1920s (Schumaker 2008). Judging by the percentage of young people under the age of eighteen who had lost their fathers, 8.4% on the Copperbelt, the majority of the population dying while of productive work age are men (CSO 2007, 300). Of this age group 1.9% of respondents had lost their mother, with 4.4% having both parents dead (CSO 2007, 300). These figures matched what I found. During my fieldwork in Luanshya, I observed that many of those who were having a harder time making a living, and who were adopting precarious livelihoods, were women, children, and youth (see Chapter 4). For these groups, and in the general social scene of the Copperbelt, death was rarely explicitly discussed, but discourses of death were to be found in the popular scene (cf. Lwanda 2003).

The fact that there is little philosophical writing in Zambia does not mean that places for thinking models and theorising about death and life in Zambia do not exist. These places are indeed everywhere. Fiona Ross, writing of a post-apartheid community in South Africa, noted that the residents had innovated ways to speak indirectly of their difficult experiences of HIV and suffering (2010, 183). In Zambia, too, this creativity was to be found in popular culture, music, and drama and in the general conversational spheres of public life, such as public transport, bars, kitchen parties, and blogs. A number of academics writing on similar places in southern central Africa, such as Malawi and Zimbabwe, and on Zambia itself have drawn attention to the importance of taking theoretical steps in the very places they study. For example, Bawa Yamba (1997, 218), writing on cosmologies of turmoil and death and HIV/AIDS in a rural setting in Zambia, argues that it is important to take seriously discourses that seek to make sense of life and hardship in place, before making the analytical leap to a structural battle opposing modernity, colonialism, or globalisation. Maurice Vambe's (2008) study of popular music and death in Zimbabwe and Filip de Boeck's film *Cemetery State*, made in 2010, emphasise that the analysis of place goes beyond text and discourse, and that the performative, in rhythm, dance, and sound, are inseparable from the activity of living and theorising life. Yamba's (1997) study narrates various stories about inviting a witch-finder to a village in Chiawa whose divinatory method resulted in several deaths and local power struggles. John Lwanda's (2003) study explores the perception of secrecy in HIV/AIDS discourse in Malawi. Lwanda found that rather than looking to the official discourse on HIV/AIDS, which implied an invisible subject, one had to look to oral discourses, in particular popular music and vernacular language, which, he argues, allowed for greater flexibility in the creation of meaning for words than English, the business language, which is seen as more utilitarian. It is from these studies that I draw to talk about how Zambians theorise their lives amidst hardship and uncertainty.

WE ARE SUFFERING

Common responses to the greeting *mulishani* ("How are you?") from the young men who hang around the bus stations trying to make a living are *twa chula ba sister* ("We are suffering, sister"), *ya, tulekosa* ("Ah, we are getting strong"), and *fili bad* ("Things are bad"). Suffering was not a temporal state; it meant a "trying"[5] life. This was a state that many Copperbelt residents and indeed many Zambians lived in. In illness and on the cusp of death, it meant a trip to the hospital as a last option, because of a lack of money to pay for consultation or medication. It meant finding food to prepare meals for the patient admitted to hospital and sitting by a sick relative's bed all night to feed and bathe the patient and change bedpans because of the limited number of nursing staff in the low-cost hospital wards (McPake et al. 2004, 14). It also meant working even when very ill, as I found in August 2008 with John, one of the few adult males working illegally on a copper dump site in Luanshya. He was clearly weak, having just been put on treatment for tuberculosis. In conversations with my informants, many struggled to articulate an optimistic future. This sense of a less than hopeful future was well captured in the title of Miles Larmer's (2004) article "If We Are Still Here Next Year," on the mine-workers' union in Luanshya and on the difficulty of carrying out research amongst people experiencing great difficulty. James Ferguson, writing on the young Zambian intelligentsia's musings on a newly market-orientated and democratising Zambia, noted that writers toward the end of the brief lifespan[6] of an online magazine struggled to imagine a hopeful future for the country (Ferguson 2006, 147). The experience of life in the present was often articulated as a struggle or a life of suffering. Fiona Ross, writing on life, illness, and death in a post-apartheid community in South Africa, argues that even in speaking of illness, words often do not convey the "full weight of experience" that may be transferred into the "body of another" (2010, 186). This view, if we draw from Devisch's (1993) work on healing cults among the Yaka in the Congo, sees illness, and in turn suffering, not just as something going functionally wrong, but as a dissonance in the entanglement of relationships and the multitude of things that sustain them, which include the social, spiritual, and material (1993, 17). It is within this view that one sees that the transposition of a discourse of illness and suffering to the popular realm, such as in music and dance, is not only about its articulation, but also about healing. Devisch in his work on healing amongst the Yaka argues that "rhythm, dance and melody give the body over to the sense and the life world. They form a primary source of healing devices or crafts. Healing originates in rhythm that intertwines with intimate fellow feeling" (1993, 259). In addition, "Dancing seeks to regenerate, re-empower and re-order the lifeworld" (Devisch 1993, 72).[7] My argument here is that it is through the popular scene of music and dance that one gets the experience of life amidst hardship in Zambia. One perceives, not that people have given up and have no future, but a rhythm that ties together the difficult experiences of trying to earn a living, one that urges people to "take out their strength" (as the musician Dalisoul's lyrics have it) and go on into an uncertain future.

WE TRY

> *Most times we are running*
> *But today we still have to find*
> *Those with luck build houses*
> *And money to sell cigarettes*
>
> *But why*
> *Us every single day we try*
> *Everything we do turns bad*
> *Suffering every single day we cry*
> *But we try*
>
> *Oh no, I do not want to look*
> *I just want to close my eyes*
> *My soul-life suffers*

As in the lyrics above of Petersen's song "Oh No" (2005), trying was evident everywhere I looked on the Copperbelt town of Luanshya where I did most of my fieldwork. Mr Mubita, with his backyard "experiments" and "pilots," a laboratory of agricultural experimentation presented in Chapter Three. There was Mr Chilufya who after two failed attempts to establish a fish farm waited an extra year to see if modification to the lining of the pond would make a difference to how much water seeped from the pond. Then there was single mother, Jane, who kept looking for new contacts within the mines to gain leverage into the male-dominated and network-based mine-supply business. Aaron, who after the chickens he was rearing died from disease because he could not afford the medicated chicken feed on the market, took to making his chickens drink aloe vera as an alternative remedy. "Besides," he said, "maybe doing away with these chemicals will make us live longer." Then there was my neighbour who kept trying to find reasons for me to cut the trees in my backyard, not specifying why he wanted me to do so, until I discovered that he wanted to fire the bricks he was moulding in his backyard.

It became clear during the course of my fieldwork that a notion of agency which presupposed that a neat line of intention and action would not work.[8] Many of my informants were aware of this. Many of the activities that Copperbelt residents engaged in were trying, that is, they were frustrating, demanding and difficult, and required numerous attempts. Repetition and trying new combinations, what was referred to as *ukusankanya*—a creative mixing of things (the tangible and intangible), became commonplace. The practice of making a living in this context of uncertainty took on an experimental nature in the way in which livelihood was sought. As one informant in Luanshya told me, "You can't plan life in these conditions" (see Chapter 2), referring to how he was looking after his late daughter's child, and two young girls from his wife's side of the family, all orphans. The implication was that if at some time in the pre-privatisation past of the mine one could plan for a future, that time had gone. It was also in the notion that people found it increasingly difficult to establish stable patterns. As one news item quoted on the loss of copper jobs that ensued following the global economic crisis of 2008: "Life is very hard. I have to pay bills and rentals. I am living like I don't know what tomorrow will bring, as if I was not employed. My children have been sent back from school [because I cannot pay the fees]."[9]

The most stable thing I found in my interaction with Copperbelt residents was their memories of the past. Many hungered for the good old days.

The past was not as David Lowenthal argues a "foreign country" (1985). For Copperbelt residents the past was in the lived-in remnants of the town's dilapidated infrastructure and in the incongruity of a well-spoken and obviously highly-skilled person trapped in an emaciated body draped in tatty clothes. As an editorial in *The Post* newspaper highlighted:

> Luanshya is in crisis and deserves serious government attention. It is very difficult for workers, retrenched or otherwise, to go for more than six months without any source of income. Workers are not like peasants who can survive on nature—roots. Workers depend on wages and without that they are literally condemned to death.[10]

It was not just wages that the mines had provided. Mr Mubita, and other former mineworkers told me how the mines had provided milk and large buns for food at work, and how medical check-ups for chest problems that were concomitant with working in mines were regular. The end of these facilities, especially for the few who went on to get jobs in the newly privatised mines,[11] had a negative effect on their health. They talk about how their entertainment was taken care of in the recreational sports offered by the mines and the social clubs that not only catered for employees but their families too. Mr Mubita and other Copperbelt residents pointed out to me in various ways, how the absence of these benefits in the present had a negative somaesthetic on their bodies.[12] Lucky Zulu, a Luanshya-born artist, told me that when his brother could no longer afford to buy Mosi Lager at the mine club he used to frequent before being laid off from the mines, he took to drinking cheaper, illicit brews. This eventually damaged his brother's liver and resulted in his death. The lack of safe recreational facilities, such as those that had been provided by the mines, was blamed for risky social behaviours. At the time of my research, the former squash club had become a nightclub and drinking place frequented by adults, but also underage children. The cinema had become a Pentecostal church, the tennis club's courts had become overgrown by an itchy weed, and its clubhouse catered to a drinking crowd.

An overwhelming majority of the residents of Luanshya whom I talked to during the research period blamed the withdrawal of the mines, not only for the physical dilapidation of the town, but also for the degradation of their society as a whole. Drunken young people loitered in the neighbourhood at night, and there were violent incidents that residents claimed were unheard of in the town's mining heyday. In some of these stories, physical and social degradation merged to highlight the loss of order. I was told that a former ZCCM employee had used explosives pilfered from the mines to kill himself and blow up the house he had been instructed by the courts to share with his estranged wife. Another story was of a crazed man who murdered his ex-girlfriend after breaking into her parents' home through a door so weathered that it could easily be kicked in. This account drew a contrast between the girl, who attempted to maintain her virtue by using both hands to prevent a wrap she was wearing from slipping in front of her father, and the former boyfriend, who took advantage of her defencelessness to stab her.

In these tragic stories, the integrity of the body is affected by changed social and material circumstance. If we are to draw from Richard Shusterman (2000) and look at the corporeality of life, not just as body and mind, but body in mind and mind in body, we can understand nostalgia not as a shadowy fragment of mind, but as part of a body shaped by changed circumstances. The big fear for parents was that in the absence of streetlights "children could do whatever they wanted." For young people, it was not just about doing what one wanted, but also about the difficulty of avoiding the dangers of life. Peter, a seventeen-year-old praise singer and dancer I met practicing for a nativity play, mused on the narrative for a short film he planned to produce based on a young woman who was raped by her teacher and infected with HIV: "Corruption is everywhere, even for those that try to lead a God-filled life. They get dribbled" (literally translated, "get their ball taken away from them)."

This loss of control, an inability to steer one's life, underlay an anxiety about the possibility of seeing another day—"Another Day," a track by the popular Zambian musician K'Millian (2006). This was a generalised fear among Copperbelt residents, a "chronic condition" that fed on uncertainty (Green 1994, 230). It is the kind of anxiety that Danny sings about in the lyrics of in his song "Kaya" ("I Don't Know," 2005):

> *The friends I grew up with, I do not see, even that one.*
> *When I ask about this one and ask about that one*
> *They are all finished, finished and overturned.*
> *It gives me great fear when I look into my future.*
> *Will I see this coming year?*
> *I don't know.*

Popular Copperbelt musicians Macky 2 and Dandy Krazy describe this uncertainty as a difficulty in steering one's life. They sing, *life yandi ila nshupa ukwensha* ("My life gives me difficulty driving") in their song "Life Yandi"

(2010). In steering their lives, the musicians are also referring to the "moving around" required to find a job (Gough 2008, 248). Another Copperbelt musician, DY2K, describes it as a fear of the loss of control in the lyrics of the song "Nyamuka, Nyamuka" ("'Get Up, Get Up" (2009):

> *My heart rises and rises over things I did not want,*
> *Over things I did not want.*
> *My eyes are looking, looking at things I did not want,*
> *Over things I did not want.*
> *My hands are touching, touching,*
> *Making me touch things, I did not want them,*
> *Over things I did not want.*
>
> *My heart that likes Marias*[13]
> *It has brought me troubles my dear.*
> *Now look, I stay with fear.*
> *Now what I am to do?*

A common response to addressing uncertainty and the awareness of not being in control was readily discernible in the public in the practice of praying. Often before the embarkation for a long-distance bus journey, a "briefcase" clergyman would pray with the passengers and "pledge" their lives to "God's hands." People prayed in other public spaces; in the hospitals visitors prayed loudly by a patient's bedside; heads bowed quietly in prayer at a fast-food joint before a meal of chicken and chips.

Another way in which young people dealt with anxiety was the oblivion to be found in *tujilijili*, little packets with lethally high alcohol content priced the same as lollipops. *Tujilijili* were to be found in the very same places that sweets were sold, the bus stations and markets, where it was not uncommon to see young men breaking out in dance to the songs mentioned here as they blared over a cacophony of loudspeakers. Both of these activities, prayer and drinking alcohol, implied a fatalistic attitude toward life, one where agency, the intentional ability to influence outcomes, was not in the hands of subjects, but lay beyond them.

Senseless Death

I had not heard from Lackson Mwale, one of my key informants in Luanshya, for several days after having arranged for him to introduce me to a metal fabricator for some work I was doing. I called his wife, Rosemary, who told me that he had travelled to see his brother, who had been involved in a work accident in the northwestern region of the country. When I caught up with him a few weeks later, he told me in great grief and frustration that his brother had died. He recounted the events leading up to his brother's death. His brother had been injured in a work accident, apparently as a result of an epileptic incident, and he decided to take him to a generally well-run mission hospital in the region. At the hospital his brother had been placed on a ventilator to aid his breathing and had been making a good recovery. Lackson decided, having seen the rough conditions his brother was living in and the danger manual labour posed for an epileptic, that when his brother recovered fully, he would stay with Lackson in Luanshya, where he need not engage in physical labour. It was not to be, because one night, as Lackson sat by his brother's bedside, there was a power blackout. The ventilator that was aiding his brother's breathing shut down. In panic Lackson called a nurse for help as he watched his brother struggling to breathe. The nurse could do little other than hope that the hospital's backup generator kicked in on time. It did not, and his brother died.

Deaths such as these were not uncommon. They highlighted for many a nation that had "lost the plot." Elias Chipimo, a presidential candidate in Zambia's 2011 tripartite elections, entered politics after witnessing the ineptitude of the country's accident emergency services and the sorry state of health facilities following a car accident that had claimed his mother's life and seriously injured his father (Chipimo 2010, 9–10). The agenda of the political party Chipimo formed, the National Restoration Party (NAREP), was to rebuild a nation that, in the eyes of many Zambians, had gone renegade on the promise of the early independence period.[14]

Letters to the editor of the main independent newspaper, *The Post*, described what they saw as the country's malaise. In one, titled "Zambia: A Nation of Defeat and Hopelessness,"[15] the author says:

> Living in this country is scary and depressing. It is like living in a house where no one is working but somehow you are managing to pay the rent and utility bills. Grace of God? I don't think so. It's just over Kaponya culture.

The editor, in response to this letter, offered a view on what was ailing the country:

It would have been better if our country was on autopilot. We say this because the autopilot machine on a plane is able to steer the aircraft in the right direction. What we have is not a government running on autopilot, it is a government in free-fall. In fact, if it was a fighter jet, one would be excused for suspecting that the pilots had ejected and were allowing the plane to fall.[16]

While these two letters paint a fatalistic picture of a country in free fall, the reference to "Kaponya culture" in the first letter indicates that there is an inventive, unplanned striving for survival embodied in the character of the *Kaponya*.

The chaotic and disorderly life in Zambia is represented for many in the person of the *Kaponya*. These are the young, male call boys, bus conductors, street traders who run the country, many agree efficiently, albeit in a way that is hard to place in a linear sequence of activity. Hazel Zulu, writing in the state national newspaper, the *Times of Zambia*, provides a decent description of what the *Kaponya* does:

> I was driving into town two months ago when I got caught up in the capital city traffic jam. All the parking spaces were full to capacity. I was in a state of panic and confusion when suddenly one *Kaponya* came to my rescue. *Apa ba sister* [here my sister], he showed me a parking slot that he had "reserved" for anyone who was ready to give him some "lunch" money.[17]

The *Kaponya* are the young persons who perceive tiny gaps that offer an opportunity to make a living on the margins. They are stylised by musicians such as Dandy Krazy for the manner in which they talk, an unfiltered straight talk, usually in the slang of Copperbelt's lingua franca, Bemba. They are also the embodiment of uncertain livelihoods and the staving off of hunger that Dandy Krazy (2010) sings about in the song "Tubombela Akabwali" ("We Work for an Nshima").[18]

Trying amidst Hunger

The *Times of Zambia*,[19] in a story titled "Man Gets 20 Years for Murder," reported on two brothers, the children of a Luanshya mineworker who had been laid off and imprisoned for murdering a man who had refused to share his nshima. Cases of murder involving food often made the home-news section of the *Times of Zambia*,[20] and in these, hunger was, just as Filip de

Boeck found amongst the Aluund in Zaire, seen as an overturning of trans-corporeal relations of reciprocity and conviviality around food (1994, 257). When stories such as those reported in the *Times of Zambia* were recounted, people tended to express their dismay by talking about how things had gone mad (*ifunti fya li pena*) or how things were turned upside down (*fyali pen-damuka*). As in Chapter 3, they also offered an opportunity for people to talk about how some people were doing better than others.

The privatisation of ZCCM was preceded by the development of stark inequities amongst Copperbelt residents, especially former mine employ-ees who had enjoyed a wide range of social benefits across all ranks. Those perceived as doing well felt under pressure to be generous to less well-off neighbours. The Phiris, for example, a relatively well-off family in Luanshya described earlier, told me that, during the worst periods that followed the sale of the mines, they took to having their meals in secret and outside reg-ular hours to avoid having to share with neighbours, who tended to drop by at meal times. An inability to share food was frowned upon. I was informed that a man who had kept pigs in the backyard of his home in a low-density former mining suburb in Luanshya had been reported to the local authorities for creating a public health nuisance. He was reported not for the slaughter of pigs in his backyard, but allegedly for not having shared the pork with his neighbours. Apart from of the immorality of not sharing food, its absence experienced as hunger has often been used in Zambian political rallying, for example Dandy Krazy's song "Tubombela Akabwali" (2010). The music video to this song offers snapshots of the pragmatic reality of youth trying a life amidst hardship. Dandy Krazy draws on the imagery of those employed in the informal sector, such as marketeers, public transport bus conductors, window cleaners, stone crushers, and shoe menders. Lyrically, Dandy Krazy draws on the experience of hunger, highlighting the corporeality of the expe-rience of working for little:

> *We work for akabwali.*
> *We get paid on Sunday only a mealie meal ata.*
> *Now you are killing us.*
> *You deflate our stomachs we suffer.*
>
> *The children cry of hunger:*
> *"Mummy, mummy, my strength is finished, I am hungry*

Yesterday just nshima.
In the morning I sponged porridge without salt.
Doesn't daddy keep some salt?
Just that night he got paid."

The use of the expression "We only work for an nshima" ties historical experiences of revolt against the state and employers, such as in the food riots that began on the Copperbelt in 1986 and 1990. Opposition politicians have also used the affective and corporeal experience of hunger as a rallying call for revolt. The song "Tomato Balunda" ("Tomato Is Expensive," 2000) by the Zambian artist Cullen Chisha (also known as 2wice) became a rallying song for those opposed to President Chiluba's standing for an unconstitutional third term in office in 2001. The same song appeared on a programme for campaign songs for the Patriotic Front (PF), which enjoyed popular support, especially among youth on the Copperbelt and Lusaka prior to the 2008 presidential by-elections. In the campaign the PF, which won the 2011 national elections, unseating the Movement for Multi-Party Democracy (MMD), which had been in power since 1991, poached Dandy Krazy's song "Donchi Kubeba" ("Don't Tell Them," 2011). The PF used it to imply that supporters, mainly poor young urban youth, could receive handouts that normally included clothes, food, cash, and alcohol freely from the MMD, but kept silent on *donchi kubeba*, who they would vote for.

Youth and Fatalism

"Young people need to be active" was a comment made in reference to the dilapidation of the sports centre. Churchgoing children were seen as worryingly secretive, while those going to bars were viewed by an older generation as nihilistic. For young people themselves, these activities were better than "doing nothing at home." They were also acutely aware of their own fragility. As one young man put it, "Everyone wants to live, but it is difficult. Things are overturned." Metaphor is often used by youth, as previously noted by Bajaj, to describe the precarious and "random" nature of life, usually in relation to contraction of HIV/AIDS (2008, 321). Youth also say often with irony that "to stay/live" these days, one has to be a *tamanga* (a runner), be quick and alert. This alertness, quickness, sits in contrast to the miner, who did not need to "run after his life" but go through the routine of going to work and wait for a salary at the end of the month. As one shopkeeper in Luanshya told me:

The miners should not have been given their benefits all in one go; they did not know what to do with the money. It should have been given in instalments, like a salary, what they were used to. Instead, they would go to the bank and demand their money whenever they wanted. . . . They would come into my shop, spend big with their children, holding two sausages in each hand. . . . Now [when] I see them no longer who they were, I feel very sad for them. Some even come to ask me for some bread, saying, "I spent a lot of money in your shop."

Apart from poorly managing their finances, I heard how miners' families had broken down, with parents turning a blind eye to their children's activities. One former miner told me how he had chastised the daughter of one of his former colleagues whom he had found soliciting money in a bar.

My own sense initially and the view of my adult informants in Luanshya was that, overall, young people seemed bent on a trajectory of destruction. This view is not uncommon in sociological writing on youth in Africa (Leclerc-Madlala 1997; Mufune 2000; Meyer-Weitz 2005; Bajaj 2008; Pugh 2010). It presumes that young people living in difficult economic circumstances have a death wish and mindlessly live a hedonistic lifestyle of drink and multiple sexual partners—activities that they should clearly know lead to an early grave. In addition, this view assumes that youth in these situations passively let go, giving in to an inertia that allows for exploitative situations, and fail to take responsibility. These assumptions have fuelled the development of projects in behavioural change and empowerment, the first to curb what is seen as a death drive, and the latter to animate young people to take responsibility. These discourses are gendered, especially in HIV/AIDS campaigns that attempt to control men's excesses and shake women's docility. While these views may ring true, they paint a myopic picture, one that does not take into account the visible empirical evidence of how people, including the residents of the Copperbelt, try to sustain their lives through numerous economic activities. Despite the fact that many do not make it beyond the breadline every day, even with failures such as the loss of goods through fire,[21] confiscation of goods by local authorities, clamping down on illegal trade, the demolition of housing and little shops,[22] security forces' brutality against illegal copper mining (see Chapter 4), and the theft of crops, many do not give up. It is hard to see fatalism or passivity in these actions. It is also hard to miss, for those who have spent any time on the Copperbelt or indeed in any African city, the energy and sounds of people carting trolleys of goods, pushing goods through bus windows in sweltering heat and in rain, women who carry their sick children on their backs for the lack of transport money or spend hours going house to house looking for piecework like washing clothes. Popular Zambian musician Dalisoul, in his song "Shansa" (2009), captures this reiteration of life:

Be optimistic, stick with the [wheel]barrow till you find.
Be optimistic, stay till you arrive.
Take out your strength because it is the only thing the world wants.
Don't be scared to go further.

For example, a lizard will fall from a tin roof but do it again!
A thief will steal, get caught but when he comes out will do it again!
Chisokone [the market] will burn, people will cry, but goods will return again!
Don't leave good things to go by you, try again!

Sound and Rhythm in Trying

By drawing on resonant sound, evocative words, images, and bodily movements, social commentary on life in Zambia through music provides a linking narrative on the experience of living. It is these reverberant experiences, the songs of political rallying, the jubilation of dance, and the sounds of death through wailing that remind many Zambians, without recourse to an explicit discourse of death, of the fragility of their lives. If we draw from Lefebvre, Régulier, and Zayani's (1999) "rhythmanalytical" project, popular music in Zambia can be seen as attempting to make sense of what has become a disruptive, disorderly rhythm of life that throws up too many unpleasant surprises. Just as Judith Brown (2001) notes of the expansion of the possibilities in information technologies, in their morale-boosting songs Zambian musicians urge people to keep on trying, to attempt not one but different paths to explore and open up the world. Contemporary Zambian music thus should be seen not only as an articulation of the experience of life, but also as metaphorical evocations of life, even in the context of death. Nowhere is this more apparent than in the celebratory funeral song "Bakalila" ("They Will Cry," 2007) by the artist Mozegater.

I first heard the music of Mozegater in a club in Kitwe as I saw a crowd galvanised to the dance floor to move in a parody of suffering. The club drew an intergenerational crowd, and I observed as young and old men and women in variation lifted their hands to their heads, shaking them as one would who had received terrible news. They limped and clutched their stomachs, and at the chorus of the song wailed as one would at a funeral. The song, as I found out later in interviews with Mozegater, is his creative attempt to make "noise," what he calls *chiunda* music. It is a sound that combines the morale-boosting songs heard at sports events, known as *boostele*, and the sounds and speech narratives heard at funerals. The song evoked the experience of death for the living that was all around. It reminded me of an expression I had heard in explanation of the general tendency not to leave wills, *bushe ukailosha pa ku fwa*, "Will you dream of yourself at your death?" In *Bakalila*, Mozegater sings:

> *They won't believe it, they will come crying*
> *Some, the gossips will come to see how thin I got.*
> *Listen, the ones who care, crying, "Come back and take me too."*
> *Myself, I am dead.*
> *I am resting, it's all quiet, and you busy crying.*
>
> *Oh, this child you cry of is gone today.*
> *The children will be crying and looking sorrowful.*
> *The child of life and air has gone today . . .*
>
> *Iyelele iyelele [wailing]*
> *You should take me to the grave . . .*
>
> *Please don't stop me.*
> *You don't know how much I have suffered.*
> *When the time for death arrives in Zed,*
> *There is no rising from the dead*
> *You cry Zambia, ama guys and ama girls, it is crying*
> *Kitchen party, chachacha, weddings and all, in the clubs, no size.*

De Boeck, writing on Kinshasa, highlights that death in contexts of great uncertainty is often collapsed into the temporal experience of presence, as a space of not there, but of now (2005, 20–21). To make noise is to evoke feeling and to displace the mourning of oneself, not to sometime in the future when you can't "dream of yourself" because you are dead, but to the time of the living. Raising *ichimwela*, "boosting morale" or "making vitality," and wailing link birth, death, celebratory events, success, and failure on the same continuum of life. Music, David Coplan argues, writing on Basotho migratory songs, boosts flagging morale and allows the poetic expression of situations of hardship in times of transition (2006, 226). In the Copperbelt context, where the frequency of death was a constant reminder of the fragility of life, music, in its rhythmic sounds, added energy to the body seen as vulnerable to the vagaries of life. It also allowed for the articulation of unspoken fears. The often-unspoken fear when someone close was admitted to hospital was whether or not they would come out alive. Complex conditions that required costly diagnostic tests were often not conducted. For residents on the Copperbelt this meant travelling to Lusaka to the state-run University Teaching Hospital, where one could access specialist units and surgeons. Even then, tests were often not carried out because the facilities were not operational or reagents for blood tests and other procedures were not in stock. Private health centres charged prohibitive costs for the same tests. As a result, failure to find out what was wrong in the biomedical sector led people to try out other remedies. They ranged from traditional healers to the country's burgeoning sector of alternative Chinese remedies.

Trying to Live

In health-seeking behaviours, the general experience for Copperbelt residents was one of frustration and ambiguity. This was especially so when families considered healthcare costs. This often put them in the difficult position of having to use on tests and medication meagre earnings that otherwise would have been spent on food. In cases where it was unclear what was ailing a patient,[23] I observed elliptical talk that alluded to the idea that what actually ailed a patient was some undiscovered strain of HIV, especially in cases where the patient was emaciated. A typical scenario was that of orphaned sixteen-year-old Annie, who died of a belatedly diagnosed heart condition. Annie had been staying with relatives of her father on the Copperbelt, who had taken her in following the deaths of her father and later her mother. In 2008, when I got to know her, she was always busy doing domestic chores in her uncle's household. Some months before she died in 2009 she seemed listless and complained of tiredness. Her aunt and cousins put this down to laziness and voiced suspicions that she might be pregnant, even though it was apparent from the amount of time she spent on chores that she had little time for a social life. When her condition became worse, her aunt took her to the local clinic, which ran a malaria test, usually the first line of inquiry. The test came back negative, but Annie was put on anti-malarial medication anyway. Her aunt dropped in conversation that Annie's parents were taken "by this disease that has come to finish us," the implication being that Annie might be HIV-positive. A couple of weeks later, her aunt told me that she had gathered the courage to take her for an HIV test, and this too had come back negative. Meanwhile Annie was getting weaker. Eventually an older sister of Annie's who had married and lived in another town insisted on taking her to Lusaka to see a specialist. The specialist diagnosed her with an enlarged heart. Annie died shortly after.

In the aftermath of Annie's death, rumours began to circulate about Annie's uncle, whose small-scale business, like others in the neighbourhood, had begun to pick up due to increasing copper prices. He was accused of having sacrificed Annie to satanists. Several neighbours argued that Annie's relatives on the mother's side of the family should have looked out for her and taken her to a diviner, which would have outed the culprit early on. Another said that they should have seen a Chinese doctor on the Copperbelt who was well known for treating heart conditions. The accusation was that the family should have explored various options.

The extension of the temporal experience of life is expressed in songs like Petersen's "Musiye Atoping'e" ("Leave Him/Her to Top Up," 2008), in lyrics that urge people to keep on trying to live, and literally "top up" to extend their life:

> On this earth there is plenty that kills us
> Death does not respect anyone.
> Those who wait for handouts it stirs [literally twists]
> Taking those too who dither.
> Over death there is no one who has power.
> We can hang out today,
> Tomorrow we are throwing you.
> Water kills, and cars kill too
> Life kills, it has no spare tire.
> When you get sick. it is to look for remedies
> And stick with them till the last hour.
> Just top up on your life, for long life.

Petersen's song and those of other Zambian musicians presented in this chapter direct us to think about life as a journeyed experimentation, in which one fills in along the way the possibilities of life.

LIFE AMIDST HARDSHIP

Life in places like the Zambian Copperbelt has been hard for many mired in the experience of death. While Copperbelt residents describe their lives as ones of suffering, there is also the hope that this suffering may end. This belief does not necessarily play out as a clear plan for a future, but as a precarious one. The possibilities of what the future may bring emerge from the environment and people's engagement within it and with each other. This engagement cannot be predetermined, and what Zambian popular music urges is for people to go on. Thus, when the musician Dalisoul sings, "Take out your strength because it is the only thing the world wants," he is not only talking about the movement of physical strength, but also the movement of feeling, a resonance that arises from "people's mutually attentive engagement, in shared contexts of practical activity" that lie at the heart of sociality (Ingold 2000, 196). Good luck and bad luck are in this view not abstract concepts, but occurrences that resonate and impact the body and the capabilities of people's engagement with the world. The awareness of the fragility of the body in this uncertain world has given way to morale-boosting narratives, like "Take out your strength because it is the only thing the world wants," raise *ichimwela*, or "make vitality." This vitality, in the context of hunger, suffering, and the depression of death, is what sustains the energy of places of great physical and psychosocial stress. The energy lies in the affective realm and is perceived in music and dance rhythms that imbue and literally move the body. This means scholars must look beyond the daily struggle and dangerous behaviour of youth to the sounds that animate their lives.

NOTES

1. A version of this chapter was originally published in *African Studies* 71, no. 2 (2012): 304–322.

2. In a survey I conducted in August 2009 within the low-density suburb in Luanshya, out of the one hundred households surveyed only twenty could be described as nuclear; the other eighty included extended family members: nieces, nephews, grandchildren, and, most often, mothers-in-law. Of the extended families, I observed in Luanshya, extended kin in urban households did much unpaid work, as Hansen had noted in her longitudinal study of everyday life in Mtendere from the 1970s to the early 1990s (1997, 101). In comparison to the period in which Hansen carried out her study, this

domestic relationship seems to have become more exploitative, with little of the previous era's benefits of clothes, toiletries, and education.

3. For example, eight illegal copper miners died at Chambeshi Metals Mine in Kitwe when a tunnel they were working in collapsed (*Times of Zambia* 11 June 2009).

4. The HIV/AIDS statistics on the Copperbelt are some of the highest in the country, at 17% of the population overall. The rate in Central Province is 17.5%, and Lusaka Province is the highest at 20.8% (CSO 2007, 231).

5. "Trying" here meant in the sense of "taxing, demanding, difficult, tough, hard, pressured, frustrating, fraught, arduous, gruelling, tiring . . . or simply hellish." *New Oxford American Dictionary*, 2005.

6. Main web activity from 1999 to 2003, archive found at http://wayback.archive.org/web/*/http://www.chrysalis.co.zm

7. By "lifeworld," Devisch connotes a phenomenological experience of the world.

8. A processual approach to agency that accounts for the generative movement of life, which in nature never results in exactly the same product even within the same species, puts paid to the idea of neat causal links (see Oyama 2000; Ingold 2011).

9. "Copper Loses Its Shine and Copperbelt Its Jobs," *Africa News*, 20 February 2009.

10. "Luanshya in Crisis," *The Post*, 1 October 2002.

11. The Luanshya mines were the first to be sold in the privatisation of the state-mining conglomerate, ZCCM. They were first sold to the Binani Group, later renamed RAMCOZ, in 1997. RAMCOZ was liquidated in 2000. In 2004 the Luanshya mines were taken over by JW & Enya, a Swiss-registered company; this went under care and maintenance at the end of 2008 and was eventually bought by NFC Africa, a Chinese company.

12. "Somaesthetic" is a term coined by Richard Shusterman (2000) to refer to the aesthetic cultivation of the body. In this case, I use it to refer to the negative aesthetic cultivation of the body. The term "aesthetic" is used in its broader definition as the experiential sense of life or being.

13. A common expression used to describe a funeral hearse, in this context an attractive woman who is "death walking," an elliptical way of referring to an attractive woman who may be HIV-positive.

14. The years following independence in 1964 until the mid-1970s are considered the most prosperous.

15. *The Post*, 1 March 2010.

16. "A Nation in Hopelessness," *The Post*, 9 April 2010.

17. *Times of Zambia*.

18. Nshima is a stiff maize-meal porridge, a staple of Zambian meals.

19. 7 October 2009.

20. *Times of Zambia*: "Woman Nabbed for Murder of Hubby," 20 March 2007; "Robbers Raid Ndola Filling Station," 18 August 2009; "Man Gets Three Years for Manslaughter," 28 February 2009; "Wife Killer Goes in for Four and a Half Years," 16 March 2010.

21. A fire at the biggest market on the Copperbelt, Chisokone Market in Kitwe, breaks out almost every year.

22. Much of this was carried out under the "Keep Zambia Clean and Healthy" campaign launched in 2007 by the country's late president Levi Mwanawasa.

23. The general assumption in diagnostics, recounted by those who fell ill, was that one either had malaria or was displaying symptoms of HIV infection.

Conclusion

Making Life out of Disorder

"There used to be order." Copperbelt residents who experienced life in the region prior to the re-privatisation of the Zambia Consolidated Copper Mines perceive their present circumstances as disorderly and their lives as uncertain. They talk of their lives as having been upended, with the precarity they face making it difficult for them to make concrete plans. To survive and get on has necessitated that they improvise. It has also required that they learn to be attentive to what place affords and to grab momentary opportunities (Cligett et al. 2007). They draw on an improvisational approach that requires a heightened perception, or a "tuning in" (De Boeck and Barber 2010) to the possibilities that the social and physical environment can offer.

There is also an affective dimension to this, conveyed in the ways in which residents speak of the past and their future, but also in the ways in which they perceive the changing character of the Copperbelt as a place. They point to infrastructural decline, seen in burst water and sewer pipes, potholed roads, and to the changes in the landscape that indicate self-provisioning for energy, food, water. These shifts are contrasted with what they remember as an orderly past. With a strong hint of nostalgia, they recount stories of tended gardens and parks, and the tight administration and maintenance of former mine neighbourhoods.

In this conclusion, I turn to the improvisational efforts of Copperbelt residents not only to survive but to make it, which I describe in this book as "trying"—reflecting not only the experimental, exploratory, and speculative approach they deploy, but also the effort employed and pitfalls encountered in everyday livelihood struggles. How does "trying" to get by or get on alter understandings of place among residents of the Copperbelt? What can it tell

us about the experience of other places that have gone through similar processes of socioeconomic decline, either as a result of deindustrialisation or
severe austerity? What can a focus on the stories and texture of a place illuminate about struggles of survival and the aspirations to make it in environments with deep limitations on the ability to flourish? In short, I draw on the
experience of Copperbelt residents to share some thoughts on what happens
to a people and a place when what they hold, or perceive as secure, comes to
an end.

AN ANTHROPOLOGY OF TRYING

The notion of trying brings together from the previous chapters the experimental, poetic, processual, and textural engagements with place; at the same
time it engages with the anxieties and uncertainties that come with making a
life in difficult circumstances. "Trying" reflects not only continual attempts to
do something, but also what is difficult, annoying, and hard to endure. To this
end, I would argue for an anthropology of trying that, in relation to talking
about the architectural character of a place, captures the effort (or sweat) of
our habitation within the world, rather than just the playful and poetic.

   An anthropology of trying responds to these questions. Departing from
systemic categorisation, it draws on theoretical and methodological perspectives in anthropology that emphasise performative movement and the senses,
and the political and the ethical as they are lived. It attempts to break with
systemic structural representations that often do not account for the effort
and the experimental, poetic, processual and textural engagements that residents have with place and circumstance. An anthropology of trying would
have us draw on "an ethos of experimentation and pluralism in how we think,
research, and present our human geographies" (Latham and Conradson
2003, 1904). On the Copperbelt, this approach is not out of place because it
perceives a crucial way in which residents address the curveballs thrown at
them by life. In the practice of fieldwork, this approach would mean not putting too much stock in trying to establish clear patterns of action, but to view
the field as a volume. If the volume is imagined as a liquid within which we
are contained and our movements and others reverberate through it, as the
immersed fieldworker we would be sounding out not points and networks
(Gell 1998; Latour 2005) nor lines or threads (Ingold 2007) but rhythms in
unfolding wholes (Bohm 2002; Ingold 2011). Accordingly, in thinking about

life and the end of life, there needs to be greater appreciation of people's attempts to live and to make a life, especially a reanalysis of places where it has been assumed to have ended.

LIVING WITH UNCERTAINTY

In the ZCCM past, former mineworkers could discern a path of upward social mobility by rising through the employment ranks. In today's privatised and deregulated social context, the obscurity of the path to success has left the field open to wild speculation, fantasy, and suspicion. The future thus for Copperbelt residents is not one that they can clearly map out or plan; it is one that unfolds with uncertainty. *Twala mona inga twa fika* ("We shall see when we get there") is an apt expression that Copperbelt residents use to talk of the future. For many, especially young people, speculation on what the future holds is frightening because the picture painted by formal analysis of the context is too grim: a short life, illness, unemployment, and an unstable family life. To accept this fate, this map of the future, is to deny life. Living does not go along one path; it is not centripetal but rather centrifugal, "seeking to cast wide" (Hallam and Ingold 2007, 13), and thus emanating from the body's movements and efforts to intermingle with those of others. To live life along a straight line in an uncertain and unpredictable environment is to court a collision with death. Copperbelt residents learn to improvise and to wander. By wander I do not mean that Copperbelt residents are going through life aimlessly, but that they do not necessarily follow a fixed point on the horizon. Their actions are not leisurely; they are effortful, tuned in to both hazards and opportunities. Their daily struggles to get by imply determination, but they do not suggest direct causal outcomes. They try.

Trying as Agency beyond a Plan

Bagozzi and Warshaw (1990), in a social psychological study of weight loss behaviour, outlined a theory of trying. A theory of trying is a conceptual map that seeks to anticipate the results of an individual's attempts to move toward a desired goal that is difficult to achieve. An individual's attitude and prior experiences contribute to the variation of outcomes (Bagozzi and Warshaw 1990). However, in this book I have argued that Copperbelt residents' actions are contingent not only on an individual's attitudes or desires, but also on affective resonances that go beyond the body of the individual to the wider lived environment. Trying here lies not only with the individual subject but with the intersubjective realm, which links the affective resonances of hope and despair with the lived experiences of dwelling.

The actions of Copperbelt residents are not guided by a clear plan but rather by an illusory and fragmented perception of it. I have argued that getting to know what to do in an uncertain world involves an improvisory repetition of movements to order one's partial understandings of it, as in Mr Mubita's economic activities in his yard (Chapter 3). This process requires a phenomenological understanding of the environment and not just an abstract one. Such an understanding is akin to an infant's learning to stand through a repetition of actions, such as bouncing to lever oneself off the ground, grabbing onto a table or a chair—actions that are effortful and opportunistic in the search for aids in the vicinity. There can be wider factors that themselves are unstable and interact with the practice of trying to stand. Maybe a gust of wind topples the chair or makes the child fall back to the ground, events that may not be expected.[1] When Copperbelt residents had an idea or dream, they were aware that it was not possible to maintain its singularity, as their life circumstances made this difficult. But this did not mean that they stopped trying or hoping to achieve something from it. The idea was more like a line cast wide in the hope of something concrete taking hold. Such action requires responsiveness, a tuning in to one own's conscious and unconscious abilities, but also to what the environment affords. When Copperbelt residents spoke of the future and said, "We shall see when we get there," their view was based on the awareness that the environment too unfolds in variation and that one's actions needed to be in tune with these changes. This view of action, an agency that is not based on clear intention, is not unique to the Copperbelt and is to be found in emergent writing on life in crisis, such as Johnson-Hanks's work in Cameroon. Johnson-Hanks (2005, 363) argues that in the context of uncertainty, the ability to seize opportunities rather than fulfil a prior intention allows promising outcomes. Povinelli describes it as an ability to "live the present as if it were this future" (2011, 130). Trying, from this perspective, thus goes beyond performative stylisation or positioning to engage body and environment in the process of doing.

Improvisational Livelihoods

Even though Copperbelt residents explore a variety of livelihood options, most of these involve working with their hands, such as agricultural activity in their backyards and on the outskirts of the town. A notion of self-sufficiency underpins much of this activity, a need to fend for oneself. Distinctions in the relative success of persons working for themselves are visible, highlighting how well residents are able to cope with the changed welfare situation on the Copperbelt. It is not only one's circumstances that indicate who is doing better, but also how skilfully a person is able to perceive and to draw upon the social and material resources available, as well as to negotiate moral boundaries. The skill employed in these livelihood-seeking activities is aimed at increasing knowledge and requires a willingness to try, as is illustrated in Vincent's and Mr Mubita's activities in building a lined well. Trying thus could be seen as a series of attempts towards activating opportunity. It is experimental and improvisory.

However, as illustrated in Chapter 6, it is not detached from what the body can physically do, nor from the skills and tools one can employ. These are not limiting factors, as neither the body nor skills or tools remain the same over time. They can be modified, or new combinations or energies, in the case of an ill body, can be found to allow the continued reiteration of doing something to earn a living. In this way improvisation, or rather the ability to follow the possibilities that open up in the course of going about life and making things, is increasingly characteristic of Copperbelt residents' engagements with their social and physical landscapes. Improvisation directly relates to Ingold's (2000) notion of skilful dwelling that enfolds people in the movements of life and living. It is entangled with and complementary to the notion of trying—the hopeful going on with one's aspirations and dreams, even in the face of numerous challenges and constraints that tend to throw plans off course. In the face of these challenges, as I have shown in the previous chapters, Copperbelt residents are willing to engage in riskier economic activities like informal mining.

Trespassing and Negotiating Social and Moral Boundaries

Copperbelt residents perceive that the political economy of the region and the country has been "overturned" like a pot of spilt milk, leaving a context where moral boundaries are flexible and negotiable, and where an illegal livelihood is less shameful than the experience of hunger. Through efforts to get by or get on, Copperbelt residents are increasingly opportunistic, taking advantage of places laid bare to exploitation by the weakened regulatory context that followed the re-privatisation of the mines. This way of going on is well illustrated in the modus operandi of the *Kaponya* (described earlier), who well illustrate Ingold's (2007) notion of the wayfarer or wanderer and highlight the performative basis of this way of seeking a living. Copperbelt residents' movements following deregulation became more like the *Kaponya*. In their seizing of the small gaps of livelihood opportunities, they tended to trespass, not only on private property (as was the case with the informal copper miners), but also on people's sensibilities of customary notions of respectability, while at the very same time offering possibility for life in a place of much uncertainty. I use the idea of the *Kaponya* to show what trying is as a dispositional attitude toward the world, simultaneously a reckless wander, an attempt to create chances, and a seeking for relations.

For example, when the *Kaponya* walk, they swagger as well as stagger, and when they speak, they affect a raspy, slightly broken drawl, a performance that is akin to an intoxicated man. However, in their entreaties to sell a good or offer a service, they perform suffering at the same time, drawing on the intersubjective morality of hunger and a notion of personhood whereby suffering is not individual but relational. Kathry Linn Guerts, writing on cultural logics of the Anlo in Ghana, noted that their notion of morality was sensorial, perceived both in movement and in dispositional feeling and characterised by onomatopoeic speech (2003, 189). There a person walking *lugulugu* (horsing around) indicated the possibility of becoming an "aimless irresponsible person" (Guerts 2003, 189). There are striking similarities between this view of morality and what on the Copperbelt is referred to as *ukwenda enda*, or in Zambian English, "to be *movious*," described as "moving around" (Gough 2008). The *Kaponya* thus not only displays the capacity to trespass in his aimless, slightly reckless wander, but also, in the portrayal of suffering, draws on the moral sense that one should share to prevent the other from hunger. Both affects are sensorial. This, I argue, demonstrates that trying is not something that exists separate from the body and its sensing abilities. It is not rational choice derived from a mental ability to drive oneself in a particular direction. Rather, it is from the body, as an organism inhabiting the environment, that one perceives possibilities and potential constraints.

In their engagement with ideas such as those that protect private property, Copperbelt residents, like those who work at the copper mine dumpsites, do not see rules as fixed, but rather as pliable, their boundaries open to exploration and trespass. Workers at these sites draw from alternate moral codes, like sharing, to justify their presence there. This does not mean that Copperbelt residents discard the notions of private property. Instead, the private property and its related concept of free markets are entangled with African notions of reciprocity that value sharing and communality, as well as perseverance when life gets hard. Trespass, then becomes a continuous political act. It also casts light on the moral vacuum of neoliberalism (Ferguson 2006; Povinelli 2011). In the moral void, it leaves those at the margins of capitalist extraction, such as the informal copper workers (Chapter 4), labouring, debilitated, and exhausted at the margins of global copper commodity chains, having to draw on sources of energy outside their bodies.

Willing to Go On

Relying on morale-boosting narratives and songs, as we saw in Chapter 6, Copperbelt residents urge each other to go on. This is akin to what Eleanor Wilkinson and Iliana Ortega-Alcazar (2019, 161) have described, drawing on Lauren Berlant, as a "cruel form of optimism," referring to the false sense of hope given by support workers to vulnerable young persons struggling with housing in England and Wales following cuts to their housing benefits. However, this hope, the encouragement to go on and endure, serves to distribute trying beyond the individual to the wider society of others who maybe similarly struggling. It forms a communitas of trying. Suffering, rather than being individualised, gets shifted to the collective public space, experienced through the sounds of music that evoke it, or in the daily witnessing of it. Likewise, as I have shown in Chapter 2, where the Spaitas tried to establish an ice-cream parlour based on lifestyles of the past, and the Mwenyas a used-oil business anticipating a recycling economy of the future—ideas of a better life resonate through nostalgia for a past, fantasies of a future, and the momentary possibilities of the temporal present. In this way hope and despair intermingle to provide the repertoire for the multiple improvisations to try to make a life.

Nowhere is this better illustrated than in the domestic expectations of Copperbelt residents. Here life unfolds in variation, and plans, such as the ideations of gender described in Chapter 5, are like tools that provide an exploratory extension into the world. Residents home in and attempt to reiterate symbolisms from a variety of ideational systems. As Moore argues, symbolism and its enactment in ritual are largely about managing lived experience and not just its representation. They encompass actions that are also "sensuous, physical and practical, and not simply ideational and intellectual" (1999, 8). As in female initiation rituals, Copperbelt residents are reiterating and improvising certain bodily movements and practices, not to fit with an abstract outcome but to give movement and a sense of direction so as to insert oneself into a flow of life through which pleasure and not just hardship can be found. Copperbelt women's management of the ideational codes of modernity and tradition provides an entry into understanding the ways in which ideas of place, such as those of the village, afford its residents a rural-like life in the city.

Villagisation as Manifestation of Trying in Place

Economic decline on the Copperbelt following the re-privatisation of the mines saw a period of increased movement of Copperbelt residents to the capital city, Lusaka, which offers some opportunities in trade and service sectors to eke out a living, and for some to gain formal employment in the state public sector concentrated there. These processes have consolidated Lusaka as a prime city, reflecting a characteristic pattern of African urbanisation (Pieterse and Parnell 2014). Crucially, Copperbelt residents increasingly have come to rely on urban agricultural activity in the town and on its rural peripheries. Other residents, in a trend noted by Ferguson (1999) in his work on mineworker retirees, are opting to take up farming further afield in other rural areas. They increasingly live converged lifestyles of the urban and rural, drawing on both to make a living. In their efforts, they leave traces of themselves within the environment they inhabit. Their attempts to make a living and find harmony and a rhythm or energy in life in hard times, as well as the multiple contestations they engage in, culminate in both visible and invisible efforts in the making of place. Thus, what has come to be known as "villagisation" reflects not only a representation of aspects of town resembling rural life, but more broadly a temporality in the continual becoming of place, affected by the changing rhythms of the everyday. It reflects an awareness of Copperbelt residents' views of themselves and their actions in a changing world. Rather than seeing modes of life in the town and the village as separate, a border-linking perspective (Devisch 2007, 107), linking the affective and conceptual world, is useful in reconciling what is seen and not seen in place and how they are connected (2007, 107).

Taking this view further to encompass the material entanglement of persons and their activities in place, border-linking highlights that villagisation is intercorporeal in the awareness and cultivation of body habits and intersubjective in the moral discourses that link the "distant" or invisible world of the village with the town and in turn with other places. In addition, villagisation connotes a pragmatic engagement of people and their world. As I have illustrated throughout the book, Copperbelt residents live converged lifestyles that do not always settle well and that are occasionally revealed in dissonant situations across various ideational modes of sociality. I have drawn from Lefebvre, Régulier, and Zayani (1999) to argue that the rhythm of life on the Copperbelt no longer resembles the structured monotony that the ZCCM mining system tried to foster, but wavers, and this is perceived in the contingent character of those doing well and not so well. Villagisation is a manifestation of these unpredictable rhythms of life, reflecting the recombinant, effortful, improvised attempts to make a life in a place that residents perceive has lost a sense of order.

Nostalgia for Place

Casey (1987) highlights the centrality of place in the experience of nostalgia and poses the following question: "What kind of place are we nostalgic about or over?" Casey argues that nostalgia suffuses those places to which we feel a strong attachment, and in which we have a sense of belonging. The patterns of life in the company town characterised not only the Copperbelt as a particular kind of place, but also its residents as coming from there. The unravelling and retexturing of the Copperbelt, as described in the previous chapters, has produced a collective sense of nostalgia popularised in music and culture.

To be from the Copperbelt is to have a mythologised expectation of modernity (Ferguson 1999). As described earlier in the book, the decades of a state and corporate welfare orientation that bolstered expectations quickly led to despair and a desperate hope following the reprivatisation of ZCCM. The past, for Copperbelt residents, has come to represent a time when former miners and their families could pursue leisure without the stress of the economic hardships that now characterise their lives. For many of my informants, the present entails living within the memories and traces of a life that was organised around the rhythms of mining shifts, recreational sports, and homemaker's clubs. In these aspects, nostalgia for Copperbelt residents has a concrete dimension. It is visible in the potholes, the rundown recreational facilities, the food gardens that have appeared here and there in the available open spaces, the smell of burst sewer lines and wood smoke from brick and charcoal furnaces, and the sounds of small-scale industrial activity punctuating suburban life. These afterlives texture the experience of place not only for the residents who remain, and who point to a changing landscape that they say has lost its order, but also for those who leave, as many did following retrenchments. For example, a well-known actor/comedian who moved to Lusaka spoke of his surprise at the dearth of recreational sporting facilities and artistic cultural life, as had been widespread on the Copperbelt.

To be from a certain place is also to inhabit a particular habitus, recognisable not only by oneself but also by others. Copperbelt residents, in evoking their changed circumstance, which has them increasingly turn to livelihood activities that resemble the rural, see themselves as becoming "more like peasants." It can be said that in this framing of themselves, they return to a mythological, pre-industrial, rural home. This "return of the rural," however, was not a loop into the past, but rather a representation of the current crisis. As I have shown in Chapter 1, Copperbelt residents often unrealistically imagined places that provided a canvas for their aspirations, or fantasies of their future, akin to a "nostalgia for the future" (Piot 2010). Nostalgia thus frames and provides meaning to Copperbelt residents' experience of a changing landscape. It also animates their ethical and political engagement with place. By referring to multiple pasts and possible futures, Copperbelt residents highlight the moral vacuum of their present. This is represented at worst in the values of an ideology that justifies austerity and the retreat of the state at the height of the HIV/AIDS pandemic, leaving death in its wake.

This points to the pyschosocial dimension of nostalgia, which anchors the fear of the loss of identification in the face of cataclysmic change (Mah 2010). Nostalgia then is a "structure of feeling" that gives the mood to the changes in the social organisation of the processes of production that over time may consolidate to define specific conditions (Williams 1977, 132). It directs us in the case of the Copperbelt to look at how the sale of ZCCM has changed not only the political economic landscape, but also the subjectivities of Copperbelt residents—in particular, how trying to make a living in a context of prolonged uncertainty is shaping an understanding of themselves and the place they call home.

Nostalgia provides a language for people to tell their stories of socioeconomic change (Tannock 1995; Dirksmeier 2016). As recounted earlier in this book, it is not homogeneous and has multiple narratives. It is gendered, generational, and classed. It is also shaped by the affordances of the past and the temporal present, to reflect variations in "visions, values and ideals" (Tannock 1995, 454). This means that if we are to take an ecological view of place, where persons and their environments are mutually constituting, nostalgia for place is textured by what is possible within their habitus, their ideations, and the affordances of the socioeconomic, political, and physical environment.

CHANGING PLACE

Recent work on urbanisms offers a nuanced understanding of the changing and transnational character of African cities (Piot 2010; Lindell 2010; Murray 2013; Quayson 2014; Hart 2016). These works highlight the ways in which

African cities are interconnected at various scales, from local informal networks to the wider mobility of persons and ideas—and they call for an analysis on their own terms. These studies draw attention to the processes that shape the institutions, infrastructure, and economy of Africa's cities (Simone and Pieterse 2018; De Boeck and Plissart 2014). In looking towards processes, these scholars describe the improvisational, experimental character of the African city (Simone and Pieterse 2018; De Boeck and Plissart 2006) and the ways in which unregulated capital is shaping the spatial geographies of cities (Murray 2017). This shift makes comparison possible. Jean and John Comaroff (2012) suggest how African perspectives might frame an understanding of how unregulated speculative capital and its inequalities are shaping Euro-America, for example. Other scholars (Robinson 2002; Marr 2016) have argued for a comparative lens to escape from the geographical silos of urban studies, given the ways in which varying inflections of neoliberalism (Wacquant 2012) and post-socialisms (Pitcher and Askew 2006) manifest across global cities and regions.

Across the globe, societies are living through multiple radical disruptions to their lives. Economic crisis, war, pandemics, climate emergencies, and ideological revolutions will catalyse radical change. While the Copperbelt has long been a locus for studying social change and urbanisation in Africa, placing the Copperbelt in wider global conversations of urban life offers the possibility to examine, in comparative perspective, places that have been dispossessed of state welfare and left behind by global speculative capital.

This book has attempted to describe how this change has been experienced during the period of neoliberal triumph, when the semi-socialist, post-independence government of Kenneth Kaunda, which had expanded the public sector and social welfare and increased the role of the state in business, gave way to privatisation, social spending cuts, austerity, and a limited role for the state in favour of free markets. This period has been characterised by uncertainty for the citizens of Zambia. For former mineworkers and their families on the Copperbelt, considered the most privileged of workers in the country, this period marked an end to their way of life, as they had to adapt to a life of precarity. It has seen Copperbelt residents engage in greater numbers in the informal economy. The unpredictability of their lives, as they face economic ruin and ill health due to a raging HIV/AIDS pandemic, has seen them deploy a myriad of efforts in gainful activity not only to survive, but maybe to prosper. They have learnt to try and in the process reoriented existing skills and acquired new ones to allow them to navigate the ambiguities and uncertainties of a less structured political and economic terrain. These efforts, in turn, have reshaped their social relations, their moralities, and their view of place, inflected with nostalgia for the ZCCM past.

Understanding a changing place requires both a description of its characteristics and the documentation of residents' stories in relation to the place. Stories of place capture the aspirations of the people telling them (Tuan 1979, 387), and these become particularly salient in times when people are confronting radical social change. As a site of analytical inquiry in anthropology and human geography, place provides entry to explore how changes to the political economy not only shift relationships within family, community, and different kinds of authority, but also alter the landscape itself, to reflect emergent forms of social organisation. As the site of lived experience, place also textures people's perception of themselves, their place in the world, and their engagement with it.

In the hardships that ensued in the aftermath of the reprivatisation of ZCCM, Copperbelt residents' efforts at making a living rely in large part on people's "perception of the environment" (Ingold 2000). It requires a constant engagement with the social and material landscape and a tuning in to the possibilities that place affords. Opportunities are largely perceived in situ. Perception here hints at the positionality of actors within their surroundings, and their skill in producing livelihoods by drawing from preexisting knowledge, materials, and social relations in a constant process of adaptation and experimentation. A key concept I have hinted at throughout the book is improvisation. None of these factors are fixed: skill is learnt and improved on; bodily strength is variable; social relations are constantly manipulated; and the physical environment is pliable. Thus, Copperbelt residents have to try, or in other words engage in a constant process of effortful improvisation. With the prospect of failure ever present, Copperbelt residents draw on the ephemeral resources of poetry, found in music, and stories to create a collective sense of being in it together and to animate each other so as not to give up and to go on. In reimagining possible futures of places left behind by the retreat of state and the vagaries of the free market, places like the Copperbelt offer, in its people's struggles to survive and hopes to make it, a scaffolding for the politics and welfare-orientated alternatives that can be built on in times of scarcity.

NOTE

1. The gust of wind would be what Bohm (2002) refers to as the implicit order, and the explicit order that which can be readily perceived.

BIBLIOGRAPHY

Adam, Christopher S., and Anthony M. Simpasa. 2010. "The economics of the copper price boom in Zambia." In *Zambia, Mining, and Neoliberalism: Boom and Bust on the Globalized Copperbelt*, edited by Alistair Fraser and Miles Larmer, 59–90. New York: Palgrave Macmillan.

Adams, Paul C., Steven D. Hoelscher, and Karen E. Till, eds. 2001. *Textures of Place: Exploring Humanist Geographies*. Minneapolis: University of Minnesota Press.

Bachelard, Gaston. 1969. *The Poetics of Space*. Translated by Maria Jolas. Boston: Beacon Press.

Bagozzi, Richard P., and Paul R. Warshaw. 1990. "Trying to consume." *Journal of Consumer Research* 17, no. 2: 127–140.

Bajaj, Monisha. 2008. "Schooling in the shadow of death: Youth agency and HIV/AIDS in Zambia." *Journal of Asian and African Studies* 43, no. 3: 307–329.

Bajaj, Monisha. 2009. "'I have big things planned for my future': The limits and possibilities of transformative agency in Zambian schools." *Compare* 39, no. 4: 551–568.

Bank, Leslie John. 2011. *Home Spaces, Street Styles: Contesting Power and Identity in a South African City*. London: Pluto Press.

Bateson, Mary Catherine. 2001. *Composing a Life*. New York: Grove Press.

Bateson, Gregory. 1972. *Steps to an Ecology of Mind: A Revolutionary Approach to Man's Understanding of Himself*. New York: Ballantine Books.

Bernard, H. Russell. 1994. *Research Methods in Anthropology: Qualitative and Quantitative Approaches*. Thousand Oaks, CA: Sage.

Bissell, William Cunningham. 2005. "Engaging colonial nostalgia." *Cultural Anthropology* 20, no. 2: 215–248.

Bohm, David. 2002. *Wholeness and the Implicate Order*. New York: Routledge.

Bourdieu, Pierre. 1977. *Outline of a Theory of Practice*. Translated by Richard Nice. Cambridge: Cambridge University Press.

Bourdieu, Pierre. 1993. *The Field of Cultural Reproduction: Essays on Art and Literature*. Edited by Randal Johnson. Oxford: Polity Press.

Bradley, Kenneth. 1952. *Copper Venture: The Discovery and Development of Roan Ante-*

lope and Mufulira. London: Mufulira Copper Mines Limited and Roan Antelope Copper Mines Limited.

Brown, Judith O. 2011. "Dwell in possibility: PLAR and e-portfolios in the age of information and communication technologies." *International Review of Research in Open and Distributed Learning* 12, no. 1: 1–23.

Burawoy, Michael. 1972. *The Colour of Class on the Copper Mines: From African Advancement to Zambianization*. Manchester: Published on behalf of the Institute for African Studies, University of Zambia, by Manchester University Press.

Burawoy, Michael. 1998. "The extended case method." *Sociological Theory* 16, no. 1: 4–33.

Burnell, Peter. 1994. "Zambia at the crossroads." *World Affairs* 157, no. 1: 19–28.

Butler, Judith. 1993. *Bodies That Matter: On the Discursive Limits of "Sex"*. New York: Routledge.

Carsten, Janet, and Stephen Hugh-Jones, eds. 1995. *About the House: Lévi-Strauss and Beyond*. Cambridge: Cambridge University Press.

Casey, Edward S. 1983. "Keeping the past in mind." *Review of Metaphysics* 37, no. 1: 77–95.

Casey, Edward S. 1984. "Origin(s) in (of) Heidegger/Derrida." *Journal of Philosophy* 81, no. 10: 601–610.

Casey, Edward S. 1987. "The world of nostalgia." *Man and World* 20, no. 4: 361–384.

Casey, Edward S. 1997. "Smooth spaces and rough-edged places: The hidden history of place." *Review of Metaphysics* 51, no. 2: 267–296.

Casey, Edward. 2001a. "Body, self, and landscape." In *Textures of Place: Exploring Humanist Geographies*, edited by Paul C. Adams, Steven D. Hoelscher, and Karen E. Till, 403–425. Minneapolis: University of Minnesota Press.

Casey, Edward S. 2001b. "Between geography and philosophy: What does it mean to be in the place-world?" *Annals of the Association American Geographers* 91, no. 4: 683–693.

Castells, Manuel, and Alejandro Portes. 1989. "World underneath: The origins, dynamics, and effects of the informal economy." In *The Informal Economy: Studies in Advanced and Less Developed Countries*, edited by Alejandro Portes, Manuel Castells, and Lauren A. Benton, 12, 11-37. Baltimore: John Hopkins University Press.

Cattell, Maria G. 2003. "African widows: Anthropological and historical perspectives." *Journal of Women and Aging* 15, nos. 2–3: 49–66.

Central Statistical Office (CSO). 2003. *Migration and Urbanization 2000 Census Report*. Lusaka: Central Statistical Office.

Central Statistical Office (CSO). 2005. *Living Conditions Monitoring Survey Report 2004*. Lusaka: Central Statistical Office.

Central Statistical Office (CSO). 2006. *Living Conditions Monitoring Survey*. Lusaka: Central Statistical Office.

Central Statistical Office (CSO). 2007. *Zambia Demographic Health Survey 2007*. Lusaka: Central Statistical Office.

Central Statistical Office (CSO). 2011. *Census of Population and Housing: Preliminary Population Figures*. Lusaka: Central Statistical Office.

Chauncey, George, Jr. 1981. "The locus of reproduction: Women's labour in the Zambian Copperbelt, 1927–1953." *Journal of Southern African Studies* 7, no. 2: 135–164.

Chipande, Hikabwa D. 2016. "Mining for goals: Football and social change on the Zambian Copperbelt, 1940s–1960s." *Radical History Review* 2016, no. 125: 55–73.

Chipimo, Elias. 2010. *Unequal to the Task? Awakening a New Generation of Leaders in Africa.* Johannesburg: June Vijeon Print Consultancy.

Cliggett, Lisa, Elizabeth Colson, Rodrick Hay, Thayer Scudder, and Jon Unruh. 2007. "Chronic uncertainty and momentary opportunity: A half century of adaptation among Zambia's Gwembe Tonga." *Human Ecology* 35, no. 1: 19–31.

Cole, Jennifer, and Lynn M. Thomas, eds. 2009. *Love in Africa.* Chicago: University of Chicago Press.

Coleman, Francis. L. 1971. *The Northern Rhodesian Copperbelt, 1899–1962: Technological Development up to the End of the Central African Federation.* Manchester: Manchester University Press.

Comaroff, Jean, and John L. Comaroff. 1999. "Occult economies and the violence of abstraction: Notes from the South African postcolony." *American Ethnologist* 26, no. 2: 279–303.

Comaroff, Jean, and John L. Comaroff. 2000. "Millennial capitalism: First thoughts on a second coming." *Public Culture* 12, no. 2: 291–343.

Comaroff, Jean, and John L. Comaroff. 2012. "Theory from the south: Or, how Euro-America is evolving toward Africa." In *Anthropological Forum* 22, no. 2: 113–131.

Coplan, David B. 2006. "'I've Worked Longer Than I've Lived': Lesotho Migrants' Songs as Maps of Experience." *Journal of Ethnic and Migration Studies* 32, no. 2: 223–241.

Cosgrove, Denis, Stephen Daniels, and Alan R. H. Baker, eds. 1988. *The Iconography of Landscape: Essays on the Symbolic Representation, Design and Use of Past Environments.* Cambridge: Cambridge University Press.

Cresswell, Tim. 2004. *Place: An Introduction.* New York: John Wiley & Sons.

Cresswell, Tim. 2013. "Displacements: Three poems." *Geographical Review* 103, no. 2: 285–287.

Curtis, Mark. 2015. *Extracting minerals, Extracting Wealth: How Zambia Is Losing $3 billion a Year from Corporate Tax Dodging.* London: War on Want.

Da Col, Giovanni, and David Graeber. 2011. "Foreword: The return of ethnographic theory." *HAU: Journal of Ethnographic Theory* 1, no. 1: vi–xxxv.

Dandaneau, Steven P. 1996. *A Town Abandoned: Flint, Michigan, Confronts Deindustrialization.* Albany: SUNY Press.

Danny. 2005. "Kaya." In *Kaya* [music CD]. Lusaka: Mondo Music.

Darby, H. Clifford. 1931. "Settlement in Northern Rhodesia." *Geographical Review* 21, no. 4: 559–573.

De Boeck, Filip. 1994. "'When Hunger Goes Around the Land': Hunger and Food among the Aluund of Zaire." *Man*, n.s., 29, no. 2: 257–282.

De Boeck, Filip. 1998. "The rootedness of trees: Place and cultural and natural texture in rural southwest Congo." In *Locality and Belonging*, edited by N. Lovell, 25–52. New York: Routledge.

De Boeck, Filip. 2005. "The apocalyptic interlude: Revealing death in Kinshasa." *African Studies Review* 48, no. 2: 11–32.

De Boeck, Filip. 2011. "Inhabiting ocular ground: Kinshasa's future in the light of Congo's spectral urban politics." *Cultural Anthropology* 26, no. 2: 263–286.

De Boeck, Filip, and Karin Barber. 2010. "Introduction: Popular culture and the city." Presented to "Tuning In to African Cities: Popular Culture and Urban Experience in Sub-Saharan Africa," 6–8 May 2010, University of Birmingham.

De Boeck, Filip, and Marie-Françoise Plissart. 2006. *Kinshasa: Tales of the Invisible City*. Ghent: Ludion.

Debord, Guy. 1967. *The Society of the Spectacle*. Detroit: Black and Red, 1983.

Devisch, René. 1993. *Weaving the Threads of Life: The Khita Gyn-Eco-Logical Healing Cult among the Yaka*. Chicago: University of Chicago Press.

Devisch, René. 1996. "'Pillaging Jesus': Healing churches and the villagisation of Kinshasa." *Africa* 66, no. 4: 555–586.

Devisch, René. 1998. "Colonial state building in the Congo, and its dismantling." *Journal of Legal Pluralism and Unofficial Law* 30, no. 42: 221–244.

Devisch, René. 2006. "A psychoanalytic revisiting of fieldwork and intercultural border-linking." *Social Analysis* 50, no. 2: 121–147.

Devisch, René. 2007. "Intercultural borderlinking, intersubjectivity, and Bantu healing cults." *Medische Antropologie* 19: 97–114.

Dirksmeier, Peter. 2016. "Providing places for structures of feeling and hierarchical complementarity in urban theory: Re-reading Williams' *The Country and the City*." *Urban Studies* 53, no. 5: 884–898.

Dlamini, Jacob. 2009. *Native Nostalgia*. Auckland Park, South Africa: Jacana Media.

Englund, Harri. 2002. "Ethnography after globalism: Migration and emplacement in Malawi." *American Ethnologist* 29, no. 2: 261–286.

Englund, Harri. 2008. "Extreme poverty and existential obligations: Beyond morality in the anthropology of Africa?" *Social Analysis* 52, no. 3: 33–50.

Epstein, Arnold Leonard. 1958. *Politics in an African Urban Community*. Manchester: Manchester University Press.

Epstein, Arnold Leonard. 1981. *Urbanization and Kinship: The Domestic Domain on the Copperbelt of Zambia, 1950–1956*. London: Academic Press.

Epstein, Arnold Leonard. 1992. *Scenes from African Urban Life: Collected Copperbelt Essays*. Edinburgh: Edinburgh University Press.

Escobar, Arturo. 2001. "Culture sits in places: Reflections on globalism and subaltern strategies of localization." *Political Geography* 20, no. 2: 139–174.

Ettinger, Bracha Lichtenberg. 1996. "Metramorphic borderlinks and matrixial border-space." In *Rethinking Borders*, edited by John Welchman, 125–159. London: Palgrave Macmillan.

Evans, Alice. 2014. "'Women can do what men can do': The causes and consequences of growing flexibility in gender divisions of labour in Kitwe, Zambia." *Journal of Southern African Studies* 40, no. 5: 981–998.

Faber, Michael. 1971. "The Mshiri-Thomson meeting of November: A note." *African Social Research* 12: 129–143.

Feeley-Harnik, G. 1996. "Against the motion." In *Key Debates in Anthropology*, edited by Tim Ingold, 201–248. London: Routledge.

Ferguson, James. 1990. "Mobile workers, modernist narratives: A critique of the historiography of transition on the Zambian Copperbelt [part 1]." *Journal of Southern African Studies* 16, no. 3: 385–412.

Ferguson, James. 1992. "The Country and the City on the Copperbelt." *Cultural Anthropology* 7, no. 1: 80–92.

Ferguson, James. 1999. *Expectations of Modernity: Myths and Meanings of Urban Life on the Zambian Copperbelt*. Berkeley: University of California Press.

Ferguson, James. 2003. "Stillborn chrysalis: Reflections on the fate of national culture in neoliberal Zambia." *Global Networks* 3, no. 3: 271–297.

Ferguson, James. 2006. *Global Shadows: Africa in the Neoliberal World Order*. Durham, NC: Duke University Press.

Fisher, Tom H. 2004. "What we touch, touches us: Materials, affects, and affordances." *Design Issues* 20, no. 4: 20–31.

Foucault, Michel. 1975. *Discipline and Punish: The Birth of the Prison*. Translated by Alan Sheridan. London: Allen Lane.

Fraser, Alistair. 2010. "Boom and bust on the Zambian Copperbelt." In *Zambia, Mining and Neoliberalism: Boom and Bust on the Globalised Copperbelt*. Edited by Alistair Fraser and Miles Larmer, 1–30. New York: Palgrave Macmillan.

Fraser, Alistair, and John Lungu. 2007. *For Whom the Windfalls? Winners and Losers in the Privatisation of Zambia's Copper Mines*. Lusaka: Civil Society Trade Network of Zambia.

Friedrich, Paul. 1988. "Eerie chaos and eerier order." *Journal of Anthropological Research* 44, no. 4: 435–444.

Geiser, Thorsten. 2008. "Embodiment, emotion and empathy: A phenomenological approach to apprenticeship learning." *Anthropological Theory* 8, no. 3: 299–318.

Geisler, Gisela. 1992. "Who is losing out? Structural adjustment, gender, and the agricultural sector in Zambia." *Journal of Modern African Studies* 30, no. 1: 113–139.

Gell, Alfred. 1988. "Technology and magic." *Anthropology Today* 4, no. 2: 6–9.

Gell, Alfred. 1998. *Art and Agency: An Anthropological Theory*. Oxford: Clarendon Press.

Geschiere, Peter. 1997. *The Modernity of Witchcraft: Politics and the Occult in Postcolonial Africa*. Charlottesville: University of Virginia Press.

Gewald, Jan-Bart, and Sebastiaan Soeters. 2010. "African miners and shape-shifting capital flight: The case of Luanshya/Baluba." In *Zambia, Mining and Neoliberalism: Boom and Bust on the Globalized Copperbelt*, edited by Alistair Fraser and Miles Larmer, 155–184. New York: Palgrave Macmillan.

Gluckman, Max. 1961. "Ethnographic data in British social anthropology." *Sociological Review* 9, no. 1: 5–17.

Goebel, Allison. 2002. "'Men these days, they are a problem': Husband-taming herbs and gender wars in rural Zimbabwe." *Canadian Journal of African Studies / Revue Canadienne des Études Africaines* 36, no. 3: 460–489.

Goffman, Erving. 1959. *The Presentation of Self in Everyday Life*. Garden City, NY: Anchor.

Gough, Katherine V. 2008. "'Moving around': The social and spatial mobility of youth in Lusaka." *Geografiska Annaler, Series B, Human Geography* 90, no. 3 (2008): 243–255.

Green, Linda. 1994. "Fear as Way of life." *Cultural Anthropology* 9, no. 2: 227–256.

Guerts, Kathryn Linn. 2003. "On rocks, walks, and talks in West Africa: Cultural categories and an anthropology of the senses." *Ethos* 30, no. 3: 178–198.

Haglund, Dan. 2008. "Regulating FDI in weak African states: A case study of Chinese copper mining in Zambia." *Journal of Modern African Studies* 46: 547–575.

Haglund, Dan. 2010. "From boom to bust: Diversity and regulation in Zambia's privatized copper sector." In *Zambia, Mining and Neoliberalism: Boom and Bust on the Globalized Copperbelt*, edited by Alistair Fraser and Miles Larmer, 91–126. New York: Palgrave Macmillan.

Hallam, Elizabeth, and Tim Ingold. 2007. *Creativity and Cultural Improvisation*. London: Bloomsbury Academic.

Hann, Christopher M., ed. 2002. *Postsocialism: Ideals, Ideologies, and Practices in Eurasia*. New York: Routledge.

Hansangule, Michelo, Patricia Feeney, and Robin Palmer. 1998. *Report on Land Tenure and Insecurity on the Zambian Copperbelt*. Lusaka: Oxfam Great Britain in Zambia.

Hansen, Karen Tranberg. 1984. "Negotiating sex and gender in urban Zambia." *Journal of Southern African Studies* 10, no. 2: 219–238.

Hansen, Karen Tranberg. 1987. "Urban women and work in Africa: A Zambian case." *Transafrica Forum* 4, no. 3: 9–24.

Hansen, Karen Tranberg. 1989. "The black market and women traders in Lusaka, Zambia." In *Women and the State in Africa*, edited by Jane L. Parpart and Kathleen A. Staudt, 143–160. London: Lynn Rienner.

Hansen, Karen Tranberg. 1997. *Keeping House in Lusaka*. New York: Columbia University Press.

Hansen, Karen Tranberg. 2000. *Salaula: The World of Secondhand Clothing and Zambia*. Chicago: University of Chicago Press.

Hansen, Karen Tranberg. 2004. "Who rules the streets? The politics of vending space in Lusaka." In *Reconsidering Informality: Perspectives from Urban Africa*, edited by Hansen Karen Tranberg and Mariken Vaa, 62–79. Uppsala: Nordic Africa Institute.

Hansen, Karen Tranberg. 2005. "Getting stuck in the compound: Some odds against social adulthood in Lusaka, Zambia." *Africa Today* 51, no. 4: 3–16.

Hansen, Karen Tranberg, and Mariken Vaa, eds. 2004. *Reconsidering Informality: Perspectives from Urban Africa*. Uppsala: Nordic Africa Institute.

Haram, Liv. 2005. "AIDS and risk: The handling of uncertainty in northern Tanzania." *Culture, Health & Sexuality* 7, no. 1: 1–11.

Hart, Keith. 2008. "Afterword: Malinowski's heirs." In *How Do We Know? Evidence,*

Ethnography and the Making of Anthropological Knowledge, edited by Liana Chua, Casey High, and Timm Lau, 201–209. Newcastle: Cambridge Scholars.

Hart, Keith, and Horacio Oritz. 2008. "Anthropology in the financial crisis." *Anthropology Today* 24, no. 6: 1–3.

Harvey, Penny. 2009. "Between narrative and number: The case of Arup's 3D Digital City model." *Cultural Sociology* 3, no. 2: 257–276.

Haynes, Naomi. 2012. "Pentecostalism and the morality of money: Prosperity, inequality, and religious sociality on the Zambian Copperbelt." *Journal of the Royal Anthropological Institute* 18, no. 1: 123–139.

Heidegger, Martin. 1962. *Being and Time*. Translated by John Macquarrie and Edward Robinson. New York: Harper.

Heisler, Helmuth. 1971. "The creation of a stabilized urban society: A turning point in the development of Northern Rhodesia/Zambia." *African Affairs* 70, no. 279: 125–145.

Hinton, Jennifer, Marcello M. Viega, and Christian Beinhoff. 2003. "Women and artisanal mining: Gender roles and the road ahead." In *The Socio-economic Impacts of Artisanal and Small-Scale Mining in Developing Countries*, edited by Gavin M. Hilson, 149–188. London: CRC Press.

Home, Robert. 1996. *Of Planting and Planning: The Making of British Colonial Cities*. New York: Routledge.

Hunter, Mark. 2010. *Love in the Time of AIDS: Inequality, Gender, and Rights in South Africa*. Bloomington: Indiana University Press.

Ingold, Tim. 1993. "The temporality of the landscape." *World Archaeology* 25, no. 2: 152–174.

Ingold, Tim. 2000. *The Perception of the Environment: Essays in Livelihood, Dwelling and Skill*. Abingdon: Routledge.

Ingold, Tim. 2007. *Lines: A Brief History*. Abingdon: Routledge.

Ingold, Tim. 2009. "Against space: Place, movement, knowledge." In *Boundless Worlds: An Anthropological Approach to Movement*, edited by Peter Wynn Kirby, 29–43. New York: Berghahn Books.

Ingold, Tim. 2011. *Being Alive: Essays on Movement, Knowledge and Description*. New York: Routledge.

Institute for Security Studies. 2009. *Illegal mining in the Copperbelt*. Organised Crime Watch Issue no.2. July. Cape Town: ISS.

Jesuit Centre for Theological Reflection (JCTR). 2009a. *Luanshya, Basic Needs Basket*. November. Lusaka: JCTR.

Jesuit Centre for Theological Reflection (JCTR). 2009b. *Mufumbwe, Basic Needs Basket*. October. Lusaka: JCTR.

Jesuit Centre for Theological Reflection (JCTR). 2010. *Lusaka, basic needs basket*. December. Lusaka: JCTR.

Johnson-Hanks, Jennifer. 2005. "When the future decides: Uncertainty and intentional action in contemporary Cameroon." *Current Anthropology* 46, no. 3: 363–385.

Johnson-Hanks, Jennifer. 2007. "Women on the Market: Marriage, consumption and the internet in urban Cameroon." *American Ethnologist* 34, no. 4: 642–658.

Kalusa, Walima T. 1997. "African health at Roan Antelope Mine during the Second World War." *Journal of Humanities* 1, no. 1: 18–38.

Kalusa, Walima T. 2011. "Death, Christianity, and African miners: Contesting indirect rule in the Zambian Copperbelt, 1935–1962." *International Journal of African Historical Studies* 44, no. 1: 89–112.

Kasonka, Ernest. 2008. *Getting Back to God's Plan for Man*. Sermon. Luanshya.

Kaunda, Francis. 2002. *Selling the Family Silver: The Zambian Copper Mines Story*. KwaZulu-Natal: Interpak Books.

Kaunda, Kenneth David, and Colin Manley Morris. 1966. *A Humanist in Africa: Letters to Colin M. Morris from Kenneth D. Kaunda, President of Zambia*. London: Longmans.

Kayira, Victor. 1998. "Roan Miner Rampage," *Times of Zambia*, October 28.

Kazimbaya-Senkwe, Barbara Mwila, and Simon C. Guy. 2007. "Back to the future? Privatisation and the domestication of water in the Copperbelt Province of Zambia, 1900–2000." *Geoforum* 38, no. 5: 869–885.

Kihato, Caroline. 2013. *Migrant Women of Johannesburg: Everyday Life in an In-Between City*. Springer.

Larmer, Miles. 2004. "If we are still here next year." *History in Africa* 31: 215–229.

Larmer, Miles. 2007. *Mineworkers in Zambia: Labour and Political Change in Postcolonial Africa*. New York: IB Tauris.

Larmer, Miles, and Alistair Fraser. 2007. "Of cabbages and King Cobra: Populist politics and Zambia's 2006 election." *African Affairs* 106, no. 425: 611–637.

Latham, Alan, and David Conradson. 2003. "The Possibilities of Performance—Guest Editorial." *Environment and Planning A* 35: 1901–1906.

Latour, Bruno. 2005. *Reassembling the Social: An Introduction to Actor-Network-Theory*. Oxford: Oxford University Press.

Lawrence, Peter. 1971. *Road Belong Cargo: A Study of the Cargo Movement in the Southern Madaang District New Guinea*. Manchester: Manchester University Press.

Leclerc-Madlala, Suzanne. 1997. "Infect one, infect all: Zulu youth response to the AIDS epidemic in South Africa." *Medical Anthropology* 17, no. 4: 363–380.

Lee, Ching Kwan. 2010. "Raw encounters: Chinese managers, African workers and the politics of casualization in Africa's Chinese enclaves." In *Zambia, Mining and Neoliberalism: Boom and Bust on the globalized Copperbelt*, edited by Alistair Fraser and Miles Larmer, 127–154. New York: Palgrave Macmillan.

Lee, Ching Kwan. 2018. *The Specter of Global China: Politics, Labor, and Foreign Investment in Africa*. Chicago: University of Chicago Press.

Lefebvre, Henri. 1992. *The Production of Space*. Translated by Donald Nicholson-Smith. Oxford: Wiley-Blackwell.

Lefebvre, Henri, Catherine Régulier, and Mohamed Zayani. 1999. "The rhythmanalytical project." *Rethinking Marxism* 11, no. 1: 5–13.

Lévi-Strauss, Claude. 1963. *Structural Anthropology*. Translated by Claire Jacobson and Brooke Grundfest Schoepf. New York: Basic Books.

Lindell, Ilda. 2010. "Informality and collective organising: Identities, alliances and transnational activism in Africa." *Third World Quarterly* 31, no. 2: 207–222.

Lindstrom, Lamont. 1993. *Cargo cult: Strange Stories of Desire from Melanesia and Beyond.* Honolulu: University of Hawai'i Press.

Lowenthal, David. 1985. *The Past Is a Foreign Country.* Cambridge: Cambridge University Press.

Lungu, John. 2008. *The politics of reforming Zambia's tax regime.* Resource Insight Issue no. 8. August. Johannesburg. *Southern African Resource Watch.*

Lungu, John, and Alistair Fraser. 2006. *For Whom the Windfall? Winner and Losers in the Privatization of Zambia's Copper Mines.* Lusaka: Civil Society Network of Zambia and Catholic Centre for Justice Peace and Development.

Lwanda, John. 2003. "The [in] visibility of HIV/AIDS in the Malawi public sphere." *African Journal of AIDS Research* 2, no. 2: 113–126.

Macmillan, Hugh. 1993. "The historiography of transition on the Zambian Copperbelt: Another view." *Journal of Southern African Studies* 19, no. 4: 681–712.

Macmillan, Hugh. 2005. *An African Trading Empire: The Story of Susman Brothers & Wulfsohn, 1901–2005.* New York: IB Tauris.

Mah, Alice. 2010. "Memory, uncertainty and industrial ruination: Walker Riverside, Newcastle upon Tyne." *International Journal of Urban and Regional Research* 34, no. 2: 398–413.

Mahlck, Paula. 2009. "Bodies at work in Volvo plants in Sweden and South Africa." In *Body Politics and Women Citizens: African Experiences,* edited by Ann Schlyter, 48–56. Stockholm: SIDA.

Makasa, Paul Lombe Kasonde. 2010. *The 1996 Zambia National Housing Policy.* Delft: Delft University Press.

Makgetla, Neva Seidman. 1986. "Theoretical and practical implications of IMF conditionality in Zambia." *Journal of Modern African Studies* 24, no. 3: 395–422.

Marr, Stephen. 2016. "Worlding and wilding: Lagos and Detroit as global cities." *Race & Class* 57, no. 4: 3–21.

McPake, Barbara, Pamela Nakamba, Kara Hanson, and Bernard McLoughlin. 2004. "Private wards in public hospitals: Two-tier charging and the allocation of resources in tertiary hospitals in Zambia." Health Economics and Financing Programme Working Paper No. 05.

Meyer-Weitz, Anna. 2005. "Understanding fatalism in HIV/AIDS protection: The individual in dialogue with contextual factors." *African Journal of AIDS Research* 4, no. 2: 75–82.

Mills, Greg. 1992. "Zambia and the winds of change." *World Today* 48, no. 1: 16–18.

Milner-Thornton, Juliette. 2011. *The Long Shadow of the British Empire: The Ongoing Legacies of Race and Class in Zambia.* Berlin: Springer.

Mitchell, J. Clyde. 1954. *African Urbanization in Ndola and Luanshya.* Lusaka: Rhodes-Livingstone Institute.

Mitchell, J. Clyde. 1957. "Aspects of African marriage on the Copperbelt of Northern Rhodesia." *Rhodes-Livingstone Journal* 22: 1–30.

Mitchell, J. Clyde. 1961. "Social change and the stability of African marriage in Northern Rhodesia." In *Social Change in Modern Africa*, edited by Aidan Southall, 316–329. Oxford: Oxford University Press.

Mitchell, J. Clyde. 1969. *Social Networks in Urban Situations: Analyses of Personal Relationships in Central African Towns*. Manchester: Manchester University Press.

Mitchell, J. Clyde, and Arnold L. Epstein. 1959. "Occupational prestige and social status among urban Africans in Northern Rhodesia." *Africa* 29, no. 1: 22–40.

Money, Duncan. 2015. "The world of European labour on the northern Rhodesian Copperbelt, 1940–1945." *International Review of Social History* 60, no. 2: 225–255.

Moore Henrietta L. 1986. *Space, Text and Gender: An Anthropological Study of the Marakwet of Kenya*. Cambridge: Cambridge University Press.

Moore, Henrietta L., Todd Sanders, and Bwire Kaare. 1999. *Those Who Play with Fire: Gender, Fertility and Transformation in East and Southern Africa*. London: Athlone Press.

Moore, Henrietta L., and Megan Vaughan. 1994. *Cutting Down Trees: Gender, Nutrition, and Agricultural Change in the Northern Province of Zambia, 1890–1990*. Portsmouth, NH: Heinemann; London: James Currey; and Lusaka: University of Zambia Press.

Moser, Caroline O. N. 1978. "Informal sector or petty commodity production: Dualism or dependence in urban development?" *World Development* 6, nos. 9–10: 1041–1064.

Mozegater. 2005. "Chikokoshi." In *Kale Twa Amba* [music CD]. Lusaka: Self-produced and self-distributed.

Mufune, Pempelani. 2000. "Street youth in southern Africa." *International Social Science Journal* 52, no. 164: 233–243.

Murray, Martin J. 2013. "The quandary of post-public space: New urbanism, Melrose Arch and the rebuilding of Johannesburg after apartheid." *Journal of Urban Design* 18, no. 1: 119–144.

Murray, Martin J. 2017. *The Urbanism of Exception*. Cambridge: Cambridge University Press.

Mususa, Patience. 2009. "Contesting illegality: Women in the informal copper business on the Zambian Copperbelt." In *Body Politics and Women Citizens: African Experiences*, edited by Ann Schlyter, 25–36. Stockholm: SIDA.

Mususa, Patience. 2010a. "'Getting by': Life on the Copperbelt after the privatisation of the Zambia Consolidated Copper Mines." *Social Dynamics* 36, no. 2: 380–394.

Mususa, Patience. 2010b. "Contesting illegality: Women in the informal copper business." In *Zambia, Mining, and Neoliberalism: Boom and Bust on the Globalized Copperbelt*. edited by Alistair Fraser and Miles Larmer, 185–208. New York: Palgrave Macmillan.

Mutale, Emmanuel. 2004. *The Management of Urban Development in Zambia*. Aldershot: Ashgate.

Mutamba, Manyewu. 2007. "Farming or foraging? Rural livelihoods in Mafulira and Kabompo districts of Zambia." Center for International Forestry Research and Rhodes University.

Mwaba, Andrew. 2004. "Privatization of state-owned enterprises in Zambia: Lessons for other African countries." In *Private and Public Sectors: Towards a Balance*, edited by Karl Wohmulth, Achim Gutowski, and Tobias Knedlik, 351–376. Munster: LIT Verlag.

Myers, Garth. 2003. *Verandas of Power: Colonialism and Space in Urban Africa*. Syracuse: Syracuse University Press.

Negi, Rohit. 2013. "'You cannot make a camel drink water': Capital, geo-history and contestations in the Zambian Copperbelt." *Geoforum* 45: 240–247.

Njoh, Ambe. 2007. *Planning Power: Town Planning and Social Control in Colonial Africa*. London: CRC Press.

Nyamnjoh, Francis B. 2001. "Expectations of modernity in Africa or a future in the rearview mirror?" *Journal of Southern African Studies* 27, no. 2: 363–368.

Oyama, Susan. 2000. *The Ontogeny of Information: Developmental Systems and Evolution*. Durham, NC: Duke University Press.

Palmer, Robin. 2000. "Land tenure insecurity on the Zambian Copperbelt: Anyone going back to the land?" *Social Dynamics* 26, no. 2: 154–170.

Parpart, Jane L. 1986. "The household and the mine shaft: Gender and class struggles on the Zambian Copperbelt, 1926–64." *Journal of Southern African Studies* 13, no. 1: 36–56.

Parpart, Jane L. 1994. "'Where is your mother?': Gender, urban marriage, and colonial discourse on the Zambian Copperbelt, 1924–1945." *International Journal of African Historical Studies* 27, no. 2: 241–271.

Parpart, Jane L. 2001. "Wicked women and respectable ladies: Reconfiguring gender on the Zambian Copperbelt, 1936–1964." In *Wicked Women and the Reconfiguration of Gender in Africa*, edited by Dorothy L. Hodgson and Sheryl A. McCurdy, 274–292. Portsmouth: Heinemann.

Petersen. 2005. "Oh no." Featuring Jay. In *Munyaule* [music CD]. Lusaka: Supershine Investments.

Phimister, Ian. 2011. "Workers in wonderland? White miners and the Northern Rhodesian Copperbelt, 1946–1962." *South African Historical Journal* 63, no. 2: 183–233.

Pieterse, Edgar, and Susan Parnell. 2014. *Africa's Urban Revolution*. London: Zed Books.

Pitcher, M. Anne, and Kelly M. Askew. 2006. "African socialisms and postsocialisms." *Africa* 76, no. 1: 1–14.

Potts, Deborah. 1995. "Shall we go home? Increasing urban poverty in African cities and migration processes." *Geographical Journal* 161, no. 3: 245–264.

Povinelli, Elizabeth. 2011. *Economies of Abandonment: Social Belonging and Endurance in Late Liberalism*. Durham, NC: Duke University Press.

Powdermaker, Hortense. 1962. *Copper Town: Changing Africa. The Human Situation on the Rhodesian Copperbelt*. New York: Harper and Row.

Prain, Ronald L. 1956. "The stabilization of labour in the Rhodesian Copper Belt." *African Affairs* 55, no. 221: 305–312.

Pugh, Sarah A. 2010. "Examining the interface between HIV/AIDS, religion and gender in sub-Saharan Africa." *Canadian Journal of African Studies / Revue Canadienne des Études Africaines* 44, no. 3: 624–643.

Quayson, Ato. 2014. *Oxford Street, Accra: City Life and the Itineraries of Transnationalism.* Durham, NC: Duke University Press.

Rakopoulos, Theodoros. 2013. "Responding to the crisis: Food co-operatives and the solidarity economy in Greece." *Anthropology Southern Africa* 36, no. 3–4: 102–107.

Rasing, Thera. 2001. *The Bush Burnt, the Stones Remain: Female Initiation Rites in Urban Zambia.* Leiden: Africa Studies Centre and Lit Verlag.

Richards, Audrey. 1956. *Chisungu: A Girl's Initiation Ceremony among the Bemba of Zambia.* London: Faber and Faber.

Rights and Accountability in Development (RAID). 2000. *Zambia: Deregulation and the Denial of Human Rights.* Submission to the Committee on Economic and Social Rights. Oxford: Queen Elizabeth House.

Robinson, Jennifer. 2002. "Global and world cities: A view from off the map." *International Journal of Urban and Regional Research* 26, no. 3: 531–554.

Robinson, Jennifer. 2006. *Ordinary Cities: Between Modernity and Development.* New York: Routledge.

Rodaway, Paul. 1994. *Sensuous Geographies: Body, Sense and Place.* New York: Routledge.

Ross, Fiona. 2010. *Raw Life, New Hope: Decency, Housing and Everyday Life in a Postapartheid Community.* Cape Town: Juta.

Sandercock, Leonie. 2005. "Out of the closet: The importance of stories and storytelling in planning practice." In *Dialogues in Urban and Regional Planning,* edited by Bruce Stiftel and Vanessa Watson, 299–321. Abingdon: Routledge.

Sautman, Barry, and Yan Hairong. 2016. "The discourse of racialization of labour and Chinese enterprises in Africa." *Ethnic and Racial Studies* 39, no. 12: 2149–2168.

Schlyter, Anne. 1999. *Recycled Inequalities: Youth and Gender in George Compound, Zambia.* Uppsala: Nordic Africa Institute.

Schlyter, Ann. 2004. *Ageing in Zambian Cities.* Goteborg: Centre for Global Gender Studies.

Schumaker, Lyn. 2008. "Slimes and death-dealing dambos: Water, industry and the garden city on Zambia's Copperbelt." *Journal of Southern African Studies* 34, no. 4: 823–840.

Seidman, Ann. 1974. "The distorted growth of import-substitution industry: The Zambian case." *Journal of Modern African Studies* 12, no. 4: 601–631.

Shusterman, Richard. 2000. *Pragmatic Aesthetics: Living Beauty, Rethinking Art.* Lanham, MD: Rowman and Littlefield.

Sichone, Owen. 2001. "Pure anthropology in a highly indebted country." Special issue on fertility in southern Africa. *Journal of Southern African Studies* 27, no. 2: 369–379.

Simone, AbdouMaliq. 2004. *For the City Yet to Come: Changing African Life in Four Cities.* Durham, NC: Duke University Press.

Simone, AbdouMaliq, and Edgar Pieterse. 2018. *New Urban Worlds: Inhabiting Dissonant Times.* New York: John Wiley & Sons.

Simutanyi, Neo. 2008. "Copper mining in Zambia: The developmental legacy of privatisation." Institute for Security Studies Papers no. 165. Cape Town. ISS.

Spitulnik, Debra. 1998. "The language of the city: Town Bemba as urban hybridity." *Journal of Linguistic Anthropology* 8, no. 1: 30–59.

Tannock, Stuart. 1995. "Nostalgia critique." *Cultural Studies* 9, no. 3: 453–464.

Tembo, James Madalitso, Edwin Nyirenda, and Imasiku Nyambe. 2017. "Enhancing faecal sludge management in peri-urban areas of Lusaka through faecal sludge valorisation: Challenges and opportunities. *IOP Conference Series: Earth and Environmental Science* 60, no. 1. https://doi.org/10.1088/1755-1315/60/1/012025

Times of Zambia. 2009. "Illegal miner shot dead, 12 wounded," March 6.

Tuan, Yi-Fu. 1971. "Geography, phenomenology, and the study of human nature." *Canadian Geographer / Le Géographe Canadien* 15, no. 3: 181–192.

Tuan, Yi-Fu. 1977. *Space and Place: The Perspective of Experience.* Minneapolis: University of Minnesota Press.

Tuan, Yi-Fu. 1979. "Space and place: Humanistic perspective." In *Philosophy in Geography,* edited by Stephen Gale and Gunnar Olsson, 387–427. Dordrecht: Springer.

Vambe, Maurice T. 2008. "A new song? Subverting discourses of death and ancestral purity in Zimbabwe's music." *Muziki* 5, no. 1: 131–144.

Van Binsbergen, Wim. 1998. "Globalization and virtuality: Analytical problems posed by the contemporary transformation of African societies." *Development and Change* 29, no. 4: 873–903.

Van Donge, Jan Kees. 2009. "The plundering of Zambian resources by Frederick Chiluba and his friends: A case study of the interaction between national politics and the international drive towards good governance." *African Affairs* 108, no. 430: 69–90.

Wacquant, Loïc. 2012. "Three steps to a historical anthropology of actually existing neoliberalism." *Social Anthropology* 20, no. 1: 66–79.

Walker, Peter A., and Pauline E. Peters. 2001. "Maps, metaphors, and meanings: Boundary struggles and village forest use on private and state land in Malawi." *Society & Natural Resources* 14, no. 5: 411–424.

White, Luise. 1993. "Cars out of place: Vampires, technology, and labor in East and Central Africa." *Representations* 43: 27–50.

Wilkinson, Eleanor, and Iliana Ortega-Alcázar. 2019. "The right to be weary? Endurance and exhaustion in austere times." *Transactions of the Institute of British Geographers* 44, no. 1: 155–167.

Willerslev, Rane. n.d. "Excellence should leave a trail of death." http://vimeo.com/4072082, accessed 3 August 2013.

Williams, Raymond. 1977. *Marxism and literature.* Oxford: Oxford Paperbacks.

Williams, Raymond. 1980. *Problems in Materialism and Culture: Selected Essays.* London: Verso.

Wilson, Anika. 2012. "Of love potions and witch baskets: Domesticity, mobility, and occult rumors in Malawi." *Western Folklore* 71, no. 2: 149–173.

Wilson, Godfrey. 1968. *An Essay on the Economics of Detribalization in Northern Rhodesia*. New York: Humanities Press.

Woldring, Klaas. 1983. "Corruption and inefficiency in Zambia: A survey of recent inquiries and their results." *Africa Today* 30, no. 3: 51–74.

Yamba, C. Bawa. 1997. "Cosmologies in turmoil: Witchfinding and AIDS in Chiawa, Zambia." *Africa* 67, no. 2: 200–223.

Zigon, Jarrett. 2007. "Moral breakdown and the ethical demand: A theoretical framework for an anthropology of moralities." *Anthropological theory* 7, no. 2: 131–150.

Note: Page numbers in italics refer to the illustrations

Adams, Paul C., 45
Africanisation, 3, 22, 25, 80, 103n7
agency, 14, 57, 61, 86, 102–3, 118. *See also* improvisation; "trying"
agriculture: Back to the Land policies, 104n9; backyard farming, 39, 79, 84–85, 92, 103n4; commercial agriculture, 39; employment, 18; on illegal land, 116; immigrant farmers, 39; on rural peripheries, 34, 93, 103n6, 104n10, 197; subsistence farming, 20, 21–22
agroforestry, 49, 75n13
alcohol, 120, 175; *tujilijili*, 177
Anglo American Corporation (AAC), 20, 24
anthropology, 56–57, 62; Copperbelt studies, 10–13; familial relations, 129–30; Manchester school, 10, 11, 80, 130, 139; of "trying," 191–92
anxiety, 170, 176–77

Bachelard, Gaston, 44, 66
backyard activities, 39, 79, 84–85, 88, 91–92, 103n4
Bagozzi, Richard P., 192
Bajaj, Monisha, 80–81, 170
banachimbusa (marriage counsellor), 131, 134, 141, 155
Banda, Mr (maître d'hôtel), 51–52
Banda, Rupiah, 28

Bateson, Gregory, 8–9, 64, 132
behaviour: risky social behaviour, 54–55, 175–76; traditional vs modern customs, 131–32, 140–45, *144*, 156–58, 161–62. *See also* "trying"
Binani Group, 27, 86, 103n3, 107, 115, 127n2
Bissell, William, 26
bodily comportment, 136, 137–40, 156, 167n8
Bohm, David, 63
Bourdieu, Pierre, 12, 44, 62, 67, 72–73, 77n28, 81, 126
British South Africa Company (BSAC), 20, 23
Burawoy, Michael, 80
Burnham, Frederick, 20
business ventures: backyard activities, 39, 79, 84–85, 88, 91–92, 103n4; cross-border trade (*makwebo*), 150; currency exchange, 110, 127n4, 154; ice cream parlour, 58; *kantemba* store, 91; mine supplier, 86–7; restaurant, 160, 161, 162; small-scale enterprises, 39, 79, 88–89, 91–92, 103n4; used-oil refinery, 59; well construction, 93–96. *See also* informal economy
Butler, Judith, 12, 164–65

capitalism, 56
carbon markets, 49, 57n14

Carsten, Janet, 7
case studies: Annie (healthcare), 185–86; Bana Jane (childcare), 122–23; Beauty (with expat Craig), 160–63; David (widower), 155–8; Gibson Musonda (living well), 86–87; Idess (someone to look after her), 158–60; Mr Kabemba (expecting return to normal), 57–58; Katherine (copper ore), 121–22; Margaret (senior civil servant), 137–38; Matilda (desperate single mother), 122; Theresa Miti (suffering), 88–89; Susan Mubita (household finances), 148–50; Nathan Mubita (livelihood improvisation), 53–54, 90–92, 97–101, 102, 148–49, 174; Lackson Mwale (construction company), 52–53, 54, 87–88, 177–78; Mwenya family ambition, 59, 152; Nsofu family (domestic workers), 54–55, 113; Phiri family prosperity, 112–13, 153–55, 180; Sarah (*lutuku* brew), 120; Spaita family (ice cream parlour), 58; Vincent (well construction business), 93–101; Mrs Ziyembe (widow), 116–17
Casey, Edward, 32, 44, 67, 68, 198
Chauncey, George, 130
children: copper-mine dumps, 34, 106–7, 115, 117, 118, 120; importance of parenthood, 141; mine trust schools, 82; orphans, 117
Chiluba, Frederick, 26, 27, 181
China Non-Ferrous Metal Mining Company (CNMC), 36–37
Chingola, 46–47
Chipimo, Elias, 178
chisungu initiation rites, 133–36, 155, 164
Christianity, 153
class: high-cost vs low-cost housing areas, 79, 81–82, 86; lifestyle distinctions, 81–82, 85; and social mobility, 80–81; and ZCCM career progression, 70–71, 78. *See also* living conditions
Cligget, Lisa, 56, 61
colonial era, 6, 17n5, 20, 23, 23–24, 41n5
Comaroff, Jean, 56, 200

Comaroff, John, 56, 200
communication: multiple types, 132–33; within marriage, 131
construction industry, 51, 76n17; flux stone, *31*, 34, 53, 101, 115, *119*, 128n8
consumer goods, 5, 43, 56, 74n1, 85, 87, 147
Copperbelt: ethnographic studies, 10–13; historical emergence, 19–20, 41n3; map, *21*; phenomenological engagement, 44–6; as textured place, 44–45
Copperbelt residents: future imaginary, 45, 50, 55–56; life's opportunities, 61, 81, 86; macroeconomic issues, 50; prosperous lifestyle, 23; unrealistic expectations, 43–44, 57–58, 74n2, 115; wayfaring/stepping out taking chances, 50, 52. *See also* improvisation; living conditions; retrenched miners; "trying"
copper dump sites: copper ore, 105, 121; dangers, 117, 124, 128n17; flux stone, *31*, 34, 53, 101, 115, *119*, 128n8; formalisation proposals, 123–24; gender inequalities, 106–7, 125; illegality a legitimate survival strategy, 106, 123; power contestation, 126; preferred informal work for women, 117–18; "rurban slums," 34–35; women's pragmatism, 116–17; women's work, 15, 88, 109, 124–25; young men, 15. *See also* Kalengwa dump site
copper mining companies: asset stripping, 86; benefits and welfare provision, 4–5, 6–7, 13–14, 23, 26–27, 78, 111, 149, 175; diversification efforts, 38; effects of withdrawal of welfare provision, 30, 36, 89, 149, 175–76; farming encouragement, 104n9; training and education sponsorship, 4, 16n2, 25, 82, 87. *See also* Zambia Consolidated Copper Mines (ZCCM)
copper price fluctuations, 23, 25, 28, 29, 49, 108
Cosgrove, Dennis, 45
cost of living, 35
courtship, 159–60
Cresswell, Tim, 8, 66

crime, petty thieving, 113
Cullen Chisha, "Tomato Balunda"
("Tomato Is Expensive"), 181

Dalisoul (musician), 187; "Shansa," 183
Dandy Krazy (musician): "Donchi
Kubeba" ("Don't Tell Them"), 181; "Life
Yandi," 176–77; "Tubombela Akabwali,"
179, 180–81
Danny (musician), 90; "Kaya," 176
Darby, Clifford, 20
death: hospital fears, 178, 185; of parents,
171; ubiquity, 170–71
De Boeck, Filip, 33, 67, 70, 171, 184
developmental systems theory, 126
Devisch, René, 24, 33, 135, 136, 139, 172–73
diamond mining, 38
Dlamini, Jacob, 6, 69
domestic workers, 54–55
dreams: of formal re-employment, 57–58.
See also business ventures
DY2K, "Nyamuka, Nyamuka" ("Get Up,
Get Up"), 177

economic recession, 5–6, 25–26, 103n7
education: mining company sponsorship, 4,
16n2, 25, 82, 87; school fees, 83, 88, 104n8
education policy, 4–5
Englund, Harri, 126–27
Epstein, Arnold Leonard, 11, 65

families, cost of living, 35
family relations: breakdown of extended
family, 152–53, 154; *chisungu* training,
135; exploitation of unpaid kin, 40, 154,
187n2; extended family, 158–59, 160–61,
168n28, 187n2; inheritance issues, 46,
75n8, 151–52; Western ideals, 129–30.
See also marriage
Feeley-Harnik, Gillian, 81
Ferguson, James, 11, 62, 72, 172; *Expectations of Modernity*, 5, 10, 13, 33, 45,
74n3, 80, 112, 129; "The Country and
the City on the Copperbelt," 60
fertility, 141

fieldwork: active participation, 74; house
purchase and renovation, 7–8, 46–48,
50–51, 75n7. *See also* research methods
finance: client reliability, 94–96; credit
loans, 54, 59; foreign investment, 36–
38, 108; threats to non-payers, 96–97
First Quantum Minerals (FQM), 37, 38
flux stone, *31*, 34, 53, 101, 115, *119*, 128n8
food, entertaining, 138
food shortages, 25–26, 33, 35, 179–80
foreign investment, 36–38, 108
forestry, 49, 75n13
Foucault, Michel, 62
Fraser, Alastair, 28, 108
free market ideology, 1, 16n1, 106, 110–11

Geiser, Thorsten, 55, 71, 77n30
Gell, Alfred, 14, 61, 71, 76n24
gender, performativity, 163–66
gender inequalities: expectations of
domesticity, 132; household finances,
148–51, 164; informal copper business,
106–7, 120, 125; women's provision of
basic family needs, 39, 120
gender relations, and power, 133, 139–40,
149
getting by, small-scale enterprises, 39, 79,
88–89, 103n4
Gluckman, Max, 79
Goffman, Ervin, 8–9
gold mining, 38
Guerts, Kathryn Linn, 195

habitus, 12, 67, 72, 77n28, 81
Haglund, Dan, 28
Hallam, Elizabeth, 79
Hansen, Karen Tranberg, 69, 69–70, 85,
110, 130, 158, 164
Harvey, Penny, 73
health, ill-health, 22, 172–73
health services, 178, 185–86
HIV/AIDS: campaigns, 182; effects,
88–89; fear, 160; indirect references,
90, 171–72; risks, 117; statistics, 104n11,
188n4; suspected cases, 185–86

Hoelscher, Steven D., 45
hope, 43–44, 60
hospitals, 172, 178, 185
household finances, 148–51, 153, 164
housing, *31*; author's house purchase
    and renovation, 7–8, 46–48, 53, 75n7;
    improvements for mineworkers, 3, 23;
    none planned post-privatisation, 36;
    rental income, 84; as retrenchment
    benefit, 27, 29, 34, 78; settlement pat-
    terns, 9, 79, 81–82, 83–84
Hugh-Jones, Stephen, 7
humanist philosophy, 19, 24
hunger, 25–26, 35, 114, 179–81
Hunter, Mark, 69

improvisation: Copperbelt residents,
    53–54, 193–94, 201; livelihood possi-
    bilities, 193–96; Mr Mubita's backyard,
    90–92, 97–101; and opportunity, 81; for
    survival, 190; in uncertain world, 193;
    Vincent's well-making, 94–101. *See also*
    uncertainty
income, 35, 89, 104n13. *See also* wages
inequalities: Copperbelt residents, 85–86,
    180; and jealousy, 58, 112–13, 153, 154,
    180; Zambia, 35–36, 114
informal economy: backyard farming, 39,
    79, 84–85, 92, 103n4; colonial era, 109;
    illegality a legitimate survival strat-
    egy, 106, 118, 125–26; interdependence
    with formal sector, 69–70, 125; moral
    dimension, 106, 112–14, 118, 125–27,
    194–96; popular music representation,
    180; power contestation, 126; primary
    income source, 108; start-up capital,
    149–50; and trespass, 69; women,
    69–70, 145, *146*; women's networking,
    147, 150, 154. *See also* business ventures;
    copper dump sites
infrastructure: decline, 29–30, *31*, 190;
    transport infrastructure, 25, 41n6;
    ZCCM provision, 27
Ingold, Tim, 7, 44, 63, 71–72, 74, 77n32, 79,
    85–86, 194

inheritance, 46, 75n8, 151–52
initiation rites, 133–36, 155, 164
Intestate Act (1989), 151–52

jealousy, 58, 112–13, 153, 154, 180
Johnson-Hanks, Jennifer, 61, 193

Kalengwa, settlement, 108–9
Kalengwa dump site: copper ore sales,
    121; gang labour, 109; informal mining
    (*pa illegal*) era, 119–20; men during
    high profit margins, 120; mine owner
    rules, 121–23; power contestation, 126;
    women and children, 118
Kalulushi, 3, 4
Kalusa, Walima, 22
Kaponya (young people), 179, 194–95
Kaunda, Kenneth: education policy, 4;
    "Heaven on Earth" vision, 44, 75n6;
    humanist philosophy, 19; nation-
    building, 4–5; removal from power, 26;
    on theft, 114
kinship ties, 52, 53; respect (*umuchinshi*),
    136–40. *See also* family relations
kitchen parties, 145–47, 148, 150
Kitwe, 46
K'Millian, "Another Day," 176
Konkola Copper Mines (KCM), 47–48

labour: colour bar, 103n7; Zambianisa-
    tion, 2, 3, 22, 25, 80, 103n7
Land Act (1995), 51, 76n18
land rates, 89
land rights, customary tenure, 37–38, 51,
    76n18
land use, small-scale and illegal mining,
    34–35
Larmer, Miles, 9, 28, 172
Lefebvre, Henri, 66–67, 183, 197–98
leisure. *See* recreation
Lévi-Strauss, Claude, 62
livelihood: diverse options, 48–49;
    diversification, 18–19, 39; foraging,
    69; improvisation, 193–96; material
    aspects, 71–72; perseverance, 182–83;

uncertainty, 6–7, 56, 61, 70, 174, 192–93. *See also* informal economy; privatisation, socio-economic effects; "trying"
living conditions: chaotic and disorderly, 178–79; first ten-year development plan, 22; getting by, 39, 79, 88–89, 103n4; golden era (1950s–70s), 23; "living well" (*abale ikala bwino*), 85, 86–87, 156; okay (*abali fye*), 85, 87–88; post-independence difficulties, 5–6; suffering (*abale cula*), 15–16, 85, 88–89, 114, 172–73, 183–84
love potions, 157, 168n21
Luanshya: author's house purchase and renovation, 7–8, 46–48, 53, 75n7; economic crisis, 78–79; environmental controls, 64; high-cost neighbourhood (*kuma yard*), 79, 81–82, 86; limited population growth, 34; livelihood difficulties, 1; low-cost housing area (*ku komboni*), 81; as place, 2–3
Luanshya mines, 27–28, 36–37, 103n3, 107, 188n11
Lumwana Mines, 36
Lungu, John, 28, 108
Lusaka, 18; economic growth, 35; informal economy, 110–11; informal settlements, 52, 76n19; socioeconomic constraints, 85; street vendors, 110
Lwanda, John, 171–2

Macky 2 (musician), 176–77
macroeconomic issues, 50
maize, 25–26, 113
Manchester school, 10, 11, 80, 130, 139
marriage: *chisungu* training, 135; courtship, 159–60; economic secrecy from husbands, 150–51, 153, 164; extramarital affairs, 135, 140, 141, 161–63, 166n7; gifts for wife, 152; kitchen parties, 145–47, 148, 150; traditional vs modern expectations, 131–32, 140–45, *144*, 156–58, 163–64
marriage counsellors (*banachimbusa*), 131, 134, 141, 155

Marr, Stephen, 65
maternal figure, 141
mbusa clay models, 134, 136, 166n4, 167n8
middle classes, 5, 14–15, 87
migrant workers, 161, 161–63, 168n29
migration: internal migration, 11, 12–13, 18–19, 34, 40; transient Europeans, 19–20, 22, 24
mineworkers: declining numbers, 18; unions, 28. *See also* retrenched miners
Mitchell, J. Clyde, 11, 65, 130
Moore, Henrietta, 130, 133, 136, 164–65, 196; *Space, Text and Gender*, 66
Mopani Copper Mines, 28, 47, 75n9
morality: "Get embarrassed but get full" (*sebana wikute*), 112–13, 140, 169–70; and the informal economy, 106, 112–14, 118, 125–27, 194–96; and trespass, 69, 126, 195–96
Movement for Multi-Party Democracy (MMD), 27, 28, 181
Mozegater (musician), 90; "Bakalila" ("They Will Cry"), 183–84
Mpongwe, 34
Mufulira, 3, 47, 93, 94
Mufumbwe, 35–36
multinational companies: taxation, 22–23, 25, 28, 29; tax evasion, 38, 42n18
Mutamba, Manyewu, 69
Mwale, Lackson, 52–54, 87–88
Mwanawasa, Levy, 28, 123
Myers, Garth, 19

nation-building, 4–5, 24
Nchanga Consolidated Copper Mines, 4
neoliberalism, 56; and free market ideology, 1, 16n1, 106, 110–11
Nkoloso, Edward, 44, 74n5
North Western Province, 37–38
nostalgia: Copperbelt residents, 68–69, 196; for the future, 57; layered experience, 68; for the past, 26, 81–83, 174–75; for place, 198–99; for simple pleasures, 5, 6
Nyamnjoh, Francis, 12, 74n3

older people, respect (*umuchinshi*), 136–37, 138, 167nn10–11
opportunity, 61, 81, 86
optimism, 183, 196
Ortega-Alcazar, Iliana, 196
Oyama, Susan, 126

Parpart, Jane, 80, 130
Patriotic Front (PF), 28, 181
Pentecostal church, 39, 59, 76n16
performativity, 12, 59–60, 163–66, 171–72
Petersen (musician): "Musiye Atoping'e" ("Leave Him/Her to Top Up"), 186; "Oh No," 90, 173
Piot, Charles, 57
place: and aspects of life, 45; character, 13; Copperbelt "two-ness," 32, 198; cultural text, 66; and empathy, 71, 77n30; performativity, 12, 171–72; provisional moments, 8; and space, 67; texture, 55, 66–67, 76n21. *See also* nostalgia
place-world, 67
platonic friendship, 157
popular music: anxiety and uncertainty, 176–77; death and life, 90, 171–72; on hunger, 180–81; life in difficult times, 15–16; love songs, 69; on precariousness, 90; relationships with Asian men, 163; on suffering, 172–73, 183–84; "trying," 90, 173, 186
poverty, 89, 104n13, 128n7
Powdermaker, Hortense, *Copper Town*, 11, 23, 64–65, 130
pragmatism, 33, 80–81, 116–17
Prain, Sir Ronald, 22
prayer, 177
privatisation: effects on infrastructure, 29–30, 31, 190; effects on recreation facilities, 30, 57–58; Luanshya mines, 27–28, 36–37, 107, 188n11; socio-economic effects, 1, 8, 28, 39–40, 89, 108, 160–61, 175–76; ZCCM, 27–28, 86, 103n3. *See also* retrenched miners

Quayson, Ato, *Oxford Street, Accra*, 8, 65

race, 163
RAMCOZ. *See* Roan Antelope Mining Company (RAMCOZ)
Rasing, Thera, 130, 133, 134, 135
recreation: found in women's daily tasks, 145, 146; kitchen parties, 145–47, 148, 150; post-privatisation, 30, 57–58; pre-privatisation, 23, 32, 82
Régulier, Catherine, 183, 197–98
relationships: dating foreign men, 160; extramarital affairs, 135, 140, 141, 161–63, 166n7; transactional sex, 159; young men's anxiety, 159–60. *See also* marriage
researcher subjectivity, 9–10
research methods: "hanging out," 8; informal interviews, 8–9; mining archives, 9; statistical data, 9; surveys, 9. *See also* fieldwork
respect (*umuchinshi*), 136–40, 153, 156–57, 162, 167nn10–12
retirement plans, 12–13
retrenched miners: benefit delays, 27–28, 83, 103n3, 112, 115, 127n3; livelihood coping strategies, 83–85; retrenchment benefits, 27, 29, 34, 43, 78, 107; spending spree, 107–8, 181–82; uncertainty, 6–7, 70, 174, 192–93; unrealistic expectations, 43–44, 57–58, 74n2, 115
Rhodes, Cecil, 20
Rhodesian Selection Trust (RST), 20
Richards, Audrey, 130, 134, 135–36
roads, 30, 31
Roan Antelope Mining Company (RAMCOZ), 3–4, 21–22, 86, 103n3, 107, 115, 127n3, 188n11
Robinson, Jennifer, 65
Ross, Fiona, 67, 171, 172
RST mines, 22, 24
rural areas: agriculture, 34, 93, 103n6, 104n10, 197; forced resettlement, 38; lifestyle, 72
rural-urban divide, 38
rural-urban migration, 11, 12, 18–19, 34, 40

salaries, 156. *See also* wages
Sandercock, Leonie, 8
Satanism, 87, 112–13, 153, 186. *See also*
    witchcraft
school fees, 83, 88, 104n8
self-sufficiency, 39, 68, 83, 88, 104n9
shame (*sebanya wikute*), 54–55, 140
Shusterman, Richard, 176, 188n12
Sichone, Owen, 12
Simutanyi, Neo, 108
single women, 150, 158
situational analysis, 12, 139
social customs: gifts, 158, 159, 168n22;
    respect (*umuchinshi*), 136–40, 153,
    156–57, 162, 167nn10–12; sharing of
    food, 180
social mobility, and class, 80–81
social propriety, 113–14, 156–58, 166. *See
    also* respect (*umuchinshi*)
structural adjustment, 56, 74n1, 109; free
    market policies, 1, 16n1
structuralist theory, 62–63
suffering (*abale cula*), 15–16, 85, 88–89,
    114; hope of an end, 187; popular music,
    172–73, 183–84

taxation, mining companies, 22–23, 25,
    28, 29
tax evasion, by multinationals, 38,
    42n18
theft, 113–14
Till, Karen E., 45
trade unions, 6, 28
traditional authorities, 37–38
traditional healers, 156–57, 185
training, 4, 16n2, 25, 82, 87
transport infrastructure, 25, 41n6
trespass, 69, 126, 195–96
"trying": anthropology, 191–92; Cop-
    perbelt residents, 13, 55, 174, 182–83;
    definition, 188n5; fieldwork, 73–74;
    popular music, 173, 183–85, 186, 187;
    small business plans, 58–59; variations
    in success, 58, 70–71, 173–74
tujilijili, 177

umuchinshi (respect), 136–40, 153, 156–57,
    162, 167nn10–12
uncertainty, 6–7, 56, 61, 70, 174, 192–93
uranium mining, 38
urbanisation, 35
urban poverty, 19, 40

Vaa, Mariken, 69
Vambe, Maurice, 171
Van Binsbergen, Wim, 33, 134
Vaughan, Megan, 130
villagisation, 30–33, 40, 72, 197–98
violence, 175–76, 180, 188n20
voluntary work, 57–58

wages, 23, 35, 84. *See also* salaries
Warshaw, Paul R., 192
water supplies: drinking water, 97; lack
    of access, 89; shortages, 30, 33, 40, 55;
    well construction business, 93–96; well
    construction techniques, 97–101
wealth, 59–60, 87
welfare provision: by ZCCM, 4–5, 6–7,
    26–27, 78, 111, 175; family giving, 19;
    mining town improvements, 20, 22;
    negative effects of privatisation, 30,
    36, 89, 108, 149, 175–76; retrenchment
    benefits, 27, 29, 34, 43, 78, 107; training
    and education sponsorship, 4, 16n2,
    25, 82, 87
well construction business, 93–96
well construction techniques, 97–101
whiteness, 161, 168n31
Wilkinson, Eleanor, 196
Willerslev, Rane, 63
Williams, Raymond, 44–45, 66
Wilson, Godfrey, 11, 130
witchcraft, 68–69, 152, 171. *See also*
    Satanism
women: business networking, 147, 150,
    154; and class, 80; cleverness, 164–65;
    female initiation rites, 133–36, 155, 164;
    household finances, 148–51, 153, 164;
    informal alternatives to dump sites, 117;
    informal economy, 69–70, 109–10;

women (*continued*)
   involvement with mine companies,
   111–12; kitchen parties, 145–47, 148,
   150; labour strike activity, 6; life before
   mine privatisation, 82; main family
   breadwinner, 87, 115, 117, 152–53, 165;
   poverty, 89; property-grab by relatives,
   115–16; respect (*umuchinshi*), 136–40;
   single women, 150, 158; subsistence
   farming, 21–22; supplementing the
   family income, 82; traditional char-
   acterisations, 15, 130; traditional vs
   modern expectations, 131–32, 140–45,
   144, 156–58, 163–64; widows, 115–16,
   117, 128n11. *See also* copper dump sites;
   families; marriage

Yamba, Bawa, 171
young people: anxiety and uncertainty,
   176–77; fatalism, 181–83; *Kaponya*, 179,
   194–95. *See also* popular music

Zambia: economic growth, 35; economic
   recession, 5–6, 25–26, 103n7; malaise,
   178–79
Zambia Consolidated Copper Mines
   (ZCCM): modernisation failure, 111;
   privatisation, 27–28, 103n3, 107; socioeconomic changes following privatisation, 1, 8, 28, 39–40, 89, 108, 160–61,
   175–76; welfare provision, 4–5, 6–7,
   26–27, 78, 111
Zambianisation, 3, 22, 25, 80, 103n7
Zayani, Mohamed, 183, 197–98